A PROMISE of HOPE

A PROMISE *of* HOPE

BOOK TWO

AMY CLIPSTON

ZONDERVAN®

ZONDERVAN

A Promise of Hope
Copyright © 2010 by Amy Clipston

This title is also available as a Zondervan ebook.
Visit www.zondervan.com/ebooks.

This title is also available in a Zondervan audio edition.
Visit www.zondervan.fm.

Requests for information should be addressed to:
Zondervan, Grand Rapids, Michigan 49546

Library of Congress Cataloging-in-Publication Data

Clipston, Amy.
       A promise of hope / Amy Clipston.
          p. cm. - (Kauffman Amish bakery series ; bk. 2)
       Summary: An Amish widow with newborn twins discovers her deceased husband
    had disturbing secrets. As she tries to come to grips with the past, she considers
    a loveless marriage to ensure stability for her young family ... with her faith in God
    hanging in the balance.
       ISBN 978-0-310-28984-5 (softcover)
       1. Amish — Fiction. I. Title.
    PS3603.L58P76 2010
    813'.6 — dc22   2009051036

Cover design: Thinkpen Design, Inc
Cover photography: iStock / Shutterstock
Interior design: Christine Orejuela-Winkelman

ISBN:978-0-3103-4408-7 (repack)

Printed in the United States of America

15 16 17 18 19 20 21 22 /RRD/ 17 16 15 14 13 12 11 10 9 8 7 6 5 4 3 2 1

In loving memory of my father-in-law,
Joseph Martin Clipston Jr., who left us too soon.
You're forever in our hearts.

NOTE TO THE READER

While this novel is set against the real backdrop of Lancaster County, Pennsylvania, the characters are fictional. There is no intended resemblance between the characters in this book and any real members of the Amish and Mennonite communities. As with any work of fiction, I've taken license in some areas of research as a means of creating the necessary circumstances for my characters. My research was thorough; however, it would be impossible to be completely accurate in details and description, since each and every community differs. Therefore, any inaccuracies in the Amish and Mennonite lifestyles portrayed in this book are completely due to fictional license.

GLOSSARY

ack: Oh
aenti: aunt
appeditlich: delicious
boppli: baby
bopplin: babies
danki: Thank you
dat: dad
Dietsch: Pennsylvania Dutch, the Amish language
    (a German dialect)
dochder: daughter
Englisher: a non-Amish person
fraa: wife
freind: friend
freindschaft: relative
gegisch: silly
gern gschehne: You're welcome
grossdaddi: grandfather
gut: good
Gut nacht: Good night
Ich liebe dich: I love you
kapp: prayer covering or cap
kind: child
kinner: children

kumm: come
liewe: love, a term of endearment
maedel: young woman
mamm: mom
mei: my
mutter: mother
onkel: uncle
Wie geht's: How do you do? or Good day!
wunderbaar: wonderful
ya: yes
zwillingbopplin: twins

PROLOGUE

Luke Troyer blew out a sigh and wiped his brow. The sweltering heat of the carpentry shop choked the air. The heaviness of sawdust, the pungent odor of stain, and the sweet smell of wood filled his nostrils. Tools and loud voices blared while a dozen other men created custom cabinets in the large work area surrounding him.

He placed his hammer next to the cabinets he'd been sanding and headed toward the small break room in the back of the shop. It held a long table with chairs, a refrigerator, and a counter with a sink. He fetched his lunch pail from the large refrigerator and pulled out a can of Coke.

"How are those cabinets coming along?" Mel Stoltzfus asked, leaning in the doorway.

Luke shrugged and gulped his cool, carbonated beverage. "All right, I guess. I'm about halfway through." Lowering himself into the chair at the small table, he glanced across at a folded copy of *The Budget*, the Amish newspaper, and sudden memories of his father gripped him. Pop had read *The Budget* cover to cover every Wednesday.

"You have plans tonight?" Moving into the room, Mel sat on the chair across from Luke and opened his bottle of iced tea. "Sally told me to invite you for supper. She's making her famous chicken and dumplings."

1

"*Danki*, but I have plans." Luke unfolded the paper and skimmed the articles.

"*Ya*. Sure." Mel snorted. "I can imagine what your plans are. You're going to work three hours past closing, go home, make yourself a turkey sandwich, and then putter around your shed until midnight. Then you'll go to bed and start all over again tomorrow."

Grimacing, Luke met his friend's pointed stare. "I don't do that every night."

"*Ya*, you do. You've done the same thing every night since your *dat* passed away." Mel set his bottle down and tapped the table for emphasis. "You nursed your *dat* for eight years. It's time you started living again. You're young, so start acting like it."

Luke blew out a sigh and turned his attention to the paper. He'd heard this lecture from Mel several times since Pop passed away eight months ago. Although Luke knew his friend was right, he just didn't know how to move on. He'd nursed Pop since he was twenty-one, so Luke didn't know how to "act young."

"You know I speak the truth," Mel said. "You should leave work on time tonight and come to my house. Enjoy an evening of friends, not solitude."

Luke shook his head and opened his mouth to respond, but the whooshing of the door opening derailed his train of thought. He gaped when he found a ghost from his past standing in the doorway.

"DeLana?" Luke stood, examining the tall, thin woman dressed in jeans and a black leather jacket. Her long, dark hair framed her attractive face, which was outlined with makeup.

"Long time, no see." She gave him a wry smile, her brown eyes sparkling. "How long has it been? Eight years?"

Luke nodded. "I reckon so." He motioned toward Mel. "DeLana Maloney, this is my good friend Mel Stoltzfus."

She smiled at Mel. "Nice to meet you."

Mel nodded, speechless.

She honed her gaze in on Luke. "Any chance we can talk? Alone?" She looked back at Mel again. "No offense."

"Uh, it's no trouble at all." Mel stood and started toward the door. He glanced back at Luke, looking puzzled, then closed the door.

Luke turned his attention to DeLana. "How have you been?" he asked.

"Good." She nodded. "How about you?"

"*Gut*." He cleared his throat. "It's a surprise to see you here."

"I bet you thought you'd never see me again, huh?" She adjusted her leather purse on her shoulder.

Luke motioned toward the table. "Would you like to have a seat? I have a spare Coke if you're thirsty."

"No, thanks. I can't stay long." DeLana rooted around in her purse and pulled out an envelope. "I wanted to ask you about Peter."

"Peter?" Luke narrowed his eyes in question. "What do you mean?"

"I haven't heard from him in a few months. I've written him a few times, but the letters from him have stopped." She handed him the envelope. "I was going to mail this to him, but I was wondering if it's even worth it since he's cut me off. Do you know why?"

Luke stared down at letters addressed to Peter Troyer in Bird-in-Hand, Pennsylvania. "No, I don't. I haven't heard from him in years."

"It's strange." She shook her head, her diamond-studded earrings sparkling in the light of the gas lamps. "I heard from him every month like clockwork and then it all stopped about five months ago."

He glanced at the envelope again, his mind clicking with questions. "Bird-in-Hand? Is that where he's living?"

"Yeah. He said he worked at some Amish furniture place in town." She folded her arms, pondering. "Shoot, I can't remember the name of it."

His brow furrowed in disbelief. "He's working in an Amish furniture store? Are you certain?"

"Oh, yeah, I'm certain. He mentioned it often, talking about the different projects he was working on." She pursed her lips. "So you don't know anything?"

Luke shook his head, processing the information. Peter was living in Pennsylvania and working in an Amish furniture store.

Is he still Amish?

"I'm sorry," he said. "Like I said, I haven't heard from him in years."

She pulled her car keys from her purse, and they jingled in response. "If you hear from him, would you ask him to contact me?"

"Of course." He held the envelope out to her.

"Would you please give that to him if you find him?" She glanced at her watch. "I'd better run."

"Let me walk you out." Luke followed her through the shop and out the front door to the parking lot, his mind flooded with questions about Peter. He shivered in the crisp autumn air.

"It was good to see you," she said.

"*Ya*, it was." He gripped the envelopes in his hand.

"If you hear from him, would you ask him to write or call me?" she asked. "He has my number."

"*Ya*, I will." He nodded.

"Thanks. Take care." She started across the parking lot.

"What was that about?" a voice behind Luke asked.

"Peter," Luke said, glancing toward Mel. "Letters from him have stopped, and her letters to him have gone unanswered."

"I'm confused," Mel said, coming up to glance at the envelopes in Luke's hand. "Why would Peter be exchanging letters with her?"

Luke waved as DeLana's SUV sped past, beeping on its way to the parking-lot exit.

"Apparently he's living in Pennsylvania and working in an Amish furniture store," Luke said.

"Amish furniture store?" Mel sounded as surprised as Luke felt. "He's still Amish?"

"That's what I said." Luke studied the envelopes again. "It looks like I'm heading to Pennsylvania."

"Why would you do that?"

"To find out what's happened to Peter. It's time for me to use the vacation time I've been saving for years." He headed toward the office to ask his boss for an extended leave of absence.

1

Smoke filled Sarah Troyer's lungs and stung her watering eyes. Covering her mouth with her trembling hand, she fell to her knees while flames engulfed the large carpentry area of the furniture store.

"Peter!" Her attempt to scream her husband's name came out in a strangled cough, inaudible over the noise of the roaring fire surrounding her.

Peter was somewhere in the fire. She had to get to him. But how would she find her way through the flames? Had someone called for help? Where was the fire department?

A thunderous boom shook the floor beneath Sarah's feet, causing her body to shake with fear. The roof must've collapsed!

"Sarah!" Peter's voice echoed, hoarse and weak within the flames.

"I'm coming!" Sobs wracked her body as she crawled toward the back of the shop. She would find him. She had to!

Turning her face toward the ceiling, Sarah begged God to spare her husband's life. He had to live. She needed him. He was everything to her. They were going to be parents.

Their baby needed a father.

Standing, she threw her body into the flames, rushing toward the crumpled silhouette on the floor next to the smashed remains of the roof ...

Sarah's eyes flew open, and she gasped. She touched her sweat-drenched nightgown with her trembling hands. Closing her eyes, she breathed a sigh of relief.

It was a dream!

Stretching her arm through the dark, she reached across the double bed for her husband of three years; however, her hand brushed only cool sheets.

Empty.

Oh, no.

Sarah cupped a hand to her hot face while reality crashed down on her. Peter had died in the fire in her father's furniture store five months ago. He was gone, and she was staying in her parents' house.

Taking a deep, ragged breath, she swallowed a sob. She'd had the fire dream again—the fourth time this week.

When were the nightmares going to cease? When was life going to get easier?

She rested her hands on her swelling belly while tears cooled her burning cheeks. It seemed like only yesterday Sarah was sharing the news of their blessing with Peter and he was smiling, his hazel eyes twinkling, while he pulled her close and kissed her.

It had been their dream to have a big family with as many as seven children, like most of the Amish couples in their church district. Sarah and Peter had spent many late nights snuggling in each other's arms while talking about names.

However, Sarah had buried those dreams along with her husband, and she still felt as bewildered as the day his body was laid to rest. She wondered how she'd ever find the emotional strength to raise her baby without the love and support of her beloved Peter.

She'd believed since the day she married Peter that they would raise a family and grow old together. But that ghastly fire had stolen everything from Sarah and her baby—their future and their stability. Her life was now in flux.

Closing her eyes, she mentally repeated her mother's favorite Scripture, Romans 12:12: "Be joyful in hope, patient in affliction, faithful in prayer." But the verse offered no comfort. She tried to pray, but the words remained unformed in her heart.

Sarah was completely numb.

She stared up through the dark until a light tap on her door roused her from her thoughts.

"Sarah Rose." Her mother's soft voice sounded through the closed door. "It's time to get up."

"*Ya*." Wiping the tears from her face, Sarah rose and slowly dressed, pulling on her black dress, black apron, and shoes. She then parted her golden hair and twirled long strands back from her face before winding the rest into a bun. Once her hair was tightly secured, she placed her white prayer *kapp* over it, anchoring it with pins.

Sarah hurried down the stairs and met her mother in the front hall of the old farmhouse in which she'd been raised. "I'm ready," she said.

Mamm's blue eyes studied her. "Aren't you going to eat?"

"No." Sarah headed for the back door. "Let's go. I'll eat later."

"Sarah Rose. You must eat for the *boppli*." Her mother trotted after her.

"I'm not hungry." Sarah slipped out onto the porch.

"Did you have the dream again?" *Mamm*'s voice was filled with concern.

Sarah sucked in a breath, hoping to curb the tears rising in her throat. "I'm just tired." She started down the dirt driveway toward the bakery.

Mamm caught up with her. Taking Sarah's hand in hers, she gave her a bereaved expression. "Sarah Rose, *mei liewe*, how it breaks my heart to see you hurting. I want to help you through this. Please let me."

Swallowing the tears that threatened, Sarah stared down at her mother's warm hand cradling hers. Grief crashed down on her, memories of Peter and their last quiet evening together flooding her. He'd held her close while they discussed their future as parents.

Rehashing those memories was too painful for Sarah to bear. She missed him with every fiber of her being. Sarah had to change the subject before she wound up sobbing in her mother's arms—again.

"We best get to work before the girls think we overslept," Sarah whispered, quickening her steps.

"Don't forget this afternoon is your ultrasound appointment," *Mamm* said. "Maybe we'll find out if you're having a boy or a girl. Nina Janitz is going to pick us up at one so we're at the hospital on time."

At her mother's words Sarah swallowed a groan. The idea of facing this doctor's appointment without Peter sharpened the pain that pulsated in her heart.

Pushing the thought aside, Sarah stared at the bakery her mother had opened more than twenty years ago. The large, white clapboard farmhouse sat near the road and included a sweeping wraparound porch. A sign with "Kauffman Amish Bakery" in old-fashioned letters hung above the door.

Out behind the building was a fenced-in play area where a few of the Kauffman grandchildren ran around playing tag and climbing on a huge wooden swing set. Beyond it was the fenced pasture. *Mamm's*, Peter's, and Timothy's large farmhouses, along with four barns, were set back beyond the pasture. The dirt road leading to the other homes was roped off with a sign declaring Private Property—No Trespassing.

A large paved parking lot sat adjacent to the building. The lot—always full during the summer months, the height of the tourist season—was now empty. Even though temperatures had cooled off for autumn, the tourist season had ended a month ago in Bird-in-Hand.

Mamm prattled on about the weather and how busy the bakery had been. Sarah grunted in agreement to give the appearance of listening.

After climbing the steps, Sarah and *Mamm* headed in through the back door of the building. The sweet aroma of freshly baked bread filled Sarah's senses while the Pennsylvania *Dietsch* chatter of her sisters swirled around her.

The large open kitchen had plain white walls, and in keeping with their tradition, there was no electricity. The lights were gas powered, as were the row of ovens. The long counter included their tools—plain pans and ordinary knives and cutlery.

Even though the air outside was cool, Sarah and her sisters still did the bulk of the baking in the early morning in order to keep the kitchen heat to a minimum. Five fans running through the power inverters gave a gentle breeze. However, the kitchen was warm.

Nodding a greeting to her sisters, Sarah washed her hands before pulling out ingredients to begin mixing a batch of her favorite sugar cookies. She engrossed herself in the task and shut out the conversations around her.

"How are you?" Lindsay, her sister-in-law's young niece, asked after a while.

"*Gut*," Sarah said, forcing a smile. "How are you today?"

"*Gut, danki.*" The fourteen-year-old smiled, her ivory complexion glowing. Although she'd been raised by non-Amish parents, Lindsay had adjusted well to the lifestyle since coming to live with Rebecca, Sarah's sister-in-law. Her parents had died in a car accident, leaving custody of her and her older sister to Rebecca. Lindsay quickly adopted the Amish dress and was learning the Pennsylvania *Dietsch* language as if she'd been born into the community.

Lindsay tilted her head in question and wrinkled her freckled nose. "You don't look *gut*, *Aenti* Sarah. Is everything okay?"

"I'm fine, but *danki*." Sarah stirred the anise cookie batter and wracked her brain for something to change the subject. "You and Rebecca got here early this morning, no?"

"*Ya*." Lindsay began cutting out cookies. "*Aenti* Rebecca was having some tummy problems this morning." She gestured toward her stomach, and Sarah knew the girl was referring to morning sickness. "She was up early, and I was too. So we just headed out. We had a couple of loaves of bread in the oven before *Aenti* Beth Anne and *Aenti* Kathryn got here."

Sarah glanced across the kitchen to where *Mamm* was whispering to Beth Anne and Kathryn, Sarah's older sisters. When her mother's gaze met Sarah's, her mother quickly looked away.

Sarah's stomach churned. She hoped her mother wasn't talking about her again. She was in no mood for another well-meaning lecture from her sisters. They were constantly insisting Sarah must accept Peter's death and concentrate on the blessing of her pregnancy. Over and over they told her it was God's will Peter had perished and the Lord would provide for her and her baby.

What did they know about loss? They both had their husbands and children, living and healthy.

"I best go check on the *kinner* on the playground," Lindsay said, wiping her hands on her apron.

Sarah picked up the cookie cutter. "I'll finish cutting out your cookies."

"*Danki*." Smiling, Lindsay crossed the kitchen and disappeared out the back door toward the playground set up for Sarah's young nieces and nephews.

"Sarah," a voice behind her said. "How are you today? *Mamm* mentioned that you had a rough night."

Sarah glanced over at Beth Anne and swallowed a groan. "I'm fine, *danki*. And you?" *I wish you all would stop worrying about me.*

Beth Anne's blue eyes mirrored her disbelief, and Sarah braced herself for the coming lecture.

"You can talk to me. I'll always listen." Her older sister squeezed her hand.

"I appreciate that, but there's nothing to say. I didn't get much sleep last night, but I'm *gut*. Really." Sarah turned back to her cookies in the hopes Beth Anne would return to work and leave her alone with her thoughts.

"I know you're hurting," Beth Anne began, moving closer and lowering her voice. "However, you must let Peter's memory rest in peace. You need your strength for your *boppli*."

Sarah gritted her teeth and took a deep breath, trying in vain to curb her rising aggravation. Facing her sister, she narrowed her eyes. "I know you mean well, but you can't possibly know what I'm thinking or what I'm feeling. I lost my husband, and you have no idea how that feels. I know I need to let go, but how can I when Peter's *boppli* is growing inside me? Grieving is different for everyone, and it can't be rushed."

Beth Anne's expression softened. "I just want what's best for you."

"Then leave me alone and let me work." Sarah faced the counter. "I have a lot of cookies to make. We sold out yesterday."

"If you need to talk, I'm here." Beth Anne's voice was soft.

"*Ya. Danki.*" Sarah closed her eyes and prayed for strength to make it through the day.

❦

Late that afternoon, Sarah lay on the cool, metal table at the hospital and stared at the monitor while a young woman moved her instrument through the gel spread on Sarah's midsection.

Sarah watched the screen and sucked in a breath while the ultrasound technician pointed out anatomy. Sarah wondered how many years of schooling it had taken for the young woman to figure out which was the spinal cord and which was the heart when it all resembled a bunch of squiggly lines.

Miranda Coleman, Sarah's midwife, interrupted the technician and moved over to the monitor. "Do you see that?" Miranda asked the young woman in a hushed whisper. "I believe that's …"

"Yeah, you're right," the technician said with a grin. "I think so."

"This is something." Miranda folded her arms and shook her head. "Well, that explains her sudden weight gain."

"What?" Sarah started to sit up, her heart racing with worry. "What's wrong with my *boppli*?"

Her eyes full of concern, *Mamm* squeezed Sarah's shoulder. Miranda chuckled. "Nothing's wrong, Sarah."

Sarah held her breath and wished Peter was by her side to help her shoulder the news. "Please tell me what's going on."

"Sarah Troyer, you're doubly blessed," Miranda said with a smirk. "You're having twins. I guess one was blocking the other when we did the last ultrasound."

"*Zwillingbopplin?*" Sarah gasped. Lightheaded, she put her hand to her forehead.

How would she ever raise twins alone?

❋

Later that evening, Sarah stood on the porch and studied the rain falling in sheets on the fields across from her parents' farmhouse. Rubbing her swollen abdomen, she swallowed the sorrow surging through her.

Zwillingbopplin.

The word had haunted her since it left Miranda's lips. Sarah had tuned out Miranda's voice while she discussed Sarah's prenatal care for the remainder of the pregnancy. She'd heard the midwife say Sarah was now "high risk" and would be referred to an obstetrician for further care. Beyond that, Sarah had just stared at her midwife and pondered the news.

Twin babies.

Two mouths to feed. Two babies for which to care.

Two children without a father.

How would Sarah bear the load? Of course, her family would help her, for it was the Amish way to care for one another. However, raising two children without Peter would be daunting, regardless of help from the extended family.

"Sarah Rose." Her mother's voice interrupted her thoughts. "How are you?"

"*Gut*," Sarah whispered, still rubbing her belly.

"*Zwillingbopplin*." *Mamm* shook her head. "The Lord is *gut*. You are blessed."

"Am I?" Sarah snorted. The shock seemed to have deflated the blessing from the news.

"Why do you say that?" *Mamm*'s eyes probed Sarah's. "*Bopplin* are a blessing. Daniel and Rebecca have waited fifteen years to have one of their own."

Sarah touched *Mamm's* warm hand. "*Ya*, I know *bopplin* are a blessing. You forget Daniel and Rebecca have each other." She gazed down at her stomach. "I'm alone. These *bopplin* will have no *dat*. They only have me."

"You're not alone. You have your *dat*, me, and the rest of our family. The community will take care of you. We'll all love and care for you and your *kinner*."

"But it's not the same." Sniffing, Sarah wiped a lone tear. "They'll know love but not their *dat's* love."

"You can tell them how much Peter loved them. We have many stories that will make them smile, and you'll smile again too." Leaning over, *Mamm* looped her arm around Sarah's shoulders. "You'll find joy again, Sarah Rose. God will make sure of that."

Nodding, Sarah wiped her eyes and cleared her throat in an effort to suppress her tears. She had to hold herself together. Dissolving into sobs wouldn't help the situation.

"When the time is right," *Mamm* began, "you may marry again."

"I doubt that." Sarah shook her head with emphasis. "I don't think I'll ever love any man as much as I loved Peter. That only happens once in a lifetime."

"Sarah Rose." *Mamm* took Sarah's hands again. "You're young. You may love again. Give your burdens up to God, and

He'll see you through. Right now, just concentrate on your *kinner*. It will all come in time, God's time."

Sarah breathed deeply, hoping to stop the emotions that threatened. "Maybe someday, but not anytime soon. My heart still belongs to Peter." She stepped toward the door. "I'm going to go to bed. Good night."

"Good night." *Mamm* reached for Sarah's hand. "Don't rush yourself, Sarah Rose. God will see you through this. He's in control."

Sarah pulled her hand back and opened the screen door. "*Ya*," she whispered. "Good night."

Climbing the stairs to her room, Sarah closed the door and lowered herself down onto her bed, hoping to keep the world out. Lying there, she prayed for her family to stop nagging her. She needed room to breathe and figure out her way without their constant unsolicited opinions. She needed strength and guidance to make the right decisions for her twins.

As she moved her gaze to the ceiling, she let go of her breath and finally allowed her tears to flow, her sobs cutting through the painful silence of her bedroom. She opened her heart to God, begging Him to raise Peter as He raised Lazarus. If He'd done it once, why couldn't He do it again for Sarah, enabling her twins to have the father they needed and deserved?

She wiped her face with a trembling hand and closed her eyes. Why was she forced to live this lonely life? Didn't she deserve to be blessed with a loving husband and father to her children, like her sisters?

She tried to open her heart to God and beg again for guidance and patience, but her prayers jammed in her throat. Like so many nights in the past five months, she cried herself to sleep.

2

"How was your appointment?" Kathryn asked while standing at the counter with Sarah the following morning.

"*Gut.*" Sarah nodded and turned her attention to straightening the containers of baked goods before her.

"Just *gut*?" Kathryn moved closer to her. "Is that all?"

Hearing the rustling of skirts, Sarah turned to find Beth Anne and Rebecca standing behind her. Sarah wondered if her mother had already broken the news of her twins. Feeling as though she were backed into a corner, Sarah narrowed her eyes with the suspicion that they were pouncing on her like the stray cats she often found wrestling each other in the barns.

"How was your appointment, Sarah Rose?" Beth Anne asked, folding her arms in front of her apron.

"We hope it was *gut* news." Rebecca smiled.

"*Zwillingbopplin,*" Sarah whispered, self-consciously rubbing her belly.

Her sisters and Rebecca shrieked, pulling her close for a group hug and cooing about how blessed Sarah was. Sarah closed her eyes and wished she could find the joy her sisters felt. She prayed the cold, foreboding feeling currently enveloping her would loosen its grasp on her soul.

The bell signaling a customer's entrance into the bakery ended the group hug.

"This is wonderful *gut*, Sarah." Beth Anne's grin was wide as she stepped back toward the kitchen. "We must talk more when the shop is quiet."

"*Ya*." Sarah forced a smile. "*Danki*."

"I'm so happy for you." Rebecca gave Sarah one last squeeze. "Let me know if you need to talk," she whispered in her ear before heading into the kitchen.

"You don't look as happy as you should," Kathryn said under her breath in Pennsylvania *Dietsch* as a customer perused the containers of pastries lining the long counter in front of them.

"It's a shock," Sarah said.

"But it seems like something more. What's weighing on your mind?" her oldest sister asked.

"I don't think we should speak of it now," Sarah said, gritting her teeth with annoyance.

Kathryn jammed her hands onto her hips. "They can't understand us, Sarah Rose. They're English."

"I don't want to talk about it." Sarah faced her sister and lowered her eyes. "I'm still processing the news. I'm having *zwilling-bopplin*, and my husband is gone."

"May I please pay for these?" the English woman asked with an unsure smile.

"Of course, ma'am." Sarah scurried from behind the bakery counter and over to the register by the door. She felt her sister's judgmental stare while she rang up the pastries and took the woman's money.

When the sale was complete, Sarah busied herself with arranging the items at the cashier's station. Feeling watched again, she glanced up to find her older sister studying her.

"You can talk to me," Kathryn said, her expression warming. "I know you're scared, but you must remember your family will see you through this." Kathryn took Sarah's hand in hers. "We love you, Sarah Rose, and we'll help you and the *kinner*."

Sarah's eyes filled with tears. "*Danki*." She hoped she wouldn't cry, not here in public.

"Excuse me, miss?" an English voice asked. "Do you have more whoopie pies?"

Saved by the Englisher! Sarah blew out a sigh of relief. While Kathryn helped the English woman, Sarah lost herself in organizing the postcard rack in an attempt to calm her anxiety.

❊

Sarah sipped a glass of cool water while gazing out over the field to where her nieces and nephews played at her parents' house.

Mamm squeezed Sarah's hand. "Before you know it, your *kinner* will be out there too."

"*Ya.*" Sarah touched her stomach and forced a smile. "Soon they will."

The clip-clop of a horse and crunch of buggy wheels on the drive stole Sarah's attention from her mother. "Who could that be?" she asked as the buggy headed for *Dat*'s barn.

"I think we have a visitor." Standing, *Mamm* patted Sarah's hand. "I'll get some iced tea." She stepped toward the door.

Glancing toward the barn, Sarah spotted Norman Zook chatting with her father and her brothers, and she smiled. Norman, who had lost his wife in childbirth a couple of years ago, had become a dear friend since she'd lost Peter. He seemed to be the only person in her church district who truly understood her grief.

Despite her protruding belly, she popped up to her feet and followed her mother through the door to the kitchen where they joined Beth Anne and Kathryn. It was only proper to have dessert when a guest visited.

"*Mamm*, do we still have some chocolate-chip cookies or cake left?"

"We have cookies." *Mamm* reached for a plate of cookies on the counter. "Let me put some on a tray for you."

"You have a visitor?" Beth Anne asked.

"*Ya*, Norman's here." Sarah lifted the tray of cookies.

"He's a *gut* man," Kathryn said with a smile.

"*Ya*," Beth Anne chimed in, coming to stand beside Kathryn. "He's a good *dat* too."

Sarah nodded. "He is, but we're just friends."

"Of course you are," *Mamm* agreed, pulled two glasses from the cabinet. "You two have a lot in common."

"It's *gut* to have a friend who understands," Rebecca said.

A slam yanked Sarah's attention to her brother, Daniel, standing with Norman by the back door. Norman's lips formed a tentative smile as his gaze met hers.

"Norman!" *Mamm* padded over to the widower. "It's *wunderbaar gut* to see you. Would you like to have a glass of iced tea on the porch?"

"*Danki*." Norman nodded. "That would be nice, Elizabeth." His eyes turned to Sarah. "How are you?"

"*Gut*." She held up the tray. "I hope you like chocolate-chip cookies."

"My favorite." He smiled.

Norman followed Daniel through the back door to the porch while *Mamm* grabbed the two glasses of iced tea from the counter. Sarah followed her out to the porch, where Norman sat on a chair next to the swing. His brown eyes met hers and then darted to the field where his children ran around, shrieking and playing with her nieces and nephews.

Sarah placed the tray of cookies on the small table in front of them and gingerly lowered herself into the swing.

"Here's some fresh-brewed iced tea," *Mamm* said, handing a glass to Norman. "Would you like a whoopie pie too? We have plenty left from the bakery. We always bring some leftovers home for the *kinner* to enjoy."

"No, *danki*." Smiling, Norman rested his hand on his abdomen. "We had a large dinner. I couldn't eat another crumb."

They sat in silence for a few moments, sipping their drinks, and Sarah relaxed. She appreciated their comfortable friendship. It was nice to not have someone telling her to let go of her grief. Norman understood her better than anyone, including her well-meaning family members.

"It's a beautiful evening," he said, breaking the silence.

"*Ya.* Beautiful. How was your day?" Sarah watched the youngest of Norman's four children, Gretchen and Marian, chase her nieces, and she wondered how the two girls were faring without their mother. Her chin trembled at the thought of children without a mother to cuddle and kiss them. His children were as needy without a mother as hers would be without their father.

"*Gut,*" he said. "How was yours?"

"Long but *gut.*" She absently rubbed her tummy, and her gaze moved to Norman, who was studying her.

"How are you feeling?" he asked, the warmth of his voice reflecting in his brown eyes.

The tenderness in his face caught her off guard, and for a moment she couldn't speak. "*Gut,*" she whispered. "I've been a bit tired, but that's to be expected."

"Your *mamm* mentioned you'd been to see the midwife recently."

"*Ya.*" She settled back in the swing.

"And it went well?" he asked.

"*Ya.*" She fingered the condensation on her glass. "I'm having *zwillingbopplin,* so I have to see a specialist now."

"*Zwillingbopplin.*" He smiled and pulled on his beard. "What a blessing. The Lord is *gut.*"

Sarah glanced down at her belly while her thoughts moved to Peter. How her heart cried for him now. She should be sitting on the porch discussing her pregnancy with him, not Norman.

"You will have your hands full when the *bopplin* arrive," he said, breaking through her musings.

"*Mamm* and I will manage," she said.

He was silent, and she glanced over to see him gazing at the children again, his mouth forming a thin line instead of the wide smile she'd seen moments ago. She assumed he was remembering the difficult time he'd had adjusting to single parenthood after Leah had died.

She lifted the glass to her dry lips and took a long gulp of the cool water.

While Norman made mundane small talk about the weather and his busy dairy farm, Sarah's mind turned to Peter and their courtship. She'd met him at a youth gathering when she was nineteen, and she was smitten the moment she laid eyes on his handsome face and gorgeous hazel eyes.

Peter was mysterious, explaining only that he'd been raised by an older Amish couple in Ohio after his parents died in an accident, and he had no siblings. He'd sold his adopted parents' farm to pay off their debts after they died and then moved to Lancaster when he was eighteen to be closer to his adopted father's brother, who lived in a neighboring Lancaster County town. After moving to Lancaster County, he had mostly kept to himself.

Sarah knew nothing more about his background, and she'd never met his uncle before Peter died. But it didn't matter to her. She'd quickly fallen madly in love with Peter.

They'd courted for two years while he gathered enough money to build a small house on her parents' farm. During that time, Peter went to work in her father's store, where he impressed her family with his carpentry skills.

Once their small home was built, they'd married. For the first year, Sarah felt as if she were living in a dream. Peter was loving and attentive, and they rarely quarreled. However, their second year of marriage was different. Sarah had wondered if Peter had changed or if she'd finally seen him for who he was— mysterious. She wondered if she'd ever truly known him during their courtship.

"Sarah? Are you all right?"

"*Ya.*" Sarah shook her head. "Sorry. I was lost in memories."

He gave an understanding smile. "Would you like to share them with me?"

"No, *danki*. But I appreciate it. You were saying?" she asked, hoping to bring his focus back to his discussion of his cows. Her memories were too personal to share out loud.

Norman explained the idiosyncrasies of his new cow while Sarah lost herself again in thoughts of her husband and the questions he'd left her.

In the weeks before Peter died, he'd become quiet, standoffish, almost cold to her. She'd tried several times to get him to talk to her and open up, but he was always too busy, rushing off to work or disappearing into the barn. She hadn't had a chance to uncover what was wrong before he'd died.

Turning her gaze across the field, her eyes fell on the home she and Peter had once shared. Memories crashed down on her like a tidal wave—she could see Peter pulling her by her hand over the threshold the spring after they were married. She remembered the first night they'd sat down to supper in the small kitchen, and she could still smell his musky scent and feel his warm, taut skin as they lay awake in each other's arms ...

"Sarah?"

She jumped, startled. Turning, she found Norman staring at her, his brown eyes full of concern. She flushed and covered her cheeks with her hands.

"Are you sure you're all right?" He touched her arm.

"*Ya*." Sarah cleared her throat and pushed away the painful memories of Peter.

"You looked as if you'd entered another world."

Nodding, Sarah stared down at her lap. "I supposed I had. I apologize for not hearing everything you said." Gazing up, her eyes locked with his, and guilt surged through her soul at the genuine worry shining in his eyes. "It was very rude of me to not listen to you."

A tentative smile curled Norman's lips. "You forget I lost *mei fraa*. I understand the pain you feel."

He leaned in closer, reaching for her and then pulling back. "If you ever need to, Sarah, you can talk to me. I know the pain and the loss you're facing. It's not easy. With the Lord's help, time will heal your wounds."

Overwhelmed by his kindness, Sarah teared up. "*Danki*, Norman."

He stood, gazing toward where the children played. "*Ack*, I suppose I should get these *kinner* home. School comes early in the morning."

"*Danki* for visiting." Sarah began to hoist herself up, and Norman motioned for her to remain seated.

"Please sit. I can find my way to my buggy." He patted her hand. "You take care. I'll visit with you soon."

"I look forward to it." Sarah cradled her belly while watching Norman gather up his children and say good-bye to her brothers and father. Her mind swirled with thoughts of his friendship. Norman was a kind man, and he was a good father to his children. Maybe someday soon she would feel comfortable enough to tell him how she felt about losing her husband. For now, she would enjoy his company and the easy conversation.

3

Luke stared out the window as the taxicab motored down Route 340 in Bird-in-Hand. He had submitted the paperwork for a leave of absence and set out to solve the mystery of what had happened to Peter.

He glanced around at the small stores—most of them Amish themed—and the old, modest homes. His stomach tightened with anticipation when the car slowed in front of a building displaying a sign that read Kauffman & Yoder Amish Furniture. It was the store a young man at the farmer's market had suggested Luke investigate since it was the only Amish-owned furniture store in the town.

After paying the driver, Luke fetched his bag from the floor and climbed from the car. Standing at the curb, he studied the one-story white building.

He took in a deep breath, inhaling the scent of fresh paint. It was a brand-new building, which caused him to doubt if this was the wrong furniture store. DeLana had made it sound as if Peter had worked in the store for a long time. Perhaps Luke should've asked the driver to wait until after he spoke to someone inside instead of going through the hassle of finding another cab if it turned out to be the wrong place.

A handwritten sign taped to the front window read Reopened. Please come in. He wondered if business had been booming so much that they added onto the shop.

Luke climbed the steps and wrenched open the front door, causing a bell to ring in announcement of his presence. Large windows lined the front of the shop, and the walls were covered in crisp, fresh white paint. He glanced around the open area, impressed with the quality of the sample pieces, including mirrored dressers, hope chests, entertainment centers, dining room sets, bed frames, wishing wells, end tables, and coffee tables. The familiar aroma of wood and stain permeated his nostrils. It smelled like home.

A long counter covered with piles of papers and catalogs sat at the far end of the room, blocking a doorway beyond which hammers, saws, and nail guns blasted while voices boomed in Pennsylvania *Dietsch*. Luke crossed the room, his boots scraping the floor.

A tall man stepped through the doorway. With blond hair and a blond beard, he stood an inch taller than Luke, approximately six one. His dark shirt, suspenders, and trousers were covered in dust and stains.

When his gaze met Luke's, he squinted as if to study Luke's countenance. Luke could've sworn he saw recognition flash for a split second in the man's eyes.

"*Wie geht's?*" the man asked. He extended his hand and gave a cautious smile.

Luke shook his hand. "*Gut*, and you?"

"*Gut, danki.*" The man swiped his hands across his shirt, setting off a cloud of dust. "Is there something I can help you with? Were you looking to order something? We've just reopened, so we're a bit backed up right now. However, if you're patient, we'd be happy to fill your order."

Pennsylvania *Dietsch* and nail guns continued to blast in the room behind him.

Luke cleared his throat and straightened his straw hat, mustering up the strength to ask about Peter. "Actually, I'm visiting from Ohio."

"Welcome to Bird-in-Hand." The man smiled. "What brings you here?"

"I'm taking some much-overdue vacation time." Luke yanked his straw hat from his head and fingered the brim.

"That's *wunderbaar*."

"I noticed your store has just reopened," Luke said. "Did you do some remodeling?"

"*Ya*." The man frowned, shaking his head. "We had to do some major reconstruction after the fire."

"You had a fire?"

"It was a tragic accident. One of our carpenters knocked over a lamp, igniting an oily rag. We lost everything." The man's gaze swept around the large room. "We had to completely rebuild."

"I'm sorry to hear that," Luke said. "When did it happen?"

"Nearly six months ago," the man said. "It's taken us a long time to get everything back on track with the shop. We're still sorting through missing orders."

"I was wondering if you know a man named Peter Troyer." Luke tightened his grip on the brim of the hat, anticipating the answer. "I heard he works in an Amish furniture store here in Bird-in-Hand."

"Peter Troyer?" The man's eyes widened. "Have you come here to see him?"

Luke nodded, his stomach tightening.

"I'm sorry, *mei freind*, but Peter perished in the fire."

Luke swallowed a gasp as bile rose in his throat. He fought to keep his emotions in check.

"It was a great tragedy." The man shook his head. "He was my brother-in-law."

"Your brother-in-law?" Despite his pain, Luke raised his eyebrows in surprise at the news Peter had been married.

"He was a *gut* man and husband. He also was one of our best carpenters."

Luke sucked in a breath, hoping to curb the surge of shock and grief coursing through him. "You own this shop?" he asked.

"It's a family business," the man said. "I'm Daniel Kauffman."

"It's nice to meet you. I'm Luke Troyer."

Daniel's eyes widened with shock. "Troyer? Was Peter your *freindschaft*?"

"*Ya*, he was my relative." Luke's voice was ragged with emotion.

Daniel's eyebrows knitted with confusion. "I didn't know Peter had relatives left in Ohio."

"He has relatives, mostly cousins," Luke said.

An older man, also covered in wood shaving dust, appeared in the doorway. He stepped through, followed by a man who resembled Daniel, only younger.

"Daniel, I thought Jake was running the front. Did he run to the supply yard again?" the older man asked.

"*Ya*, I think so. *Dat*, this is Luke Troyer." Daniel made a sweeping gesture toward Luke. "He's Peter's cousin visiting from Ohio. I just told him that we lost Peter in the fire." He turned to the older man. "This is my *dat*, Eli Kauffman."

Eli shook Luke's hand. "Welcome to Bird-in-Hand. Peter was a *gut* man. He was *gut* to my Sarah Rose."

"*Danki*." Luke blew out a trembling breath as the words sunk into his soul. Peter's wife was Sarah Rose—what a lovely name.

"This is my younger brother, Timothy," Daniel said, pointing to the younger man.

Luke held his hand out to Timothy, and the man hesitated before taking it. Luke thought he read shock and perhaps worry in Timothy's eyes.

Daniel patted Luke's shoulder. "Would you like to meet my sister? She can tell you more about Peter's life here in Bird-in-Hand."

Unable to speak, Luke nodded, grappling with the news Peter was dead and had left behind a widow.

"Let's take Luke over to the bakery. I'll go tell Elmer that we're leaving," Eli said, nodding toward the entrance to the shop.

❀

Sarah handed an English woman her fistful of change. After thanking the woman, she leaned back on the counter behind her and groaned in response to her throbbing temples.

"You look tired." Kathryn rested her hand on Sarah's shoulder. "You should go sit. I can walk you home if you'd like. You need to take it easy for the babies."

Sarah shifted her weight on her aching feet. "I'll be fine. It's almost time for my lunch break."

"Excuse me." An English woman approached the counter. "Do you have any shoofly pie? I just love it. I'm heading back to Jersey this afternoon, and I promised my husband I'd bring him home a few pieces."

Smiling, Kathryn stepped over to the customer. "I believe we have some over here." She nodded toward the end of the counter. "How many pieces would you like?"

While her sister and the customer moved to the other end of the long counter, Sarah sighed and leaned forward. Her feet throbbed, and her head pounded. Kathryn's offer to walk her home was tempting.

But being alone in the house wasn't relaxing.

When Sarah was alone, memories of Peter overtook her, filling her heart with sorrow and regret. Remaining at the bakery and helping English tourists kept Sarah busy and silenced her numbing thoughts.

The whoosh of the door pulled Sarah from her mental tirade. Daniel stepped through the doorway, followed by Timothy, *Dat*, and another man. Timothy's face was creased with a frown, causing her to wonder why her brother was out of sorts. The men stopped to speak with *Mamm*, who was standing across the room with a frequent English customer.

The mysterious stranger pushed his straw hat back a fraction of an inch on his brown hair. His eyes scanned the bakery, and Sarah fixated on his clean-shaven face.

Her breath caught in her throat as she took in his familiar countenance. His cheekbones, the shape of his eyes and nose, and his complexion all mirrored Peter's. It was as though she were looking at her husband's face before they were married and he grew his beard.

Sarah gripped the counter and sucked in a breath while studying the stranger's tall, lanky build, wide chest, and broad shoulders. Even his physique and light-brown hair resembled her late husband's. He looked to be six feet tall, like Peter.

Dat said something to the man, and he turned and greeted *Mamm* with a smile.

Her heart hammered in her chest, and she cupped a hand to her burning face. Was she dreaming or had God raised Peter in response to her prayer?

"Sometimes I wish our English customers would open their eyes," Kathryn muttered in Pennsylvania *Dietsch*, coming up to Sarah. "The pie was right in front of her face, but I had to lead her to it. Then I had to hear the story of her life, and how she—"

"Kathryn," Sarah's voice came in a strangled whisper. She gripped her sister's apron and yanked her over, causing her to stumble. "Do you see that man over there talking to *Mamm*?"

"Sarah Rose?" Kathryn's blue eyes were wide with worry. "Are you okay? You're so pale. Sit." She took Sarah's clammy hands and pulled her toward a stool. "I'll call *Mamm* over here, and we'll take you home so you can rest."

"No!" Sarah wrenched her hands back and gestured toward the stranger, who was chatting with the others across the bakery. "Look at him, Kathryn. Please!"

Kathryn's eyebrows careened toward her blonde hairline as her gaze followed Sarah's pointed finger.

"Tell me I'm seeing Peter. Tell me God raised him like He raised Lazarus." Sarah wiped the tears that were suddenly escaping down her hot cheeks and wished her heart would stop pounding against her rib cage.

"He does favor Peter a little." Frowning, Kathryn took Sarah's hand in hers. "Sweet Sarah Rose, Peter has gone to be with the Lord and won't come back. I'm sorry."

Sarah swallowed a sob. In her mind, she knew her sister was right, but that man looked like Peter. Taking a deep breath, she willed her tears to stop flowing. "I think I need to get some air," she said. "Will you take care of the customers for me?"

"Of course." Kathryn's lips formed a sad smile. "Tell Beth Anne to come out front, and I'll walk you home."

"I'll be fine," Sarah whispered before racing through the kitchen, past her sister, and out the back door.

She wiped her eyes as she approached the small fenced-in play area where Lindsay sat with her nieces and nephews. Leaning on the fence, Sarah wished she could stop the pain strangling her heart. She prayed her soul would heal and stop playing cruel tricks on her, such as spotting Peter in the bakery. Hadn't she suffered enough without having hallucinations?

"*Aenti* Sarah?" Lindsay asked, stepping over to the fence. "Are you okay?"

Sarah nodded. "It's been a long morning. I needed to step out to get some air."

Lindsay reached for her. "Do you need help?"

Sarah shook her head. "No. *Danki.*"

The children ran around playing tag and swinging on the elaborate wooden swing set that her brothers and father had built. Sarah contemplated the two babies growing inside her, wondering what they would look like and how much they would remind her of Peter. Would the sight of her newborns cause her more heartache or would they give her the comfort she craved?

"Sarah Rose?" a voice behind her called.

Turning, she faced her mother standing in the doorway.

"Would you please come here?" *Mamm* asked, her pretty face distraught.

Sarah headed for the door, wondering what had upset her mother. She hoped Kathryn hadn't told their mother that she was having a breakdown. The last thing she needed was another lecture about allowing Peter to rest in peace. It was much easier said than done.

Mamm stepped out onto the concrete. When the mysterious man followed her, Sarah stopped, frozen in place as she assessed him. He seemed to study her also, his brown eyes fixed on her as he sauntered toward her, the swing of his arms echoing Peter's movements.

Sarah remained cemented in place, feeling as though her shoes were sinking in quicksand. Her mouth dried, and her heart thumped madly in her chest. Was she hallucinating again, or was this man who resembled Peter advancing toward her?

Mamm and the man stopped near Sarah, and Sarah's gaze never left his. While Peter's eyes had been a deep hazel, the mystery man's were the color of mocha, reminding her of the milk-chocolate pies she loved to bake.

"This is Luke Troyer," *Mamm* said, breaking through Sarah's reverie. "Peter's cousin."

Sarah gasped and clasped her mother's arm to steady herself. She opened her mouth to speak, but no sound escaped. After clearing her throat, she tried again. "That's impossible," she whispered. "Peter had no family. There must be some mistake. *Troyer* is a common Amish name."

"He was my kin," Luke said. "His full name was Peter Jacob Troyer, and he was born on May 25 in Middlefield, Ohio. He had a strawberry birthmark on his upper left shoulder blade, and he was a talented carpenter."

Sarah's hands trembled as she stared into Luke's deep brown eyes. In her heart, she knew he was telling the truth, but doubt still filtered through her mind.

But why would Peter lie?

She wondered if this man who claimed to be Peter's relative was really just someone posing as a Troyer in order to gain something. But what could he be after?

"Anyone could've confirmed that information," Sarah said, hoping to sound more confident than she felt. "That doesn't prove you're his *Freindschaft*."

He folded his arms across his broad chest. "Your brothers and father agree there's a family resemblance between Peter and me."

Unable to disagree, Sarah nodded.

"I'll leave you two alone to talk," *Mamm* said, her voice shaking with emotion. She disappeared into the bakery.

Sarah opened her mouth to protest her mother's desertion and then stopped. She cut her eyes to the tentative smile growing on Luke Troyer's lips, and her body tensed.

Suddenly her mother's favorite verse from Romans 12 echoed in her mind: *"Be joyful in hope, patient in affliction, faithful in prayer."*

She bit her lip while the words soaked through her being. Was Luke the source of hope she'd been begging God to send her?

No!

The internal response sent a jolt through her soul. He couldn't be the tranquility she craved. Having Luke here sent her already-crumbling confidence sinking into a black hole of doubt.

Who was this man? Why was he here when Peter had said he had no family left in Ohio?

She put her hand to her throbbing temples. "This is all too much," she muttered.

"Sarah Rose?" He stepped toward her. "Are you all right?" He held a hand out to her.

"Please don't touch me." She took a step back.

His eyes widened with shock, and he raised his hands. "I'm sorry. I didn't mean to make you feel uncomfortable."

"This is just a lot to take in." She gestured toward him. "I'm feeling a bit overwhelmed."

He glanced back toward the bakery and then at her. "Would you like to go for a walk?"

She hesitated and then nodded. "I guess it would be okay for a few minutes, but then I need to get back to work."

"That sounds fair."

FASTNACHTS (RAISED DONUTS)

2 cups milk
1/3 cup lard
3/4 cup sugar
1–1/2 tsp salt
2 eggs
1 yeast cake/package
1–1/2 Tbsp warm water
About 7 cups sifted flour
Oil for frying
Powdered sugar

Bring milk and lard to boiling point, but do not boil. Stir in sugar and salt and let cool to lukewarm. Beat eggs and add to the mixture. Soak yeast cake in warm water and keep warm. Sift and measure the flour. Combine yeast and mixture. Add enough flour until able to handle easily. Knead well by stretching and folding it over itself. Let rise overnight.

The following day roll dough out to 1/4–inch thickness. Cut into 2–inch squares and make a slit in the center. Cover and let rise for 45 minutes. Fry in deep fat until brown. While warm, roll in powdered sugar.

4

Timothy glanced out the kitchen window to where Sarah Rose and Luke stood talking. He gritted his teeth and swallowed a groan.

This can't be happening!

Ever since Peter's death, Timothy had worried he'd be caught in the lie of knowing about Peter's past. Now with this relative from Ohio showing up, the truth would be revealed, making Timothy look like a liar. His stomach roiled as he paced around the kitchen in front of his siblings.

"What's wrong with you?" Kathryn asked. "You got ants in your pants?"

While his siblings snickered, Timothy huffed. "We've got to be careful of this man. We can't know who he is for sure, and he's only going to upset Sarah Rose by bringing up the past—a past that Peter can't defend."

Daniel's brows furrowed with question. "What are you saying?"

Timothy gulped. *I said too much.* "I just meant that this man is coming at the worst possible time. Sarah Rose is in a very delicate condition. We don't need her upset right now. How can we even be sure he's truly Peter's *freindschaft*?"

"He's family," Beth Anne said. "You can see it in his eyes. He's a Troyer in search of other Troyers."

37

"Timothy has a point." Kathryn tapped her finger on the counter. "Why would he suddenly show up after his cousin is dead? Is he going to take advantage of Sarah in her fragile state?"

Timothy swallowed a sigh of relief. *Danki, Kathryn! Finally someone is listening to me.*

"No, he won't take advantage of her or upset her." Timothy crossed his arms. "I won't allow it. I'll watch him like a hawk. He needs to tend to his business and then leave."

"You're overreacting," Daniel said, raising his hands to calm Timothy. "We don't know if he's a liar, and we don't know what he's after. We need to give him a chance."

"We need to protect Sarah," Kathryn said. "She's still grieving for her husband."

Daniel lowered himself onto a stool. "He didn't even know Peter was married. I saw surprise in his eyes when I told him Peter had a widow."

"*Ya*, he seems genuine," Beth Anne said. "I'm a good judge of character."

Timothy shook his head. His siblings were always too quick to trust people. He knew all about how liars operated. Miriam Lapp, his ex-fiancée, had proved that when she shattered his trust along with his heart. He needed to make sure that Luke left and left soon, before he hurt Sarah Rose or, worse yet, convinced her to come to Ohio with him to be with the rest of the Troyer family. Sarah needed to be with the Kauffmans, not the Troyers.

"He could be a good actor," Timothy said. "People like that take you by surprise."

Meeting his gaze, Kathryn nodded with understanding. "*Ya*. It's the truth."

Beth Anne waved them off with a frown. "You two were always the skeptics of the family."

"And rightfully so," Timothy said, turning his stare toward the door. "I'll make sure he doesn't hurt Sarah. She's been through enough, and it's our job to protect her."

❁

Luke fell in step with Sarah as they moved across the parking lot toward a pasture beyond the bakery. He closed his eyes for a split second, checking to see if he'd been dreaming. However, when his eyes reopened, the blonde was still walking beside him, the sweet aromas of the bakery emanating from her like an invisible cloud. Luke shook his head with astonishment at the revelation.

Sarah was beautiful. No, she was stunning, almost angelic. Her skin was porcelain, and the hair peeking from beneath her prayer *kapp* was honey blonde, even lighter than her siblings'. Her eyes were powder blue and her lips a deep pink. When she spoke, her voice was soft and sweet, reminding him of the treats lining the counters and shelves inside the bakery.

He couldn't help but wonder how Peter had managed to court and marry such a delicate beauty.

Jealousy bubbled up inside of him. While Luke had put his own life on hold, Peter had managed to sweet-talk his way into this close family and win himself a lovely bride.

Somehow life didn't seem fair.

Sarah stood straight as an arrow, as if she were marching to her death. He could feel anxiety radiating from her.

"Peter never spoke of relatives in Ohio," she said, breaking the silence between them. "If I had known about you, I would've contacted you in time for the funeral. I'm sorry you missed it."

"It's not your fault. Daniel told me Peter claimed he didn't have any family." His eyes moved to her hands, folded across her abdomen, and he stopped short. He'd noticed her shape earlier, but the meaning of her size hadn't registered with him until that moment.

Peter was expecting a child.

No, life wasn't fair. Now Peter was gone, leaving a widow who would soon be a single mother.

"*Zwillingbopplin*," she whispered, her blue eyes full of sadness. "Our first *kinner*."

While it made his pulse kick with joy at the notion that he would still have family, a quick look at her face reminded him of her grief. "*Zwillingbopplin*," he repeated. "Sarah Rose, I'm so sorry for your loss."

She nodded, glancing down at her stomach. "I am too." Her gaze collided with his again, her crystal eyes hardening. "Why would Peter not tell me about his family? It doesn't make sense. Family is the most important thing of all—aside from God, of course."

Luke scanned the pasture while collecting his thoughts. He couldn't tell her the truth. It would hurt her too much, and her condition was already delicate at best. He could tell by the sadness and anger in her eyes that his mere presence had rocked her to her very core.

It was best to just tell her what she needed to know, which was very little.

He spotted a wooden park bench near the fence that closed off a few horses from the open pasture. "Let's sit and talk, so you can get off your feet," he said.

They walked together. After she slowly lowered herself onto the bench, he sank down beside her. She smoothed the black apron over her black dress, a sign of mourning. When his eyes met hers, his heart sank at the hurt and turmoil he found there. He vowed not to tell her anything that would upset her. Her condition was paramount.

"What did Peter tell you about his past?" Luke asked.

"He said his parents, Hezekiah and Ruth Troyer, died when he was young and an older couple named Abner and Clara Yoder raised him." She stared down at her hands. "And he didn't have any siblings. He moved here after his adoptive parents had died. He sold the family farm to pay off their debts and then came to Lancaster County to be closer to his Uncle Ephraim, who lives in a neighboring town. I never met his uncle, but I understood he was the only family Peter had left."

Luke resisted the urge to shake his head with disappointment. Peter wasn't an orphan and had been raised by his biological parents.

"And Peter came to work for the family furniture store?" Luke prompted her to move on with her story.

"*Ya.* My *dat* was very happy with his work." Sarah's eyes glistened. She cleared her throat and placed her hands back on her belly. "Peter said his foster father taught him how to make cabinets."

"How did you meet Peter?" he asked.

Her expression softened, her eyes reflecting happy memories. "He had joined the church in Ohio, but he became a member of our church district since he quickly made friends here. We met at a singing one Sunday night. He offered to take me home, and I told him no since I didn't know him. But he pursued me." She laughed. "He was relentless. He actually got a job at my father's shop in order to get to know me. It took about six months, but I finally agreed to see him."

"Why were you so unsure of him?"

"He was new to our church district."

"When did you marry?"

"Two years later. Peter wanted to save money. We built a house on my *dat*'s land, and we moved in the spring after we married." She sighed, her smile fading. "He wanted a big family. At first, we didn't think God wanted us to have *kinner*. I only just found out we were having *zwillingbopplin* after he died. He never knew."

He stared across the pasture, wondering what kind of parent Peter would've been.

"Sarah Rose!" A strident voice behind them caused them both to jump.

Turning, Luke found Timothy charging toward them, his

expression serious. He wondered if the guy ever smiled or if he was a constant killjoy.

"Timothy?" Sarah asked. "What's wrong?"

"I think you should come back inside and rest," her brother said.

"I'm sitting on a bench, Timothy. I think I'm resting just fine." Holding her back, she hoisted herself up. Her brother reached out to help her, and she swatted his hand away. "I'm fine. Don't suffocate me!"

Luke bit back a smile at her feistiness. Not only was she beautiful, but she was also strong.

"*Mamm* says we should offer our guest something to eat," Timothy said.

She faced Luke. "Are you hungry? Would you like some lunch?"

He stood. "That sounds nice."

"Let's go find you some of my famous pork chops and scalloped potatoes," she said. "*Mamm* and I brought it for lunch today. It was left over from last night."

As they strolled back toward the bakery, Timothy motioned for Luke to hang back with him. "Your being here is not the best timing," he said through gritted teeth. "My sister has been through enough after losing her husband."

Luke flinched at the sting of the words. "I'm not going to do anything to upset her. I'm just trying to find out what happened to Peter."

"I can tell you what happened. He passed away, and now we're all trying to pick up the pieces. My sister doesn't need you here upsetting her. She didn't know Peter had a life outside of Lancaster County, and you're opening up a can of worms that doesn't matter anymore." Timothy scowled. "I think it would be best if you just left. Peter is gone, and we'll take good care of her. We don't need you or the rest of your family."

Luke studied Timothy's expression. "So you know about Peter's past?"

"I know enough. If Sarah finds out, it will crush her." He lowered his voice. "I'm going to watch your every move. My concern is my sister and her welfare. Don't do anything that will upset her. If you do, then my brothers and I will escort you to the train station and send you on your way fast enough to make your head spin."

Raising his eyebrows, Luke nodded. "I understand."

Stepping into the kitchen, Luke wondered how close Timothy had been to Peter.

More important, just how much did Timothy know about Peter's past?

❋

Sarah stepped back into the kitchen after serving lunch to Luke, Daniel, and her father on the porch outside the bakery. Worry and doubt played havoc with her emotions. She felt as if the very ground beneath her feet was shaking with the uncertainty in her heart. Who was Luke Troyer and why had he shown up now, nearly six months after Peter had died?

But the question haunting her the most was why, oh why, hadn't Peter told her he had family in Ohio? What else had he hidden from her?

Sarah had trusted Peter with her very heart and soul. Why would he lie to her?

Since she was a little girl, Sarah had dreamt of having a loving marriage modeled after her parents, who had met young and fallen head over heels in love with each other. She believed with all of her heart that there should be no secrets between a husband and a wife.

Hadn't Peter felt the same way?

Pushing the hurtful questions away, Sarah poured herself a cold glass of water from the pitcher in the refrigerator. After taking a long drink, she set the glass down on the counter. When a hand gripped her arm, she jumped, startled. She turned to face Timothy frowning at her.

"Why didn't you announce yourself?" she snapped with a glare. "I can't stand it when you sneak up on me."

"Sorry." He shifted his straw hat and wiped sweat from his brow.

"Why aren't you outside eating lunch with the rest of the men?"

"I wanted to speak with you alone." He scanned the bakery and then nodded toward the door. "Let's go outside for a minute."

Shaking her head with impatience, Sarah followed him out to the parking lot. "What's so important that we have to step outside? I have baking to do. You may get a day to goof off, but I actually work."

"This is important." Timothy leaned against the fence. "I want you to be cautious of Luke."

"Why?" Sarah's stomach roiled at the seriousness of her brother's words. She couldn't handle more distressing news of Peter's past. "What do you know about him?"

He shrugged. "It's just a feeling I have. I don't want you to upset yourself. You need to concentrate on the *bopplin* right now, not what some stranger from Ohio says."

He glanced across the pasture, and she wondered why he was avoiding eye contact with her.

"Timothy, is there something you're not telling me?" She studied his face, waiting for his gaze to meet hers, but he kept his eyes focused on the ground and kicked a pebble. "Please look at me."

Sighing, his eyes met hers. "Sarah, I'm just worried about you, is all."

She pursed her lips and studied him. Something was bothering her brother, and she was determined to get him to confess to her. "You haven't smiled once since you came into the bakery today. Has Luke upset you?"

He shook his head and repeated himself. "I'm just worried about you."

"You're not being forthright," she said. "You were Peter's best friend, Timothy, and, besides me, you knew him best."

He glanced across the pasture.

"Timothy? What is it?" She braced herself for his response. *Please, not more upsetting news about Peter's past.*

He touched her arm and trained his eyes on hers. "Sarah Rose, I miss Peter, and I also feel it's my duty to make sure you're well taken care of. I just don't want Luke to upset you or the *kinner*. That's all."

Sarah searched her brother's eyes for any hint of a lie and couldn't shake the feeling he wasn't being completely open with her.

"Sarah!" Beth Anne called. "Can you help me with this chocolate cake?"

Walking slowly back toward the bakery, Sarah sucked in a deep breath. A headache pulsed in her temple, and her body quaked with hurt and worry.

Closing her eyes, she sent up a prayer. *Please God, lead me to the truth about my husband's past. Give me faith in my future, and help me figure out who Luke Troyer is and why he's here now.*

5

Sarah's hands trembled as she puttered around her mother's kitchen later that evening. While she chopped lettuce for salad, her mind whirled with confusion caused by the afternoon spent with Luke Troyer. She kept asking herself why Peter would've claimed to be an orphan when he had family living in Ohio. Why would Peter want to hide his identity from Sarah, his wife? She and Peter had pledged to share all of their secrets and be loyal to each other.

Mamm opened the oven door, and the aroma of juicy meat-loaf penetrated the warm kitchen, tickling Sarah's taste buds.

"I think it's just about done," *Mamm* said, closing the door.

Sarah nodded and scraped the lettuce into a large bowl.

"You've hardly said a word for the last hour, Sarah Rose," her mother said, wiping her hands on her apron. "Meeting Luke has to be difficult for you. You know you can talk to me, *mei Liewe*."

"I don't know what to think, *Mamm*. Everything is a big, jumbled mess. I don't understand why Peter would tell me he had no family in Ohio if it wasn't true. I don't know how to feel. But I do know that I'm hurt." Sarah's eyes flooded with tears. "Why did he lie to me, *Mamm*? Why couldn't he trust me, his wife, with the truth?"

"Oh, Sarah Rose." *Mamm* opened her arms, and Sarah folded herself into her mother's warm hug as the tears fell. "I'm so sorry you're going through this. But remember we all love you. Perhaps God sent Luke here to help you through the rest of the pregnancy."

Sniffing, Sarah looked up at *Mamm*. "What do you mean, 'help me through the rest of the pregnancy'? How could some stranger who claims to be Peter's relative help me through a pregnancy?"

Mamm pushed back a lock of hair that had escaped Sarah's prayer *kapp*. "The Lord may have plans for you and Luke to become friends and help each other through your loss."

Sarah wiped her eyes and nose with a napkin. "How do I know he's truly family? Peter said he had no family and then this mysterious man shows up months after his death. He knows Peter's middle name and his birth date. He even knows Peter had a birthmark on his shoulder blade. But that doesn't prove anything! A former schoolmate would know those things."

Leaning back on the counter, Sarah covered her mouth to stifle a sob. The confusion swelling in her mind was making her crazy. She wished life would return to normal, and that Peter would bound through the front door with a smile and kiss for her. *Ack*, she would even be happy to hear him fuss at her for forgetting to mend his favorite shirt or for burning supper.

"*Mei liewe*," *Mamm* began, rubbing Sarah's arm. "I think you know in your heart that he's family. Just look at his face, and you'll see the truth." She nodded toward the window above the sink. "See for yourself."

Sarah gazed out the window to where Luke stood with Timothy and *Dat*. She agreed Luke resembled her late husband, but the resemblance didn't answer the questions burning in her heart.

"But Peter said he didn't have any family." Sarah watched *Dat* pat Luke on the shoulder and laugh, and her heart thumped in her chest. This mysterious man was already worming his way into her family, and his presence nipped at her nerves. Was he a symbol of the untruths Peter had told her? Had she ever known her husband at all if he would lie about his family?

"Why would he show up now?" she asked, her voice trembling like a leaf in a gusty autumn wind. She grasped for someone to take the blame for her husband's dishonesty and settled on Luke. "What is Luke after? Does he want some of our land? Or does he want money?"

Mamm chuckled. "I doubt that. It isn't our way to go around looking for money after a *freindschaft* dies."

Biting her lip, she faced her mother, needing her reassurance and guidance. "Do you think my husband lied to me when he said he was an orphan?"

Mamm sighed while straightening the ties on Sarah's prayer *kapp*. "I don't know. Luke brings up some unanswered questions. Why would a husband deceive his wife about his family? What would be the purpose in that?"

"I can't imagine a reason to do that to me." Sarah swiped at a wayward tear, her voice still quaking. "If he could lie to me about that, then he could've lied to me about anything and everything. It's not fair that I can't ask him. Why did God have to take Peter when he was so young and in the prime of his life?"

Mamm shook her head. "I promise we'll get through this. The Lord will see you through. Remember Nahum 1:7: 'The Lord is good, a refuge in times of trouble. He cares for those who trust in him.'"

Sarah nodded, hoping her mother was right and that her emotions would calm before she had to sit at the supper table with this mysterious visitor.

❋

Luke followed Timothy and Eli into the kitchen, which included a large gas oven, beautifully crafted cabinets, and a magnificent hutch in the corner. He assumed Eli had built the hutch and maybe even the cabinets; they were the products of a master carpenter.

The two men sat at the long table in the center of the large room, Eli at the far end and Timothy to his right. Timothy shot Luke another cool glance, causing Luke to wonder what Peter had said about him. Was Timothy simply overprotective of his younger sister due to her delicate condition, or had Peter told lies about Luke's character and integrity?

His attention turned to the savory smells penetrating the room. The fragrance of meatloaf awakened his appetite, causing his stomach to growl in response. He cleared his throat, hoping to shield his rude body in front of his new friends.

"I hope you like meatloaf," Elizabeth said, placing a pan on the table.

"It smells *appeditlich*," Luke said. "*Danki.*"

"Don't thank me," Elizabeth said. "Thank Sarah Rose. She's the talented chef in the family." She smiled with pride toward her daughter.

Sarah shook her head as she handed a bowl of salad to her father. "Don't be *gegisch*, *Mamm*. You taught me everything I know." After calling her mother silly, her eyes met Luke's and then quickly darted away. "Have a seat," she muttered, nodding toward the chair next to her brother.

"*Danki*," he said, wondering if she was always shy or if his presence made her uncomfortable. He hoped he hadn't overstepped his bounds with Peter's family. Jealousy bubbled up inside him at the thought.

Did Peter even realize how lucky he was to have a family like this?

Ack, what Luke would've given to be surrounded by a large, loving family like the Kauffmans.

The women finished delivering the various dishes, then sat. Luke bowed his head in silent prayer along with the rest of the family and looked up when the sounds of cutlery banging against the dinnerware broke through the silence. He began to fill his plate, putting each entree on a different corner of the dish in order to prevent the food from touching — a habit he'd learned from his father when he was young. When he felt someone's eyes boring into him, he glanced across the table to find Sarah staring at his plate. Her gaze met his, and her eyes widened with astonishment.

Luke chuckled in response to her disbelief. "It's an old habit."

She nodded, the blood draining from her pretty face.

"You all right, Sarah Rose?" Eli asked, his face full of concern. "You look like you've seen a ghost."

She blinked and lifted her glass of water to her lips. Elizabeth whispered something, and Sarah averted her eyes to her plate. Luke wished he could read Sarah's mind. He hoped he wasn't the cause of her distress. Like Timothy, he was concerned for her welfare.

"How long do you plan to stay in Bird-in-Hand, Luke?" Eli asked, slapping mashed potatoes onto his plate.

"I'm not certain." Luke stabbed his meatloaf. "I thought I'd stay at least a couple of weeks to learn about Peter's life." In his peripheral vision he spotted Sarah watching him. When he looked up, she quickly glanced back at her plate. He wished she would look at him. He couldn't bear making her uncomfortable in her parents' home.

"Do you have a place to stay?" Elizabeth asked.

Luke shrugged. "I figured I'd find something out on that main highway. What is it—Route 30?"

"Route 30 out by the English tourists?" Eli asked. "Don't be ridiculous. We have plenty of room here."

Covering her mouth, Sarah began to sputter and choke.

"Sarah Rose?" Elizabeth leaned over and held her hands while her daughter continued to cough, tears streaming down her porcelain cheeks. "Lean forward," she ordered. Once she moved, Elizabeth rubbed her back. "It's all right. Just breathe easy."

After a few deep breaths, the coughing subsided.

"Take a drink," Elizabeth said.

"Are you all right?" Luke asked.

Sarah nodded. "Something went down the wrong way."

Her glance met his for a split second, and he saw something

flash deep in her eyes—sadness or perhaps loneliness. Luke stood and picked up her glass from the table.

"What are you doing?" Sarah asked, her voice laced with annoyance.

"Refilling your glass," he said, wrenching open the refrigerator door.

"You're our guest," Sarah said. "You're supposed to sit while I refill your glass."

Luke topped off the drink and brought it back to her. "A simple thank you would suffice." He then returned to his seat.

Sarah studied Luke while Eli snickered.

"He told you, daughter," Eli said.

Sarah shot her father an evil look while Luke grinned. *Ack*, she was beautiful, especially when she was angry.

Turning toward Timothy, Luke found the man glaring at him. Luke cleared his throat and turned his attention back to his plate. He had crossed a line and gotten a cold stare for the effort. But he sure didn't regret it.

"I was thinking you could stay here," Eli repeated. "It would be wasteful to spend money on a motel when we have so much room."

Out of the corner of his eye, Luke spotted Sarah shooting her father a look of horror. His heart twisted with disappointment. He couldn't fault Sarah for being upset after hearing Peter had lied to her. However, he'd hoped they could somehow forge a friendship. He longed to be a part of her twins' lives, since they were his closest link to Peter.

Luke met Sarah's disapproving stare as he responded to her father. "Thank you for your hospitality, Eli, but I think it would be best if I stayed in a hotel."

Sarah's gaze was unmoving, challenging him. She sure was a feisty one!

"I won't allow you to waste your money," Elizabeth retorted. "You'll stay here. Why doesn't he stay at your house, Sarah

Rose? It's been empty for six months now, and I'm sure the walls would enjoy some company."

Gasping, Sarah turned to her *Mamm*. "My house?" she asked. "The house that Peter built for us?"

"*Ya*," Elizabeth said.

The women exchanged expressions, a silent and private conversation, before Sarah faced him again. "I'd be happy to host you," she deadpanned. "Please stay at my house."

"Are you certain?" Luke raised an eyebrow.

Sarah nodded and returned her attention to her supper.

"Where did you say you worked in Ohio?" Eli asked.

"A cabinet shop near my home," Luke said.

"Tell us about it," Eli said.

Luke swallowed a piece of juicy meatloaf and then told the Kauffmans about his life back home.

❀

"How could you do that to me?" Sarah snapped while scrubbing a pot after supper. "How could you put me on the spot like that?"

"Whatever are you going on about?" *Mamm* asked, wiping off the table.

"What makes you think I want that man sleeping in my house?" Sarah shook her head and rinsed the detergent off the pot. "That was our house! The house I shared with my beloved Peter. I don't need that stranger—"

"He's not a stranger." Her mother's voice was calm.

"Yes, he is!" Sarah threw down the towel for emphasis. "I don't need him coming in here and stirring things up while I'm trying to create a life for my *zwillingbopplin*."

"He was Peter's family, so that makes him the *zwillingbopplin's* family too."

"How do you really know that?" Sarah propped her hands on her hips. "What proof do you have?"

A smile curved *Mamm's* lips. "I know you saw it at supper. I witnessed the shock on your face."

Sarah shook her head. "I don't know what you're talking about."

"Sarah Rose, don't lie to me." *Mamm* wagged her slim finger. "You know exactly what I'm talking about. *Dat* even asked you what was wrong. He asked you if you'd seen a ghost."

Sarah gulped, knowing she'd been caught in a fib. "I did see it," she whispered. "He separated his food so it wouldn't touch."

"Peter did that at every meal I shared with him." Crossing the kitchen, *Mamm* pointed out the window. "Look at him, Sarah Rose. Tell me you don't see similarities in the way he walks and holds himself."

Licking her dry lips, Sarah turned her attention to the field where Luke stood by the barn, chatting with *Dat* and Timothy. Luke held onto his suspenders as he listened to *Dat*. Before speaking, he lifted his hat and smoothed back his hair.

"Peter always did that," she whispered, her voice croaking with emotion and memories. "He'd hold onto his suspenders and then smooth his hair when he was trying to remember something." Tears filled her eyes. "*Dat* was right when he asked me if I'd seen a ghost. I have seen one, and he's standing right there with my brother and *Dat*."

Mamm rubbed her back. "Embrace him as a friend. He's a connection to your Peter."

Sarah wiped her eyes. "But if I embrace him, then I embrace the knowledge that my marriage to Peter was a lie, *Mamm*," she whispered. "Don't you see how his presence here is breaking my heart? How do I know I married a man named Peter Troyer? His real name could've been something completely different. Maybe he was really an English man posing as an Amish man to run from indiscretions he committed in his former life."

Mamm pulled her into a hug. "Peter was a *gut* man with a *gut* heart. Hold onto the happy memories, Sarah Rose. He's gone, but you know he loved you and loved your *kinner*."

"But he lied," Sarah said, resting her chin on *Mamm's* shoulder as she'd done as a little girl.

"There must've been a reason. I don't want to believe the worst."

Standing up tall, Sarah swiped her hand over her hot cheeks. "Neither do I, but the lies are here in the flesh of that man who looks like Peter and shares his mannerisms. How can I come to terms with that when it's staring me in the face? And how do I know my whole marriage wasn't a sham?"

Elizabeth took Sarah's hands in hers. "I don't have the answers, but I do know one thing for certain: Peter loved you. I could see it in his eyes every time he looked at you, Sarah Rose. I don't know why he would be dishonest with you, but I know his heart belonged to you and only you." She nodded toward the sink. "I'll finish the dishes. You go wash your face, then take Luke over to your house. Let him see where Peter lived and tell him about your life with him."

Sarah heaved a deep breath and headed toward the bathroom.

6

With her heart pounding, Sarah gripped the knob to the front door of the house she and Peter had shared for three short years. For a split second, she wished she'd taken Timothy up on his offer to accompany her and Luke to the house. However, she couldn't depend on her family to shield her from the pain for the rest of her life. She had to do this in order to start down the road to healing her shattered heart, for the sake of the twins.

Her soul swelled with grief when she pushed the door open and stared at the modest living room furniture on which she and her husband would sit and talk late into the evenings.

A husband who lied to me about his family!

Sarah closed her eyes. She couldn't deal with that now. She had to get through showing Luke the house. After a tour, she would retreat to her old room in her mother's house and try to sort through the stress of the day caused by the mysterious visitor.

Luke stepped past her into the room and dropped his duffel bag onto the floor with a loud thud. "Your house is real nice," he said, scanning the room. He sauntered to the doorway separating the living room from the kitchen and ran his long fingers over the molding. "Simple, but every piece fits perfectly. The moldings fit as if they were carved out of the wall. Peter's work. I'd know it anywhere."

Sarah rubbed her belly as Luke examined the baseboards. His mannerisms were so familiar. The way his hands swept lightly over the woodwork while he frowned, deep in thought, and how he rubbed his chin and squinted his eyes—it was so much like Peter that she almost felt her late husband's presence.

Sarah cleared her throat and crossed the room. "The kitchen is small, but I liked it." She gestured toward the oak cabinets. "He made them himself."

"*Wunderbaar.*" Luke rubbed the cabinets as if they were velvety-soft kittens. "Nice craftsmanship. I always told him he could open his own cabinet shop, but he wanted to concentrate on furniture. An uncle taught him how to make tables, chairs, and bed frames. Peter was a master at it."

"Uncle?" she asked, her voice small, weighed down with more hurt. "He had an uncle in Ohio too?"

He nodded. "*Ya*, he did."

Pain shot through Sarah's abdomen like fire, and she sucked in a deep breath.

"Sarah?" Luke rushed over to her. "Are you all right?"

Unable to speak, she held her breath, praying the cramping would subside.

"Sit," he ordered, pulling out a chair. He started to reach for her but instead pointed to the chair and she sat. He then knelt next to her, his eyes full of worry. "Should I run and get your *mamm*? Do we need to take you to a doctor?"

"No." She swallowed deep breaths. The pain eased, and she leaned back in the chair. "It passed," she whispered.

He nodded, concern still reflected in his face. "Want me to go get your *mamm*?"

She forced a smile and shook her head. "I'm *gut*, but *danki*." She took short breaths in anticipation of any lingering pain. Finding none, she let her body relax. "Would you like to see the upstairs?" she asked.

He frowned. "Are you sure you can make it up the stairs?"

"I'm expecting *zwillingbopplin*. I'm not ill." She hoisted herself from the chair and started for the stairs. "Go get your bag, and I'll show you your room."

He grabbed his bag from the living room and followed.

Sarah took her time climbing the stairs and insisted she was doing fine when Luke again asked if she was okay. When they reached the hallway on the second floor, she leaned against the wall and breathed deeply, feeling as if she'd trotted across the back pasture in record time.

"Are you sure you're okay?"

"*Ya.*" She caught her breath. "I have two more months of this. I'd better make myself a bedroom on my parents' first floor."

"I think that would be wise," he said with a smile.

Sarah motioned toward the master bedroom. "This is our room." She paused. "I guess I should say this *was* our room." She scowled while studying her bed, which sat lonely and tidy, untouched since the morning Peter had perished. The beautiful green-and-blue log-cabin quilt her sister-in-law Sadie had crafted as a wedding gift seemed to mock her.

Closing her eyes, she concentrated on the last night Peter had held her close in the dark. She could almost feel his whiskers brushing her face, and she could almost smell his fresh, masculine scent.

But he lied! a small voice inside her chided. *Your precious husband died and took all of his secrets with him. You'll never know if anything he ever told you was true!*

"If this is too painful for you, we can move to another room," Luke's voice whispered close to her ear.

Sarah kept her eyes squeezed shut. If she concentrated, she could imagine the voice speaking to her belonged to Peter. She'd give anything to hear him say, "I love you, Sarah Rose" one last time.

And she'd give anything to find out why he'd been dishonest with her.

"Which room would you prefer I use?" he asked.

Sarah's eyes flew open, and she cleared her throat, forcing back the lump threatening to strangle her words. She had to find a way to let Peter rest in peace. She needed to pray for strength.

"Sarah?" he asked, stepping closer to her. "Do you need some time alone in here?"

"No," she whispered, surprised by his understanding, wondering if he could read her mind. "I need to face the memories in this house eventually, and there's no time like the present." She headed into the hall and pointed toward the room next door.

"This was my sewing room." Her eyes moved over the piles of material strewn about—the shirts and trousers she hadn't finished making for Peter, and the maternity dresses she had begun. Her sewing machine sat on a small desk in the center of the room.

"I need to clean up the mess. I'll have to tell Timothy to bring the material to *Mamm's*," she muttered, closing the door and moving to the next room, which contained a cradle and a few dressers. Bags of baby clothes from her sisters sat in the corner of the room awaiting sorting.

Her stomach twisted at the idea of being in this house, surrounded by bittersweet memories while organizing baby clothes for the twins who would never know their father.

And what would she tell her children about their father? Would she tell them they had more relatives in Ohio? Should she go to Ohio and meet the relatives herself before the babies were born?

She crossed the room and stared down at the cradle, wondering if she'd ever truly know who her husband had been.

Her thoughts turned to her own family.

"*Dat* made this cradle for my oldest brother, Robert," she said. "It's been passed down to each of the Kauffman *kinner* and *kinskinner*." Gingerly she pushed the cradle, which rocked back and forth, quietly scraping the floor.

"Eli does some nice work." Luke ran his fingers over the finish. "But you'll need a second cradle. Maybe I can make it for you."

Raising her eyebrows, Sarah met his gaze. "You want to make me a cradle?"

"Why not?" He tilted his head and shot her a crooked smile.

She noticed for the first time that Luke was handsome. Due to the strong family resemblance, she assumed he was Peter's first cousin. Perhaps their fathers had been brothers.

It didn't matter if they were first cousins or even distant cousins. How could Sarah even know for sure? What if the whole Troyer family was full of liars?

She headed for the door. "The guest room is here."

He stepped into the small bedroom and glanced around. "This is perfect."

Sarah moved to the bed and idly straightened the quilt. "It's nothing fancy, but it's functional."

"I'm Amish," he said with a chuckle. "I don't need fancy."

She lowered herself onto the edge of the bed. "Ya, that's true."

He lifted the dark-green shade and glanced out the window. "Who lives in that house across the field?"

"Timothy." Sarah held her stomach as the twins performed summersaults. "He built that house a few years ago."

"Is he engaged?" Luke straightened the shade and leaned back against the wall. His lanky physique filled the room, and she guessed he was taller than Peter by at least an inch.

"It was three years ago, but his girlfriend, Miriam, changed her mind a month before the wedding and left the community." She absently smoothed the quilt.

"She left the community?"

"Ya." Sarah glanced up, meeting his surprised look.

"I guess she was shunned, ya?"

She shook her head. "She was going to join the church before they were married, but she left abruptly. Timothy was crushed. They'd been together a long time, and it took him a few years to

61

work up the nerve to ask her to marry him. She'd always toyed with the idea of going to college, and she said she had to try to fulfill her dream. She longed to be a pediatric nurse."

He shook his head. "I'm sure he took that hard."

"He was angry for a long time. But he finally managed to move on by focusing on the furniture store." She hoisted herself up. "He works long hours and always takes on the larger projects at the shop. *Dat* tells him he's a workaholic, but that doesn't stop him. I think that's how he deals with his broken heart."

"He never met anyone else?" Luke asked, standing up to his full height, which meant he towered over her by at least six inches.

"No. I hope he does someday. He'd be a *gut* husband and *dat*." She studied Luke's face and tried to guess his age. "How old are you?"

"Twenty-nine," he said.

"Two years older than Peter," she whispered.

"*Ya*, that's right." He rubbed his clean-shaven chin.

Studying his mocha eyes, she wondered who Luke Troyer was. Part of her wanted to stay distant from him and not get to know him, but another part of her wanted the truth—the real truth. Yet she worried Luke would reveal even more painful deception Peter had left behind without explanation.

"Why haven't you married?" she asked before she could stop the words.

A grin turned up the corners of his mouth. "You get right to the point, Sarah Rose."

"I'm sorry." Her face burned.

"It's fine." He waved off the thought. "I did have someone special back before my pop got sick."

"Your father was ill?"

"*Ya*, he had a stroke several years ago, and he died about eight months ago."

"And your *mamm*, is she living?"

He shook his head. "She died in an accident when I was young."

"I'm sorry to hear that. And you took care of your father alone?"

He leaned back against the wall again. "That's right. I split my time between work and Pop. My girlfriend got sick of waiting for me, and she moved on."

"Waiting for you?" She tilted her head in question. "I don't understand."

"She wanted me to choose between my pop and her. I couldn't leave Pop. He was my responsibility."

"Was she Amish?" Sarah asked.

"*Ya*. We grew up together." He tossed his straw hat onto the peg on the wall next to the bed.

She shook her head with disbelief. "How could she abandon you when you needed her most? It's our way to care for each other. Now that Peter's gone, it seems everyone wants to take care of me whether I want their help or not."

"Millie wasn't like that. I think she was too selfish to spend her time caring for my pop. She waited for a year and then married someone else—my best friend."

"And you never met anyone else?"

"I was too busy caring for Pop and working. I didn't have time for courting."

"You've had a lot of tragedy in your life. You've lost your *mamm*, your *dat*, and your true love. That's a lot for a person to bear." She stepped toward the door. "I'll let you get settled. The bathroom is downstairs next to the kitchen. I'll go to the market tomorrow and get you some groceries. Feel free to come to my parents' house for meals."

Although Luke's presence had sent her emotions into a deep abyss of anger and hurt, she felt sorry for him and his loss. She didn't wish her sorrow on anyone, especially someone who was family.

"We'll be sitting on the porch later if you want to join us."

She studied the exhaustion in his eyes and shook her head. "You look tired, though, so I'll understand if you'd rather sleep tonight. It's been a long day for you."

He raked his hand through his brown hair. "I think I may call it a day, but I appreciate the invitation."

"You're also welcome to use our horse and buggy," she added. "Timothy may have already introduced you to Molly in *Dat's* barn. Peter bought Molly before we were married. She's a very docile horse. You can use her to venture around town."

"*Danki*," he said.

"I'll see you tomorrow," she said. "Sleep well." Turning, she stepped through the doorway.

"Sarah!" Timothy's voice rang out downstairs. "Sarah Rose! *Mamm* is looking for you back at the house."

"Wait. I want to say something," Luke said.

He ran his hand through his hair again, reminding her of Peter when he was nervous. Her mouth went dry.

"*Danki* for everything," he said. "I appreciate how your family has welcomed me here."

"Sarah? Where are you?" Timothy called, boots scraping the stairs.

"I could only dream of having a family like this," Luke said.

His words brought tears to her eyes. This poor man had lost his family. He deserved her sympathy.

But how can I know he's telling the truth?

"Sarah?" Timothy said as he came up behind her. "We were starting to get worried. You've been here quite awhile. *Mamm* is looking for you."

"I was just showing Luke the house," Sarah huffed, annoyed. "I was about to head back." Wasn't she old enough to take care of herself? She was sick of everyone hovering over her like she was a fragile little girl.

"Good night, Luke," she said. "I'll see you tomorrow."

"Let's go," Timothy said. Placing his hand on her shoulder, he steered her toward the stairs.

❁

Later that evening, Luke stepped from the shower and snatched a towel off the rack on the wall. While drying himself, he reflected on the day, and exhaustion pummeled him. He was both emotionally and physically drained. His life had taken a turn he hadn't expected after arriving at the Kauffman & Yoder Amish Furniture store this morning. He'd discovered that not only was Peter dead, but that he had left behind a family—a real family with a wife, unborn twins, and a host of in-laws who'd cared for him.

Grief mixed with anger gripped Luke. He was filled with questions, and he wanted answers. No, he *needed* answers, and they were answers only Peter could provide.

But Peter was gone. He was dead.

Luke brushed at the moisture in his eyes and cleared his throat while unanswered questions swirled like a tornado in his mind. How had Peter—who had been anti-Amish and driven to become English, and who had left home in Ohio in a fit of anger—moved to another Amish community and quickly become a part of it? It didn't make sense.

Luke could tell the Kauffmans had loved and accepted Peter as one of their own. Peter had been a lucky man—probably luckier than he'd ever appreciated.

While pulling on his clothes, anger entangled with envy surged through Luke. Peter had married sweet, angelic Sarah, and from the sound of her stories, he was a good Amish man.

He contemplated that for a moment. Perhaps Peter had rediscovered his belief in God. Peter had joined the church in Ohio before he left, and maybe he'd found renewed belief when he met the people here in Bird-in-Hand.

But still, it didn't seem fair. All Luke had ever dreamed of was a family—a real family, with a loving wife and many, many children. He'd given it all up to care for his pop. Yet Peter had walked away from his family in Ohio and into a brand-new one in Pennsylvania.

Balancing a kerosene lantern in his hand, Luke fetched his dirty clothes and moved through the kitchen toward the stairs. Scanning the room, he tried to imagine Peter and Sarah sharing a life in this house. He wondered if they'd been happy together.

The sorrow reflected in Sarah's eyes told him she missed her husband with all of her heart. Their home seemed haunted with a ghost of the love Peter had left behind. Luke's heart craved the love Sarah held for Peter. He hoped someday he could find a woman who was as sweet, loving, and kind as Sarah seemed to be.

Ascending the stairs, he focused on Sarah. Or, as her parents called her, Sarah Rose. How fitting her middle name was. She indeed was a delicate flower, but he'd also seen her thorns when she stood up to her family members. She was a complex woman. He hoped he could foster a friendship with her and be a part of her twins' lives. It was the least he could do to help her through her loss and the rough road ahead.

Luke yawned as he threw his dirty clothes into a pile on the chair near the bed. Tomorrow he would hitch up Molly and take a tour of Bird-in-Hand. Then he'd visit Eli and see if he could get some wood to start on that cradle.

He would have to tell DeLana the news of Peter's death, but first he wanted to find out more about the family Peter had left behind. He would contact DeLana when he traveled back to Ohio.

He snuffed out the lantern light and climbed into the double bed. Closing his eyes, he imagined Sarah's face. He prayed silently, thanking God for his safe passage to Bird-in-Hand and for the opportunity to find Peter's family.

7

"Sarah, is that chocolate cake ready yet?" Beth Anne asked as she crossed the bakery kitchen. "We have customers asking for one of your famous cakes."

"*Ya*." Sarah swiped the knife over the icing one more time and then placed it on the counter. "Here you go."

"*Wunderbaar*." Beth Anne lifted the cake plate. "Your best yet." She paused and turned her concerned eyes to Sarah. "How is Luke doing?"

Sarah shrugged. "*Gut*, I guess. I haven't seen him in a few days since I dropped off some groceries and supplies for him. But *Dat* says Luke's been visiting businesses and checking out Lancaster County. He's stopped in to see *Dat* every day and helps out with the projects at the shop."

"*Gut*." Beth Anne touched Sarah's arm. "How are you feeling?"

Sarah yawned. "Tired."

"You need a break. Sit for a while, and I'll bring you some ice water." Beth Anne ambled toward the front of the bakery. "I'll be right back."

Sarah lowered herself onto a chair and took a deep breath. The past few days had been long. Although her mother had suggested she cut back on her hours at the bakery, Sarah couldn't bring herself to stay home. She'd rather be with her sisters, contributing to the family business.

Lindsay appeared with a glass and placed it in Sarah's hand. "Here's your water, *Aenti* Sarah."

"*Danki*," Sarah said, lifting it to her lips. The icy liquid was just the refreshment she craved.

While running her fingers through the cool condensation, she wondered what Luke had been doing since he'd arrived at Bird-in-Hand. Truth be known, she'd avoided him as much as possible, worried if she spent more time with him, she'd find out about more lies from Peter, crushing her already-broken heart.

Timothy insisted Luke would only hurt Sarah, and he encouraged her to avoid him. But while she wanted to stay away from Luke, Sarah still couldn't stop her mind from wondering about the questions Peter had left unanswered. The biggest was why Peter had left Ohio.

As curious as she was, she was afraid of the answers.

"Sarah Rose," Kathryn said, stepping into the kitchen through the back door. "You have a visitor."

Moving to the doorway, Sarah smiled when she found Norman standing outside.

His lips formed a tentative smile as his gaze met hers. "Sarah Rose. How are you?"

"*Gut. Danki.*" Sarah wiped her hands over her apron. "And you?"

"*Gut.*" He nodded.

"I'll let you talk," Kathryn said, moving into the bakery.

"Have you had lunch?" he asked.

Facing him, Sarah shook her head.

"Would you like to go to the Bird-in-Hand Restaurant?" he offered. "I'm sure you're very busy, but I promise I'll have you back soon."

Sarah blew out a sigh of relief. Getting out of the bakery and away from her overactive thought processes would be a blessing. She needed a nice distraction. "I'd love to join you for lunch."

❄

Sarah studied the menu while sitting across from Norman at the Bird-in-Hand Restaurant and Smorgasbord. Stealing a glance over the table, she found Norman's attention fixed on her. She smiled and wondered what was going through his mind.

"Have you decided?" he asked.

She shook her head. "You?"

"I think I'll have my usual." He closed the menu and slapped it onto the table in front of him.

The server appeared with their glasses of ice water. Sarah lifted hers from the table and took a long drink while Norman gave his order—the Lancaster County Baked Ham.

"And you, ma'am?" the young Plain Mennonite woman asked.

"I'll have the same, thank you." Sarah handed her menu to the woman and sat back in the chair. "The weather has been nice, *ya*? I bet your herd is doing well."

He nodded, though his eyes seemed to be concentrating on something other than her words.

Enjoying the mundane conversation, she continued to babble. "My *dat* says it's hotter than usual this time of year. I really don't remember how hot it was last year this time. It seems normal to me." She drew imaginary circles on her glass. "An English customer the other day asked me if it was always this mild in October. I told her I thought so." She snickered. "Don't we always have a mixture of mild and cool weather in autumn? I guess she must've been from somewhere cold, like Alaska." She smiled. "You want to know something *gegisch*? I've always wanted to go to Alaska."

Norman took her hands into his. "Sarah Rose."

Glancing up, she met his gaze, and the warmth of his eyes caught her off guard. "Norman? Are you all right?"

"*Ya*, I am." He gave a sad smile. "I asked you here for a reason. I wanted to see how you're doing. I remember clearly the first half year after I lost Leah. I felt as if I were on a roller coaster. Waves of grief would drown me one moment and then the next moment I'd be remembering the happier times and laughing so hard my stomach hurt." He squeezed her hand. "How are you, Sarah Rose? How are you truly?"

Sarah licked her lips and sniffed back sudden tears while she wondered how Norman could understand her so well. The answer was obvious—he had lived through losing his own life partner, the person who was supposed to grow old with him as Peter was supposed to grow old with her.

"I'm *gut*," she whispered.

He raised an eyebrow. "Really?"

"No." Her voice croaked, and she cleared her throat. "I'm a walking time bomb, and I feel like I'll blow any moment."

He nodded. "I remember feeling that way. If you're comfortable sharing, I'd be honored to listen without judgment."

"*Danki*." She bit her lip and studied her glass, silently debating how much to share. Although she hadn't felt comfortable sharing her feelings in the past, she suddenly felt the strength of his friendship and trusted him. "My situation is a little more complicated than yours. I found out Peter omitted some information about his past."

"I'm sorry, but I don't understand."

Sarah explained how Luke had arrived from Ohio, proving that Peter in fact had family.

Their food arrived, and Sarah continued her story while they ate.

"Now I'm struggling with the realization that he lied to me," she said in between bites of ham. "It's made my grief so much deeper. I feel like my heart has been shredded. I don't know what to do with the pain."

Norman sipped his water and shook his head. "I'm sorry you're going through this. I don't know how to help you, except to say Peter did love you. It was obvious just by looking in his eyes."

Sarah studied Norman and blinked. "My *mamm* said the same thing to me."

He gave a sad smile. "Knowing and believing that won't take away the pain or the questions. But it may help you accept he's gone, and you may never know the answers. Just hold onto the belief and faith in the love you shared, a love that created your *zwillingbopplin*."

Sarah stared into his brown eyes and nodded. Norman was a good friend—a generous Christian man. God had blessed her with so many wonderful people in her life.

During the ride back to the bakery, Sarah lost herself in thought. Although *Mamm* and Norman had told her to hold onto the knowledge that her husband had loved her, their words didn't offer her any comfort. Anger and grief still surged through her. She wanted to speak to Peter face-to-face and tell him how much his lies had hurt her.

But she couldn't talk to him ever again.

Peter was dead. He was gone forever.

Sarah forced herself to concentrate on the scenery despite the renewed grief soaking through her soul.

❀

"How was lunch?" *Mamm* asked as Sarah stepped through the door to the bakery.

"*Gut*," Sarah said, moving past her to the stove. "It was nice to get out of the bakery and talk for a while. Did Beth Anne finish another chocolate cake?"

"*Ya*, she did." *Mamm* sidled up beside her, her expression expectant. "Did you have a good talk at lunch?"

"*Ya*." Sarah moved to the sink. "He just wanted to see how I was doing. He remembers what it feels like to lose a spouse." She washed her hands, careful to keep her expression nonchalant. She didn't want to rehash the whole conversation for fear of crying again. She'd cried enough tears to last a lifetime.

"I'm glad you have Norman to talk to. He's the best one to share your feelings with during this difficult time. I'm glad he's your friend. He's a *gut* man and a *gut* father." *Mamm* studied

Sarah's face. "You seem preoccupied, Sarah Rose. What's on your mind?"

"Nothing." Sarah dried her hands and turned toward the counter. "I best get going on the next chocolate cake. I took a long lunch and need to get caught up."

"*Liewe.*" *Mamm* pulled her into a warm hug, then walked toward the front of the store.

Sucking in a deep breath, Sarah prayed for strength and answers to the riddle of Peter's life.

Funny Cake Pie

Top of cake:
1 cup sugar
1/4 cup butter or lard (shortening)
1/2 cup milk
1 beaten egg
1 cup flour
1 tsp baking powder
1/2 tsp vanilla
Pinch of cinnamon

Cream together sugar and butter. Add the milk and egg alternately with flour and baking powder. Add vanilla and cinnamon and set aside until lower part is mixed.

Lower part of cake:
4 Tbsp cocoa
1/2 cup sugar
1/2 tsp vanilla
6 Tbsp water

Mix together the cocoa, sugar, vanilla, and water. Pour into an unbaked pie shell. Over this pour the top part. The chocolate will come up around the outside edge, giving a nice crusty edge on the finished product. Bake at 350 degrees for 40 minutes or until firm (toothpick test).

8

"I thought Timothy would be back in time for supper," Sarah said while filling the kitchen sink with hot water.

"He said he had to stop by Norman's on his way home from the shop," *Mamm* said.

"Oh." Sarah faced her mother, who was balancing a load of dirty dishes in her arms. She wasn't surprised to hear Timothy had gone to see Norman; the two men had been friends since they were teenagers.

She thought about her lunchtime conversation with Norman. She wished she could take to heart Norman's assurance that Peter loved her. She knew if she could put aside her anger toward Peter and get to know Luke, she could ask him about Peter's past.

However, she was still afraid of finding out information that would hurt her even more.

Mamm shook her head and placed the stack of dishes in the soapy water. "You're a million miles away tonight. Come to think of it, you've been that way all afternoon. What is wrong, *mei liewe?*"

"Nothing." Sarah waved off the question with a dishcloth, avoiding the thoughts that haunted her. "Must be hormones from the babies. What were you saying?" She turned her attention to scrubbing the dishes.

"I said I guess Timothy stayed for supper." *Mamm* grabbed a cloth from the drawer and wet it.

"*Ya*. He must've." Sarah lined the clean dishes onto the drying rack. "I'm surprised Luke hasn't joined us for supper these past few days."

"*Dat* asked him that at the shop today, and Luke said he'd been eating a quick supper at the house at night. He mentioned something about working on a project at your house. You haven't visited with him lately, have you?" *Mamm* asked.

Sarah shook her head.

"Why is that?" *Mamm's* eyes were full of concern. "Are you worried he'll tell you more about Peter?"

"You mean more lies?" Sarah crossed her arms in front of her chest as if to guard her already-broken heart.

Mamm's face softened. "Sarah Rose, I can't pretend to understand how you feel, but I can offer you the intuition I feel in my heart. I know you're grieving, and I know you're hurt by what Peter told you and by what he didn't tell you. However, the only way you're going to heal is to face Peter's past, remembering his past came before he met you, and his future was with you and still is with you." She touched Sarah's stomach. "While he isn't here to defend the choices he made by not telling you the whole truth, he left part of his heart with you and you need to hold onto that."

Sarah swallowed and blinked back tears.

"I don't mean to patronize you." *Mamm* cupped Sarah's face in her hands. "But it's breaking my heart to watch you suffer so. Luke is only going to be with us for a short time. Perhaps you should give him a chance and hear what he has to say."

"Okay," Sarah whispered before clearing her throat.

Mamm gave her a quick hug and stepped toward the table.

❦

Luke's boots crunched across the rocky driveway leading from Sarah and Peter's house to Eli's. Covering his mouth with his hand, he blew out a deep yawn. Despite his better judgment, he planned to spend a few hours visiting with the Kauffmans on the porch instead of heading to bed for some much-needed rest.

He'd begun the day riding through Bird-in-Hand, and as if pulled by an invisible magnet, he found himself in front of Eli's furniture store.

He then spent the rest of the day helping Elmer Yoder's grandson, Jake Miller, build a dresser for an English customer. The store was still backed up with orders that had been placed before the fire. He enjoyed helping the carpenters get caught up since it made him feel an even stronger connection to the Kauffman family.

He'd enjoyed getting to know the family and their friends, and he felt closer to them every day. However, he still felt a chill from Timothy. The man never smiled, and he only offered one-word answers or terse instructions when he addressed Luke. Despite his best efforts, Luke hadn't been able to get Timothy to hold a cordial conversation with him.

When they closed up the shop at suppertime, Eli invited Luke to join him for the evening meal. Luke glanced down at his dust-covered clothes and decided it would be best if he cleaned up first. He promised Eli that he would make it to the Kauffmans' house in time for dessert.

Later that evening, Luke's gaze moved up the back steps to the small kitchen window, and he wondered if Sarah was washing the dishes. Guilt washed over him; he knew he'd been avoiding her. He'd wanted to sit her down alone and tell her the truth, the whole truth, about who he was and also about Peter's past. Luke knew in his heart he owed it to Sarah, but he was worried he would hurt her, just as Timothy predicted.

Luke cared about Sarah, and he worried about how she would cope without Peter. He knew her family would look after her, but he also wanted to be a part of her twins' lives. They were the closest chance he had left to enjoying a true family.

Those feelings haunted him every day, growing more intense

each time he helped her father and brothers work in the new furniture shop. While surrounded by her brothers and father, Luke couldn't shake one thought—he longed to stay in Bird-in-Hand with the Kauffman family, even if only as a surrogate member. He'd picked up a paper during his travels through town and perused the real estate section. If he found an affordable home, he might consider staying.

He couldn't suppress the feeling that the Lord had held him in Bird-in-Hand for a reason, and he prayed about it every night. He wanted to be a part of the twins' lives, and he hoped to get to know Sarah. He prayed she would support his decision to stay.

Taking a deep breath, Luke sauntered up the path leading to the back porch of Sarah's parents' house.

The door creaked open, and his breath paused when he spotted Sarah, glowing in the low light of the kitchen behind her.

"Luke," she said, her eyes round with surprise.

"Good evening, Sarah." He stood on the bottom step. "Your *dat* invited me to come visit with him this evening."

"Oh. He had to tend to some chores in the barn." She smoothed her apron. "Would you like to sit on the porch and have some hot cocoa and some crumbly peach pie?"

"*Ya.*" He pushed his hat farther back on his head. "I'd like that very much. *Danki.*" He climbed the stairs. When she stepped back toward the door, he reached for her and then stopped. "How about you sit on the swing and I get the cocoa and pie?"

A sweet smile curved up her rosy lips. "And how will you find the cocoa and pie, *gegisch?*" she asked, her eyes twinkling with humor.

"Hmm. I guess you got me there." He rubbed his chin, trying in vain not to grin at the surprise of being called silly. Her cautious and cold demeanor seemed to have vanished, at least temporarily. Was Sarah finally opening up to him?

"*Ya.*" She laughed, the sound a sweet melody to his ears. "I do. Sit." She gestured toward the swing. "I'll be right back."

Luke lowered himself onto the swing, which creaked under his weight. Swaying back and forth, he breathed in the cool autumn air. His mind wandered with the idea of moving here and joining the community.

Since his father had passed away, he'd more than once considered selling his land to a developer who had been after his father to sell for years. Apparently the Troyer farm was prime property for an English housing development, but his father had never given in to the generous offering. However, Luke didn't feel tied to Ohio now that his immediate family was gone. He wanted to be near his only remaining Amish family: Peter's children.

The door opened and slammed with a bang, revealing Sarah balancing a tray with two mugs of cocoa topped with whipped cream, two plates with pieces of pie, forks, and napkins.

Popping up, he took the tray and motioned for her to sit. "Now I can serve you."

Pursing her lips, she let out a sigh. "You win." She lowered herself onto the swing. "*Danki.*"

He placed the tray on a small table in front of them and then sat beside her. Picking up a mug, he handed it to her. "The cocoa smells *wunderbaar.*"

"I hope you like it." Sipping the hot drink, she left a whipped cream mustache on her upper lip. She chuckled and licked it off. "*Ya,* it's *gut.*"

He sipped it and nodded. "Very chocolaty."

Her eyes twinkled in the low light of the kerosene lamp on the porch railing. "I heard you've been helping out at my *dat's* shop. *Danki* for that. They've been struggling to fill back orders taken before the fire. You're a great help."

He became sheepish. "I don't mind. I enjoy getting to know your family." He placed the mug on the table and forked a piece of pie into his mouth, savoring the rich, sweet flavor. "Wow. This is the best peach pie I've ever eaten." He met her disbelieving stare. "I mean that."

She scrunched her nose in disagreement, and he couldn't help thinking she was absolutely adorable. "No." She shook her head. "I didn't get the filling right. Too much sugar."

"I disagree, Sarah. It's heavenly." Taking another bite, he groaned. "Wow. You're an amazing cook."

"Stop." She blushed. "You're embarrassing me." She sipped more cocoa and then shivered.

"You cold?"

"*Ya.*" She cupped her hands around the mug. "The temperature is dropping."

Luke put his plate back onto the tray and then slipped out of his coat. "Here. Take this."

"No." She waved him off. "I'm fine."

"I insist." Draping the jacket around her shoulders, he inhaled her sweet scent, which reminded him of cinnamon and lilac.

"*Danki.*" She took another sip and gazed out across the dark field. "It's finally autumn. I was just telling Norman today at lunch that it had been unusually warm. We were spoiled."

His stomach twisted at the thought of her having lunch with Norman. He frowned at the involuntary reaction. Was that jealousy? Why should he care if she had lunch with another man? He hardly knew her. "You had lunch with Norman?"

"*Ya,*" she whispered, studying her half-full mug. "He's a *gut* friend. He lost his *fraa* in childbirth a few years ago, so we have a lot in common. I enjoy talking with him."

"Oh?" He studied her. Why was she avoiding his stare? Was the warm friendship he'd felt earlier dissolving back into the cold front she'd had earlier?

She looked up at him, and something flashed in her eyes. Was it sadness? Or possibly worry? Her expression softened.

She placed her mug on the tray. "How do you like Bird-in-Hand?" She lifted her plate and took a bite of the pie.

"It's a beautiful place." Leaning back on the swing, he stretched his arm behind her. "I was thinking about staying awhile." He held his breath, awaiting her reaction, hoping for her approval.

"Really?" She turned to him, her eyes wide. "How long?"

"I'm not certain." He ran his fingers along the wood back of the swing. "I like it here, so I thought I'd see how it goes."

Her eyebrows knitted with confusion. "Are you going to move here permanently?"

He shrugged. "We'll see."

She turned back to the field, and a comfortable silence fell between them. He wished he could sit next to her forever, just enjoying her company.

After a moment, she took a few more bites of the pie, then returned the plate to the tray. With her eyes trained on the field, she took a deep breath. "I need to ask you something," she whispered.

Luke nodded. "You can ask me anything."

"You told me Peter hadn't been honest about his past, and I can see that truth just by looking at your face." Her voice was soft, her eyes still focused on the field across from where they sat. "I need to know more, but yet I'm afraid to ask. I'm worried that hearing my husband lied about ... everything ... will be too much to handle."

"I understand," he said. Sitting up straight, he prepared himself for the questions. He wanted to tell her the truth, and yet he didn't want to hurt her. He vowed to frame his answers in order to not cause her more pain.

She met his gaze, her expression cautious. "Were you and Peter close?"

He nodded. "We were."

"He wasn't an orphan, was he?" She bit her lip in anticipation of the answer.

"No," he shook his head.

Closing her eyes, she brought her hand to her temple and groaned. "Oh, Luke, I don't understand why he did this to me. It doesn't make sense. Why didn't he trust me?"

Luke started to reach for her and then stopped, knowing it was inappropriate for him to touch her, even just to console her. "I'm sorry I upset you, Sarah Rose. That's the last thing I wanted to do by coming to visit tonight."

She met his gaze. "It's not your fault." She looked toward to the field again. "Did he have siblings?"

Luke paused, knowing the truth would be painful, but not wanting to withhold information. Peter had already done too much damage to her heart with his deception. "*Ya*," he said.

"Are they living?" Her voice trembled.

"*Ya*," he whispered.

Her hands framed her stomach, and her expression was pensive. "My *zwillingbopplin* will want to know them."

"I agree." He prayed her questions would end before the answers became too distressing.

She faced him, her brows furrowed in question. "Why did he leave Ohio if he had a family? Did he have a falling out with a family member?"

Luke nodded. "*Ya*."

Her eyes widened with shock. "Who?"

Luke stared at her, wanting to tell her the truth, the whole truth. But his gut told him to filter the information and give only the bare minimum that she needed to know.

"His father?" she guessed.

Luke swallowed a sigh of relief, thankful she'd guessed correctly. "*Ya*."

Sarah shook her head, her expression softening. "How sad. I wish I had gotten to meet his family." She rubbed her belly. "But maybe the *kinner* will get to meet them. They may have lost their father, but maybe they can get to know his family."

Luke nodded, wishing he could tell her more without hurting her.

"How many siblings did he have?" she asked.

The clip-clop of hooves crunching up the rock driveway traveled toward them.

"It must be Timothy." She faced the oncoming horse. "He visited Norman tonight and must've stayed for supper."

Luke silently thanked Timothy for saving him from answering her question about Peter's siblings. Instead, he watched as Timothy stopped in front of Eli's barn and unhitched the horse.

Sarah cleared her throat.

"Sarah." Luke glanced at her. "Are you okay?"

Meeting his stare, she sighed. "I'll be fine. I'm trying to convince myself not to be angry, but I keep wondering if my marriage was a mockery. I feel as if I didn't know my husband at all."

He frowned, guilt nipping at him. "I'm sorry. I never meant to upset you. I just want you to know the truth."

She gave him a sad smile. "*Danki*. I appreciate it."

"*Wie geht's?*" Timothy's voice boomed as his boots scraped up the porch steps. He gave his sister a friendly nod and then frowned at Luke. "Isn't it a bit late to be visiting my sister?"

"I was just getting ready to leave." Luke folded his hands in his lap. "Beautiful evening."

"*Ya.*" Timothy turned back to his sister. "Could I possibly speak with you before you retire for the evening?" He shot another frown at Luke. "In private, Sarah Rose."

Not wanting to wear out his welcome, Luke stood. "I guess I should be heading back to the house."

Sarah placed her hands on the swing and started to heave herself up.

"No, no." Luke shook his head. "Don't get up. We can say good night here."

She pulled the coat from her shoulders and handed it to him. "Here. *Danki*."

"You're welcome." He smiled. "Thank you for dessert and the pleasant conversation."

She nodded, and he wished he could steal the sadness from her eyes. Again, he wondered how Peter had snatched up such a lovely wife. Had Peter appreciated her? Perhaps not, since he hadn't told her the truth about his past. Or maybe he'd worried the truth would scare her away.

"I'll see you soon." He pulled on his coat. "Sleep well." Turning to Timothy, he nodded. "Have a good evening."

Timothy nodded in response.

"*Gut nacht,*" Sarah called as he headed down the stairs.

As he ambled down the rock driveway to Sarah's and Peter's home, he contemplated his evening with Sarah.

He wished he could take away the pain in her heart that the stories of Peter caused. However, he knew in the depths of his soul he was doing the right thing by telling her the truth. He hoped her questions and her openness were signs that she was beginning to trust him.

❀

Sarah's gaze remained glued on Luke's silhouette as he strode through the shadows toward her house. She hugged her arms while concentrating on the information Luke had shared about Peter's past. While the news that Peter had lied about being an orphan caused her more heartache, another question came to the forefront: could she trust everything Luke had told her about Peter? She shivered.

Timothy took off his coat and sat next to her. "Would you like my coat?"

"No, *danki.* I'm fine." She shivered again.

"Don't be *gegisch.*" He covered her shoulders with his coat. "Your lips are turning blue." He chuckled at his joke.

"It's not that cold," she muttered, snuggling into the warmth of the jacket. "You were with Norman's family, yes?"

"*Ya.*" He glanced down at the tray. "I hope you saved me some crumbly peach pie. You know it's my favorite."

"Of course I saved you some," she said. "I always do."

"What were you thinking?" he said suddenly, his tone accusing.

"What?" She gave him a confused look.

"Why were you sitting out here in the dark, sharing dessert with … *him?*" He spat out the last word.

"I was talking with our guest, Timothy. Why is that so bad?"

"Don't tell me you trust him, Sarah Rose."

"Please." She rolled her eyes and pushed an errant strand of hair back from her face. "You can let go of your *gegisch* accusations. Why wouldn't I trust him?" *At least, I hope I can trust him.*

Timothy's expression softened. "Please be careful, Sarah Rose. I don't want to see you get hurt. I'm worried about you and the *zwillingbopplin.*"

"Timothy!" *Mamm* appeared in the doorway. "Have some pie." She turned her gaze to Sarah and frowned. "Sarah Rose, get in here before you catch a cold."

Hoisting herself up, Sarah picked up the tray from the little table beside her and headed through the door. Stepping into the kitchen, she wondered if her life would somehow get easier. She yearned to squelch all of the confusing feelings that rained down on her. She hoped the Lord would lead her toward the truth about Peter's past—and also about Luke Troyer.

9

Sarah slathered cream-cheese frosting on another rhubarb cookie and yawned. The news of Peter's life in Ohio, along with her brother's words of caution about Luke, had haunted her throughout the night. Even more than before, she'd found herself doubting her marriage to Peter. Had she known him at all?

Had anything he'd told her been the truth?

Snippets of possible dishonesty flashed through her mind. She'd heard from family members that Peter had been spotted at the Bird-in-Hand post office at odd times during the day. He had also been very quiet and distant from her days before the fire.

What else had he been hiding from her?

The questions soaked her mind while she finished icing the cookies. She was wrapping the cookies in packages of three when her mother came up behind her.

"Those look absolutely scrumptious, Sarah Rose," she said. "Nice work."

"*Danki.*" Sarah wiped her hands on a towel. "I need to sit now."

"*Ya.* Let's find a quiet spot to sit and talk." Taking Sarah's arm, *Mamm* led her to the small back room that served as the bakery's office, with a desk, file cabinet, adding machine, and ledgers. A stack of receipts sat on the corner of the desk.

"Have a seat, Sarah Rose." *Mamm* gestured toward the chair in front of the desk. "Tell me what's on your mind."

Sinking into the chair, Sarah suppressed a groan at her mother's serious tone. She didn't want to be coddled. She had too much on her mind already. "I'm fine, *Mamm*."

Her mother's blue eyes were warm and supportive, breaking down the wall Sarah was building around her heart. "I can't help you unless you tell me what's going on. I know it's more than hormones, Sarah Rose. Won't you let me help you through this?"

Sarah's heart pounded in her chest, but she merely shrugged to shield her nerves.

Mamm touched her hands. "Sarah Rose, did Luke tell you something last night that upset you?"

Sarah's eyes immediately began to water. "He told me Peter wasn't an orphan. He was raised by his parents with siblings. He left Ohio and came here because he'd had a fight with his father."

"*Ack*, Sarah Rose." *Mamm* pulled her into her arms and held her close. "I'm sorry you're hurting."

"I'm trying to sort through it all, but I keep thinking my whole marriage was a lie." Her voice quavered as tears spilled down first one cheek, then the other.

"No, no. Don't say that," *Mamm* cooed in her ear.

"I'm remembering things Peter did that made me wonder if something was wrong. Perhaps the signs were there all along. He was so cold and distant the last few weeks before the fire. Maybe he was hiding more from me."

"Sarah Rose, you have to stop beating yourself up over this," *Mamm* said. He's not here to explain why he did what he did, and speculating will only cause your heart to hurt even more."

Wiping her eyes with the backs of her hands, Sarah looked at her mother. "But what about the *kinner*? What do I tell them when they ask about their father? What kind of a man do I tell them he was when I don't know for certain myself?"

"The words will come to you when the time is right." *Mamm* rested her hands on Sarah's shoulders. "The Lord will lead your lips to the right words. Have faith in that."

"What is faith, *Mamm?*" Sarah wished her voice would stop trembling. "What is it really?"

"Hebrews 11:1 tells us, 'Now faith is being sure of what we hope for and certain of what we do not see.'" She squeezed Sarah's hand. "Does that help you at all?"

Sarah nodded to appease her mother, but the questions still haunted her. "And what about Luke? How do I know if I can believe him?"

"What does your heart tell you?"

"My heart is a jumbled mess. I'm not sure what it's telling me at all." Sarah gazed down at her lap. "I just keep thinking I'm too young to be a widow and a single mother. It somehow doesn't seem fair."

"But you have a family who loves you and will take care of you. That's more than some people have."

Sarah frowned, feeling like a heel for complaining. "*Danki.* I do appreciate and love you, but I'm not sure what to think about Luke."

"Listen to what he has to tell you and then see what your heart says."

Sarah nodded, but she still needed answers. She had to figure out how to get past her grief and understand what God's plan was for her and the children. *Please God*, she prayed silently, *please show me the right path for my zwillingbopplin.*

❀

"You do good work," Luke said as he examined the triple dresser. "Your *grossdaddi* taught you well." Glancing around, he examined the shop, thinking how similar it was to his own back home.

The large, open area was divided into work areas separated by workbenches cluttered with an array of tools. The sweet scent of wood and stain filled his nostrils. The men working around Jake and him were building beautifully designed dining room sets, bedroom suites, entertainment centers, hutches, end tables, desks, and coffee tables.

Hammers banged, saw blades whirled, and air compressors hummed. Just like his shop back home, the air compressors powering the tools ran off diesel generators.

Returning Luke's nod, Jake Miller swiped the back of his hand across his brow. "Thanks for the compliment. You do good work too." He leaned back on the workbench and grabbed a bottle of water. After a long gulp, he placed it on the bench beside him. "So, you're from Ohio, huh?"

"*Ya.*" Luke sat on a bench and opened a can of Coke. "Middlefield."

"I didn't realize Peter had grown up in Ohio. I wonder why he didn't tell anyone about his family back home."

Rubbing his lower lip, Luke contemplated how much to reveal about Peter's history. "I guess you could say he was running from some things in his past."

"Why hide the past?" Jake wondered. "Peter had a great life here. He and Sarah seemed so happy. I can't see how telling where he came from would ruin that. I think it would be more detrimental and risky to create a web of lies you have to remember so you don't flub it."

A smile crept across Luke's lips. "You're a very wise young man."

Grinning, Jake stood. "I try."

"So, what's your story?" Luke asked.

"Well, I live about a mile up the road in half of a two-story house my uncle owns, and I love working on furniture. That's about it."

"Do you have a special *maedel* in your life?"

Jake shrugged. "I guess you could say I have a girl. At least, she's special to me. She moved back home to Virginia, but she's supposed to come visit in the spring."

"Oh?" Luke grabbed a can of stain.

"She's Lindsay's older sister, Jessica." Jake grabbed a paintbrush from his tool cart. "We met last summer when she came to live with Rebecca and Daniel. She wanted to go back home to live with her mom's best friend and finish high school. I'm hoping I can convince her to go to college in Pennsylvania, so we have a chance to get to know each other better. She's got another year of high school yet, though."

"She's English?" Luke asked.

"Yup." Jake grinned. "She's a great girl."

"You seem smitten." Luke shook the can of stain and then opened and stirred it.

The young man chuckled. "Yeah, I guess I am. I just wish she'd realize how smitten I am and give me a chance."

"Luke," a voice behind him called.

Turning, Luke spotted Timothy frowning near the door to the parking lot. He wondered idly if that man went through life with a dark cloud over his head.

"Can I speak with you for a moment?" Timothy asked, motioning toward the door.

"*Ya.*" Luke cut his eyes to Jake. "I'll be back to help you stain this."

Jake took the can of stain from him. "No problem. Take your time."

Luke crossed the shop and followed Timothy out to the parking lot, where they stood by a pile of scrap wood. "What's going on?" he asked.

"I'd like to know what your intentions are with my sister."

"My intentions?" Luke gripped his suspenders. "I reckon I intend to become her friend so I can be a part of her *zwillingbopplin's* lives. That's as far as my intentions go. I don't see why you have a problem with that."

"My problem is, Sarah is in a fragile state, and she doesn't need you showing up here and confusing her." He gestured wildly for emphasis. "She's suffered a huge loss, and you don't need to be sticking your nose in her business."

Luke shook his head while trying to make sense of Timothy's anger. "I don't understand why you have this resentment toward me. I lost Peter too." He studied Timothy for a moment. "How much did Peter tell you?"

Timothy shrugged and looked away. "Enough."

"Why don't you try being more specific? I'd like to know why you know more than everyone else in your family. Were you and Peter close?"

"*Ya*." Timothy met his gaze, sadness filling his eyes. "He was my best friend."

Luke's eyes widened. "Why didn't you tell me?"

"Because I can't let the rest of the family know how much Peter told me about his past. It makes me look bad."

"It makes you look like a liar," Luke finished his thought.

"Exactly." Timothy's expression softened. "You're his brother."

Luke knew he was caught. "I am."

Timothy snapped his fingers. "I knew it!"

Luke folded his arms in front of his chest. "What else do you know?"

"I know Peter left after having a horrible argument with your *dat*. And he regretted it very much."

"He did?" Luke raised his eyebrows in disbelief.

"He said he wished he'd had the courage to make things right between him and you and also him and your *dat*."

Luke scowled. "If he only knew what he put us through by leaving. Pop was so distraught that he had a stroke, and I nursed him until he died. I gave up everything to care for him. I lost my girlfriend and the chance to have a family of my own while Peter rebuilt his life here with a new family. It's hard for me to believe he had regrets when he had this." He gestured around the parking lot with his arms.

"I'm sorry. I truly am. But you have to believe Peter wanted to make amends before the *boppli* was born. He was talking about how to tell Sarah the truth." Timothy rubbed his chin and looked across the parking lot. "He was like a brother to me. We used to talk for hours."

"That's how it was before he abandoned Pop and me." Luke shook his head, disappointment mixed with resentment simmering through him. "Our address never changed. He could've written us. He had eight years to make things right."

"He wanted to make things right." Timothy shrugged. "I believed he would've done so if he'd had more time."

More questions bombarded Luke. "So why did he open up to you and no one else?"

"I told you—we were best friends."

"You knew the truth all along?"

Timothy shook his head. "No, I didn't know from the beginning. We quickly became friends when he got the job at the shop, but he didn't tell me he had family in Ohio until I met him at the post office one day about a year and a half ago. I found it strange that he had a post-office box. It seemed an unnecessary expense. Then he confided in me that he received letters there from his family in Ohio. He begged me not to tell Sarah. He said the news that he had family would crush her, and he wanted to tell her when the time was right."

"Did he say who the letters were from?" Luke braced himself, wondering if Timothy knew the truth about DeLana.

Timothy shrugged. "I had assumed they were from relatives, maybe your *dat* or even you. I never thought much about it."

Peter didn't tell him about DeLana.

"So where does that leave us now?" Luke asked. "You know who I am, but everyone else thinks I'm Peter's cousin."

Timothy's expression hardened. "It doesn't leave us anywhere different. You know I want you go to back home and let Sarah pick up the pieces of her life and move on. Your being here complicates things for her. She doesn't need to know any more about Peter's life back in Ohio. She belongs here with us."

Luke blanched. "You think I'm going to take her away?"

"I didn't say that. I don't want her to even consider leaving, which is why you need to leave."

"You also don't want me to tell the rest of the family you kept secrets from them."

Timothy frowned.

"It's up to you and your conscience to come clean with your family, but I can tell you this—those *kinner* are my family and my only connection to my brother. I have every right to be a part of their lives. They are as much my family as they are yours. You said Peter was like a brother to you and you lost him." Luke jammed a finger into his own chest. "Well, I lost him eight years ago when he chose to run out on my pop and me and start a new life without so much as telling us where he was living. I don't intend to hurt your sister. I only want to be her friend and be a part of her *kinner*'s lives. That's all."

"Sarah doesn't need you. She has the Kauffmans, and she belongs with us. You belong back in Ohio in your church district with your family. Peter must've left you for a reason."

Luke shook his head. "You're wrong. I think it's Sarah's decision if she wants me to stay or not."

Timothy's eyes narrowed to slits. "My sister is in no condition to make decisions like that. She's lost her husband and is about to become a mother for the first time. If you tell her who you really are and then ask her to decide if she wants you around, you'll hurt her even more. You'll probably crush whatever spirit she has left in her. Is that what you want?"

Knowing Timothy was right, Luke shook his head.

"Good. I'm glad we've reached an understanding. You need to start packing and head back to Ohio. That's where you belong." Timothy turned and stalked back into the shop.

The crunch of tires on gravel pulled Luke's attention to a pickup truck steering into the back lot. Eli hopped out of the passenger seat while the English driver climbed out and circled to the back of the truck.

"Luke!" Eli called. "Would you help unload some supplies?"

"*Ya*." Luke jogged over to the bed full of wood and lifted an armful.

"*Danki*, son," Eli said with a smile. "You're such a wonderful addition to our family."

Luke forced a smile. *Too bad your son doesn't agree.* "Danki, Eli."

"I hope you'll join us for supper tonight," the older man said.

"Of course." Luke suppressed a sarcastic snort. Timothy would not be glad to find him at supper once again.

10

Luke leaned back on the fence and laughed while Daniel shared another story about an English customer who'd ordered a triple dresser and wanted it within a week. It was obvious some of the customers had no concept of what went into making a beautiful piece of furniture. Creating a dresser wasn't about hammers and nails; it was creating a work of art that would be enjoyed for years and passed down through generations of families.

The aroma of livestock filled Luke's nostrils as he breathed in the crisp autumn afternoon air of the Esh family farm. Standing up straight, he righted his hat while trying to keep his focus on the men surrounding him. However, his eyes betrayed him for what felt like the hundredth time today, and he found his gaze trained on Sarah sitting on a bench across the yard and rubbing her abdomen while she watched the younger children play on the intricate wooden swing set.

He'd been fighting in vain all morning to avoid staring at Sarah, but it had been impossible. During the church service, his eyes kept moving from the bishop and ministers to Sarah sitting across the room on the backless bench with her sisters. She looked radiant—her cheeks pink and her eyes as bright a blue as the summer sky. A few times, she met his stare and graced him with a small smile, causing his heart to thump madly in his chest. He tried in vain to focus on God's Word.

Was he falling for her?

He pushed that idea away. She was his brother's widow. Any romantic feelings for her would be a sin.

However, he'd thought about her nonstop since their last meeting at her parents' house two nights ago. She invaded his head throughout the day and stole into his dreams at night.

"Did you hear me?" Daniel's voice penetrated Luke's daydream.

"*Ya?*" Luke met Daniel's questioning glance. "I'm sorry." Clearing his throat, he tried to ignore his heated face while the rest of the Kauffman men looked on with interest. "I wasn't listening."

"What has you so captivated?" Daniel asked with a smile.

"I think I know," Eli said with a sly grin. "It could be it's a certain *maedel.*"

Oh, no. Luke's stomach twisted. How could Eli know? *Is my ogling that obvious?*

Luke braced himself for a much-deserved tongue-lashing from the elder Kauffman.

"She's right over there." Eli looped his arm around Luke's shoulders and nodded across the yard toward a group of young women. "It's Naomi King, isn't it? She's a pretty thing. I tried getting Timothy to court her, but he thinks he's too good for her."

Timothy rolled his eyes. "Please, *Dat.* You know it's not that. She's too young for me. Besides, I'm through with courting. Miriam ended that for me."

"You have to move on, son. Miriam wasn't right for you."

"Let's leave the subject of my lack of a *fraa* for another day." Timothy stepped toward the house and held up his cup. "Anyone want more iced tea?"

Luke started to move toward Timothy to escape from the grilling, but Eli held him back.

"Look, Luke," he said. "She's smiling at you. You should go talk to her."

Luke glanced toward the brunette standing near the barn and found her grinning in his direction. His shoulders tensed. The last thing he needed to complicate his life was a girl with a crush on him in Lancaster County. He started toward Timothy. "I'll come with you. I could use some more iced tea."

Luke followed him into the large kitchen where more than twenty women chatted and cleaned up after the noon meal. Conversation flew through the air like confetti while they washed dishes and tidied up tables. Timothy refilled his and Luke's cups before they moved back out onto the concrete walk.

Luke stepped toward the gate leading to the playground and spotted Norman sitting with Sarah on the bench. She had been sitting alone when Luke had gone in the house.

A flicker of jealousy poked at him, and he stopped dead in his tracks. Where had that come from? Sarah and Norman were friends, which made perfect sense considering their circumstances. Why should Luke care who Sarah chose as her friends?

But his reaction made him think again: was he beginning to feel something more than friendship for Sarah?

He swallowed a groan. He didn't need the complication of feelings for his brother's widow.

"Luke," a sweet voice said. "I've been looking all over for you. I thought you'd run off."

Luke turned to find Naomi King beaming at him. She had deep brown eyes and matching brown hair that stuck out from under her white prayer *kapp*.

"Hi, there." He raised his cup as if to toast her. "I was just getting some more tea."

"*Ya.*" She smiled with a little too much mirth. "Elizabeth Kauffman makes the best iced tea." She stuck her hand out and shook his—hard, crushing his fingers in her grip. "I'm Naomi King. It's a pleasure to meet you."

"Luke Troyer." He pulled his hand back. "Nice to meet you too."

"Are you staying here in Lancaster County long?"

He shrugged. "Not sure yet." He glanced toward Sarah. She was still talking to Norman. "I guess I'll see how things go." He looked back at Naomi. The determined look in her eyes made him uneasy.

"I heard you're a carpenter."

He nodded. "That's true."

"There are plenty of carpentry businesses 'round here. You could make a nice living." When a gentle breeze blew her hair in front of her eyes, she pushed a wisp back from her face. "I bet Eli Kauffman would consider hiring you. He's short-handed since the—" She stopped short, turning pink with embarrassment at mention of the fire.

Luke sipped his tea and nodded. "Possibly. He could need help."

"I didn't mean to say—" Her face turned sad. "I'm sorry about your cousin. It was a tragedy. I heard you were close to Peter."

"*Danki.* I knew you didn't mean anything by mentioning the fire. It's quite all right." He cleared his throat and glanced toward the Kauffman men. Eli's wolfish grin annoyed him. Luke sure didn't need a matchmaker. "It was nice meeting you." He stepped toward the Kauffmans, but a hand on his arm, followed by a tug, stopped him.

His gaze collided with Naomi's bold smile.

She bit her bottom lip as if scheming. "Have you gotten a proper tour of our church district?"

"Well . . ." He searched for an excuse—anything—but came up blank. He was stuck.

"How about I give you one?" She pulled him toward the line of buggies in the field next to the second white barn. "I'll drive."

"I don't know if that's such a great idea," he began, scanning the yard for someone, anyone, to save him from an afternoon spent with an overly eager young woman he barely knew.

She stopped, blushing again. "Oh. Right." Turning, she called toward a group of young women gathered by the horse pasture. "Lizzie Anne! Lindsay! Let's go for a ride." She then faced Luke again. "We'll have two young chaperones so the rumors won't be too bad."

Before Luke could mount a protest against being kidnapped, a young woman resembling a younger Naomi trotted over, accompanied by Lindsay, Rebecca Kauffman's niece.

"Luke, this is my sister, Lizzie Anne, and you know Lindsay," Naomi said. "Okay, girls, let's give Luke a tour of our district." Turning, Naomi called to a young man, ordering him to retrieve her horse from the barn and hitch it to her buggy. Within several minutes, the horse and buggy were ready for the tour.

Plastering a smile on his face, Luke succumbed to the determined hand steering him toward the buggy. He hoped the district was small and the ride short.

❄

Sarah smiled in response to the pleasant discussion of the weather Norman was providing from the bench seat beside her. As she listened, her eyes found Naomi King smiling, laughing, and batting her eyelashes at Luke across the yard. Sarah shook her head. Didn't Naomi realize she was making a spectacle of herself by flirting with Luke in front of the whole church district?

"Sarah?" Norman's voice broke through her mental tirade. "Are you with me?"

Her cheeks flushed. "I'm sorry. I was thinking about the *zwillingbopplin* again. Sometimes I just get caught up in my dreams of the future." She rubbed her belly, feeling a kick in response. A smile broke out across her lips. "Someone is awake."

Norman grinned. "Really?" He reached his hand out, then

swiftly pulled it back and frowned. "How forward of me. I apologize."

She smiled. He was such a gentleman.

A movement behind Norman distracted her, and she watched Naomi yanking Luke back toward her. What was that girl trying to prove by manhandling him? Was she going to force him to court her?

If he courted her, would he stay in Bird-in-Hand permanently?

Sarah analyzed her feelings about that. His staying would give the twins a connection to their father. However, how did she feel about his courting Naomi King?

Why was that her business anyway?

"Sarah?" Norman asked. "I've lost you again."

"Sorry," she whispered, glancing back at him. "You were saying?"

"Is something across the yard intriguing you?" Norman glanced over his shoulder toward the area where Luke stood with Naomi and then looked back at Sarah. His eyebrows arched in question. "Did you need to talk to Lindsay? Would you like me to call her?"

"No," she said, shaking her head. "I was just wondering what they were doing."

"Oh." He cleared his throat and his expression softened. "How have you been feeling lately?"

"I'm doing okay." She smiled. "*Danki* for asking."

"I've been concerned about you. Your due date is coming up fast. Is there anything you need? Anything for you or for the *kinner*? I have plenty of supplies up in my attic. Leah seemed to save everything from clothes to high chairs for the *kinner*. I'd be happy to turn them over to you."

She shook her head. "I'm fine with supplies, but *danki* for asking. My sisters are loading me up, but I appreciate it very much. You're a very thoughtful friend."

At the word "friend" something unreadable flashed in his

eyes. However, his pleasant expression remained attentive and sweet.

Against her will, her attention moved across the yard again to find Naomi pulling Luke toward the field of parked buggies. Where was she taking him?

Sarah pushed the thought of Luke and Naomi away. How could she blame Luke for going out for a ride with a young, pretty woman like Naomi? Since he'd lost his true love when he was nursing his father, he deserved someone young and sweet like Naomi. He seemed so unhappy and alone. Perhaps Naomi would bring some joy into his life.

Sarah should be happy for him. And she should be happy her children would be born soon, putting a piece of Peter back into her life.

So why was something nagging at her? Some little, tiny feeling of unease creeping into her stomach.

Meeting Norman's gaze, Sarah smiled and patted Norman's hand. "What were you saying about the weather?"

❁

Luke yawned and guided Molly up the driveway toward the Kauffman home, the horse's hooves crunching over the rocks. After Naomi had dropped him off at the Esh farm, Luke hitched up Molly and his buggy and headed back to the Kauffmans'. He breathed in the brisk evening air. As the scent of wood-burning stoves filled his lungs, he reflected upon his long afternoon of riding around the beautiful, rolling farmlands of Lancaster County. He'd listened to Naomi pointing out farms owned by families he didn't know while Lizzie Anne and Lindsay whispered and giggled from the back of the buggy.

Naomi was sweet and kind, but she was a little too eager, with her hand frequently brushing his and her girlish giggle bursting out at odd times. She'd invited him to come to supper tonight with her family, but he declined, hoping to not hurt her feelings. She seemed to want to court, but finding a mate was not the purpose of his trip. He'd come here to find Peter and what was left of his past.

The scent of cinnamon mixed with dew washed over Luke as the buggy approached the back porch of Elizabeth and Eli's home. He spotted the lamp still glowing in the kitchen and his thoughts turned to Sarah. He'd missed his chance to speak with her after the service, and he hoped she was doing well today.

He unhitched Molly, led her to the barn, and then stowed the buggy. He was locking up the barn when the back door swung open, revealing Sarah leaning in the doorway and squinting toward the barn.

Luke ambled toward the house, and when he stepped into the light from the kerosene lamp flooding the steps, she returned a cautious smile.

"*Wie geht's?*" He pushed his hat back on his head and rested his right foot on the bottom step.

"*Gut.*" She stepped onto the porch and gingerly closed the door. "You?"

"*Gut.*" He leaned forward, resting his elbows on his bent knee.

She gestured toward the swing. "Do you have a minute to visit before you head in for the night?"

"Of course." His boots clomped up the steps before he sank onto the swing next to her.

She cleared her throat and brushed a few stray golden strands under her prayer *kapp*. "Did you enjoy the service today?"

"*Ya.*" He nodded. "It was lovely."

"*Gut.*" She stared off across the dark field, and he wished he could read her mind.

"I was disappointed we didn't get to talk after the service," he said.

She looked at him, confusion clouding her pretty face. "You were?"

"*Ya.* I had every intention of visiting with you after the noon meal, but Naomi King had other plans for me."

"How was your ride with her?" Her expression gave no hint as to her thoughts.

He blinked, surprised that she'd seen him leave with Naomi. "It was nice. She gave me a tour of the area, pointing out Amish businesses and farms. She gave me a bit of a history lesson too." He shrugged. "I'm sure she was just trying to welcome me to the area."

"Were you gone all afternoon?" she asked.

"*Ya.*" He brushed a piece of lint from his trousers. "Did you stay at the Eshes' late?"

She nodded. "Norman invited me to join him and his family for supper, but I was too tired. The *zwillingbopplin* are wearing me out sooner these days."

No sooner had she said that than a small yelp escaped from her rosy lips, and she hugged her middle.

"Sarah?" He leaned over and touched her arm. "Are you all right?"

Meeting his gaze, her crystal-blue eyes beamed with pure elation. "That was the hardest kick yet. Want to feel?" Taking his hand, she laid it on her belly.

What he felt next sent his soul soaring with a rush of joy he'd never experienced in his life. Beneath his hand, a tiny bump-bump vibrated. Gasping, he looked up at her.

"The *zwillingbopplin*," she whispered. "They're awake. Sometimes I wonder if they're wearing boots." She gave a little laugh.

His eyes misted. How blessed he was to be sharing this moment with Sarah. Love for her twins, his brother's children, swelled in his soul, deeper than the ocean.

"I say a prayer of thanks every time they kick," she whispered. "*Kinner* are a gift from the Lord."

Luke wanted to agree, but his voice was stuck in his throat.

They sat in silence for several moments while he felt the twins kick and tumble. He wished this moment could last forever.

When the screen door banged open, Luke and Sarah both

jumped back, startled. He rested his hands in his lap feeling as if he'd been caught doing something inappropriate.

"*Wie geht's*, Luke," Elizabeth said, her expression curious as her eyes darted from him to Sarah.

"Hello, Elizabeth," Luke said.

"Sarah Rose," she said. "It's late."

Luke stood and straightened his hat. "I hadn't had a chance to speak with Sarah after service this afternoon, so I stopped by after putting Molly in the barn. I was just leaving."

Elizabeth nodded and turned her eyes to her daughter. "You remember what the doctor said. You need your rest now more than ever. You really should be in bed."

Sighing, Sarah rolled her eyes. "I know, *Mamm*."

"*Ya*, but I can't help but worry." Elizabeth glanced at Luke. "*Gut nacht*." She disappeared through the door.

"I'd best go." Luke took Sarah's hand and helped her to her feet.

"You'd think I was five, the way they treat me," she said, huffing as she stood. "I'm so sick of being treated like a child. I can make my own decisions. I'm going to be a *mutter*, for goodness' sake."

"It's just because they care about you," he said. "I can't blame them."

Her expression softened. "*Danki* for stopping by."

"I enjoyed it," he said. "*Gut nacht*."

"*Gut nacht*." She released his hand.

When he climbed into bed later that evening, he grinned as he remembered the vibration of the twins' kicks against his palm. Yes, children were a blessing from the Lord, and Sarah's friendship was a blessing as well.

Closing his eyes, he silently recited his evening prayers, adding a few extra for Sarah and her twins.

11

Sarah sat on a stool and sipped a glass of ice water, observing while Lindsay rolled out another batch of peanut butter cookies. Her thoughts wandered to last night and Luke's reaction to the feel of the babies' kicks. He appeared to be consumed by the twins, and she could've sworn she'd seen tears in his eyes. Did he truly care for the children?

Of course he did. Peter was his cousin, and the twins were his relatives.

"How's this?" Lindsay's question interrupted her musings.

"What's that?" Sarah asked, wiping the condensation on the glass.

"Is this size all right?" She gestured toward the circular cookie cutouts on the counter.

"*Ya.* Perfect." Sarah ran the cold glass over her flaming cheeks. "It's hot in here."

"It's not that hot in here." Lindsay's eyes filled with alarm. "Can I walk you outside?"

"No." Sarah shook her head. "I'll be all right."

Lindsay tilted her head, unconvinced. "You sure, *Aenti* Sarah?"

Sarah nodded and smiled at the girl's concern. "I'm fine."

Lindsay frowned in disbelief, but turned back to the cookies, loading them onto a sheet.

Biting her lower lip, Sarah contemplated asking Lindsay about the tour Naomi had given Luke yesterday. Would asking about it give Lindsay the wrong idea? But what was the wrong idea anyway? After all, Sarah was just curious. "Lindsay?"

"Hmm?" the girl asked, her stare focused on a stubborn cookie stuck to the cutting board.

"How was the ride yesterday with Naomi, Lizzie Anne, and Luke?"

"Oh, it was fun," Lindsay said. The knife freed the cookie, and she tossed it onto the sheet before facing Sarah and wiping her hands on her apron. "We rode all around the county, and Naomi pointed out different landmarks. She showed him the farmer's market where she sells her quilts, and where her family farm is. It was a lot of fun."

"Oh." Sarah took another long drink and then placed the glass on the counter beside her. She wanted to know more about the tour but struggled with what to ask. It wouldn't be appropriate to ask her niece if she thought Naomi and Luke were courting. "Did Luke enjoy the tour?"

"Oh, yeah." Lindsay smiled. "He seemed to have a great time. He and Naomi talked a lot." She turned back to the task at hand, flipping more cookies onto the metal sheet.

Sarah nodded. Naomi was so young and pretty; of course Luke had had a good time. Why should Sarah be surprised?

"I think Naomi likes Luke." Lindsay placed the last cookie on the sheet, then rolled out the remaining dough and began cutting more. "After we dropped him off, she told Lizzie Anne and me that she thought he was handsome. Then she said she was going to bring him lunch at work this week since her quilt store at the farmer's market is right across the street from the furniture store. I think she has a crush."

Sarah told herself it wasn't her concern. It was Luke's business whom he courted.

And why should she care anyway?

"Lizzie Anne said Naomi doesn't give up when she sets her

mind to something." Lindsay cut out the last circle and proceeded to place the cookies onto the next sheet. "But I asked if she was sure he was even going to stay in town. Seems like she may be setting herself up to get hurt if she puts so much effort into trying to get him to court her and then he moves back home to Ohio."

"Good point," Sarah said, her voice brittle with something that felt an awful lot like jealousy.

"Done!" Lindsay smiled as she loaded the two full cookie sheets into the oven. She set the timer, hopped up on the stool next to Sarah, and grabbed her glass of ice water. After taking a long sip, she gave Sarah another concerned look. "You don't look so good. I think you should let me walk you outside or back to the house for a nap."

"I'll be fine," Sarah said, swiping the glass across her forehead.

"Lindsay's right, Sarah Rose," *Mamm* said behind her. "You should walk outside with me."

"Fine," Sarah muttered, lowering herself to the floor and schlepping outside behind *Mamm*. Her legs and feet ached, and her shoes were tight. She wished she could sleep for a week and awaken refreshed without any aches, pains, or swelling in her legs and feet.

She sank onto the bench outside of the play area. *Mamm* dropped down beside her and relieved Beth Anne from babysitting duty. They silently watched the children swinging and shrieking with delight.

After a few moments, *Mamm* turned her gaze to Sarah. "You look exhausted, Sarah Rose. You should go home and get some rest."

"No," Sarah said, shaking her head. "The house is too quiet, and it gives me too much time to miss Peter and think about the things Luke told me about his past. I'd rather stay here and keep busy. That way I can't think too much."

Sarah sank back on the bench and idly rubbed her belly. A rhythmic blip caused her to grin. "*Mamm*! Someone has the hiccups!" Grabbing her mother's hand, Sarah placed it over the bump.

"Oh, Sarah Rose." Tears filled *Mamm*'s eyes and spilled over her cheeks. "Oh, just *wunderbaar*." A faraway look shone from her eyes. "I remember so clearly. Daniel had the hiccups the same time every morning like clockwork. You had them often too. I loved all of those little bumps and kicks."

"*Ya*." Sarah smiled. "Sometimes when they're doing summersaults it feels like butterflies."

Mamm gave a soft laugh. "That's exactly how it felt."

They sat in silence for several moments, tuned in to the hiccups from the unborn twins and oblivious to the laughs and screams of the children on the playground.

When the hiccups ceased, *Mamm* sat back on the bench and sighed. "Before you know it, those little ones will be out here swinging and hollering with all of their cousins on the playground."

"*Ya*." Sarah folded her arms over her stomach. "Time moves so quickly. It seems like only yesterday I found out I was pregnant." She waited for her mother to speak. When *Mamm* didn't continue, Sarah prodded her. "What's really on your mind?"

Mamm patted her hand. "I think it's time you stopped working. You've been so tired and hot all the time. I worry you'll get ill before the *kinner* come. You heard what the doctor said. You need to save your strength. You've only got two months to go."

Sarah knew her *mamm* was right. "I just can't face being at the house alone all day. When I think too much, I feel myself falling back into a bottomless pit of grief and anger. But the good news is that the nightmares about the fire have stopped."

"That's *wunderbaar*, but you still need your rest." *Mamm* squeezed her hand. "How about we have one of Robert's girls stay with you and help you get the room ready? Your nieces would love to help you. Nancy is a very sweet girl. I bet she would love to spend her days with you. She could sew and clean for you."

"You win." Sarah sighed. "It's a good plan."

"*Mamm!*" a voice behind them boomed. "*Dat's* on the phone!"

Mamm stood and patted Sarah's leg. "I better go. Think about what I said. We can leave Sadie a message on her voice-mail and ask her if Nancy would like to come stay with you. I know she would love it."

Sarah nodded. "Sounds good."

"Did you want to come in?" *Mamm* asked.

"No," Sarah said, turning back to her nieces and nephews. "I'll stay out here and watch the *kinner*. It's nice and cool. I felt like I was going to pass out in the kitchen."

While *Mamm* ambled back into the bakery, Sarah watched her niece leap from the swing, landing in the mulch and collapsing in giggles. She imagined her children on the swings, laughing and singing with their nieces and nephews. Were her twins boys or girls or one of each? Soon she would know. A skitter of excitement coursed through her.

Her thoughts turned to Luke, and she absently wondered if Luke would sit with her someday, watching the children play. Would he stay in Bird-in-Hand long enough to see that? If so, would he perhaps be watching children play with Naomi instead?

Sarah settled back on the bench and focused on her niece dancing before her.

❄

"That's great work." Daniel slapped Luke's shoulder as he studied the finished triple dresser. "You and Jake make a *gut* team."

Luke wiped the sweat from his brow. Glancing at the clock on the wall, he found it was nearing noon. He wondered if he could hitch a ride with an English customer and sneak over to the bakery to ask Sarah to lunch. He had awakened this morning remembering the feel of the twins kicking his hand last night. It was a sensation he'd never experienced; it was heavenly.

"Luke!" Jake bellowed from up front. "You have a visitor."

"A visitor?" Luke muttered, walking toward the front. Had Sarah beaten him to the punch and come to surprise him?

Stepping out into the showroom, he frowned as his eyes fell on Naomi standing by the counter. She was chatting with Eli while holding a picnic basket. He hoped she wasn't the visitor Jake had mentioned, but he knew in his gut he was wrong.

Naomi glanced up at Luke, and a coy grin spread across her lips. "Hi!" She held up the basket. "I hope you don't have plans for lunch."

"Well, I—" Luke searched for an excuse to work through lunch. He gave Jake a pleading look, but the young man simply shrugged. He made a mental note to clue Jake in on his feelings for Naomi.

Stepping behind the counter, Eli smacked Luke's shoulder. "Go on. Take a long lunch. You've been working hard, and you deserve it." He winked as if he and Luke shared an inside joke about picnic lunches.

Luke swallowed hard as he met Naomi's expectant stare. He was trapped yet again. How did he continue to find himself backed into a corner with this woman? She was pleasant and nice looking, but he didn't want to court her. And yet here she stood holding out a picnic basket and her heart for Luke's taking. How could he possibly hurt her feelings?

"I'll go wash up," Luke muttered, heading for the back room.

"*Wunderbaar*!" she called after him. "I'll get the picnic table by the pasture behind the shop set up for our meal."

❀

"This is *appeditlich*," Luke said before biting into his chicken salad sandwich.

"*Danki*." Naomi lifted the bottle of iced tea and refilled his glass. "I thought today would be the perfect day for a picnic. It warmed up a bit." She set the bottle down and brushed a stray crumb from the tablecloth. Her brown eyes sparkled with something resembling expectation, or maybe hope. "It's *wun-

derbaar that you're working here. Maybe Eli will offer you a permanent job. I visited Robert and Sadie's farm last night after supper, and Robert mentioned his *dat* was thinking of offering you a permanent job here at the shop."

Luke wiped his chin with a napkin. "Maybe. I haven't thought about that."

"Oh, if so, then you must stay! Do you want to stay here permanently?" she asked, her smile wide and bright.

"Eli hasn't offered me a job yet." Luke lifted the cup of tea. "And I haven't decided what I want to do."

Her eyes were wide, full of urgency. "Oh, you should stay, Luke. You said yourself you like it here."

He sipped his tea. "That's true. I do like it, but I like Ohio too. Ohio's always been my home, and I'm not sure if I want to pick up and move, leaving everything behind."

Naomi pushed the remaining crumbs of her sandwich around on her paper plate. "Is there someone special in Ohio?"

"You mean a *maedel*?" he asked.

Frowning, she nodded.

He almost chuckled. She couldn't be more obvious if she wore a sign declaring "Court me, Luke Troyer."

"No," he said, trying not to grin. "There's no girl."

Her smile returned. "So, there's nothing keeping you there."

"Nothing but memories, I guess. And some good friends, a couple of cousins, aunts, and uncles." He scooped another mound of homemade potato salad onto his plate. "How's business at the quilt shop today?"

"Busy. I took six custom orders this morning, so our quilting group will have to get busy." She retrieved a plate containing half of a vanilla crumb pie from the bottom of the basket. "I hope you have room for dessert."

"Wow." The scent of vanilla enveloped him. "That looks *wunderbaar gut*."

She grinned. "It is." After cutting two large slices, she slapped one onto his plate. "Enjoy."

He forked a piece into his mouth and savored the smooth, moist decadence.

"I'm a *gut* cook," Naomi announced, cutting up her piece. "I'm great at sewing and quilting, and I keep the house and farm in order. I take *gut* care of my eight siblings too."

Luke kept his eyes trained on the hunk of pie on his plate. He couldn't look her in the eye while she recited her résumé to him. He wasn't interested in her domestic skills.

"Do you ever feel like the Lord is guiding you?" she asked. "I mean, do you ever feel His hand on your back leading you to the way He wants you to go?"

Luke nodded. "*Ya*. Absolutely. He led me here."

Her smile widened, and he regretted the words immediately. He'd meant that the Lord had led him to Bird-in-Hand and Peter's new life, not to Naomi. Hoping to change the subject, he pointed the fork at the pie. "This is outstanding."

"*Danki*." Placing her elbows on the table, she rested her chin on her hand. "I'll be sure to remember this recipe for you."

❀

An hour later, Luke walked through the back door of the shop with a full belly and a worried mind. Lunch had been delicious, but he felt guilty for giving poor Naomi the wrong idea. He would be happy to share a nice friendship with her, but he had no interest in courting her. Yet breaking the news to her would surely shred her heart. The last thing he wanted to do was hurt an innocent girl who enjoyed his company.

"Luke," Eli called, approaching. "How was lunch?" The older man waggled his bushy, salt-and-pepper eyebrows, and Luke sighed.

"*Appeditlich*." Luke hoped to leave it at that.

"She's a *gut* girl." Eli smacked his arm. "She'd be a *wunderbaar fraa*."

Luke pushed his hat back on his head and scratched his

scalp. "I hope she's not getting the wrong idea. I'm not looking to court anyone."

"Take your time, son." Eli idly pulled on his beard. "I wasn't looking to court when I met my Elizabeth. The Lord has a way of leading us to roads we never imagined we'd take. Just keep your heart and mind open to endless possibilities."

Luke nodded and then headed over to Jake's work area, where the young man studied plans for another project. "So, what are we starting now?" he asked.

"My grandpa asked me to take a look at this new design for a hope chest. It's similar to the one you helped me finish last week before you completed that triple dresser." Jake pushed the papers over to Luke.

"Hey, Troyer." A strong hand on Luke's shoulder nudged him backward.

Luke turned to find Timothy smirking.

Timothy gestured toward the back door. "I see you were getting cozy with Naomi King at lunch."

"We're friends," Luke said. "That's all. Now, if you'll excuse us, Jake and I have work to do."

"I thought you weren't going to stay here permanently," Timothy said, his expression hardening. "Don't you have a job, family, and friends to return to in Ohio?"

"I'm not sure what I'm going to do, but I know for sure I'm not ready to court anyone." Luke turned his attention back to the plans, hinting it was time for him to leave.

"Don't forget our conversation," Timothy said. "I think you know what would be best for everyone involved."

Luke met Timothy's stare. "I know what you're saying, and I'm not promising you I'm going to stay, and I'm not promising I'm going to leave. I'm going to wait and see what feels right to me. But I can promise you one thing: I won't hurt Sarah."

Timothy shook his head. "You're making a mistake if you stay here. You will hurt her, and no one in my family will be happy." He turned on his heel and stomped back over to his workstation.

Luke stared after him and gritted his teeth with frustration.

"What was that about?" Jake asked.

"Timothy is convinced my being here is detrimental to Sarah because I remind her of how Peter lied about his past. He wants me to leave, and he won't let me forget it." Luke looked back at the plans, hoping his stomach would stop churning.

"I think Timothy needs to leave the future to God and let it go," Jake said. "You're not the type of person to hurt anyone, and you know how precious life is since you've lost your parents and your cousin."

Luke met the young man eyes and smiled. "You are wise beyond your years, Jake. I wish more people thought like you." He then studied the plans. "All right, we better get to work before your grandpa gets impatient."

Apple Ring Fritters

1 cup sifted flour
1/4 tsp salt
1 – 1/2 tsp baking powder
1 egg
3/4 cup milk
4 large apples
Shortening
2 Tbsp cinnamon (For use after draining on paper towel)
2 Tbsp sugar

Sift together flour, salt, and baking powder. Add egg and milk. Beat well. Peel and core apples and slice into rings about 3/4 – inch thick. Dip rings in batter and drop into skillet containing 3/4 inch of hot melted shortening. Fry until golden brown on both sides. Drain on paper towel. Mix sugar and cinnamon together and sprinkle over fritters. Makes 18 to 20.

12

Sitting across from Naomi Friday afternoon, Luke popped another large piece of vanilla crumb cake into his mouth. The cake was superbly moist and sweet, just like it had been the previous four days this week.

He smiled while Naomi prattled on about amusing English customers and new quilt designs. She had appeared in the showroom of the furniture store precisely at a quarter of twelve each day with her basket and a delicious lunch. Each day he accepted her invitation, even though he knew by spending time with her he was leading her to believe he wanted to court her. Yet he couldn't seem to form the words "I want to just be friends" or "I don't want to court you." Extinguishing her hopes and dreams felt wrong, but so did letting her believe he wanted to be more than friends.

Today Naomi had brought a mysterious large black garbage bag, which she'd refused to allow him to carry to the table for her—and which she also refused to open. It sat next on the ground at her feet like a loyal pet.

"Would you like to join my family for supper tonight?" she asked, a tentative smile spreading on her lip. "I'm making my *appeditlich* ham loaf."

"Oh," Luke said, setting his fork down on the empty plate. "I wish I could, but I can't."

She frowned. "That's a shame. I guess you already have plans?"

"*Ya*," he said quickly, hoping a half truth wasn't too much of a sin. "I'm going to join the Kauffmans tonight. I haven't made it over to their place all week, and Eli's been asking me to come by."

It wasn't a complete lie. He hadn't had a chance to make it to Eli's because he'd been working late helping Jake with a project for a loyal customer, and he'd been working on Sarah's cradle late into the night at the house. He'd longed to see Sarah all week, and while her father hadn't invited him over, he hoped to pop in and see her around suppertime tonight.

Naomi suddenly brightened. "I plan to get on your schedule soon. Perhaps you can join us Saturday night."

"Perhaps." Luke cleared his throat and began piling up their dirty plates. "I'd best get back to work before I lose my job." He put the dirty dishes into a small bag and then added the used cups.

Smiling, she hefted the bag onto the bench beside her. "I brought you a gift." She untied the knot and pulled down the sides of the bag. "Since you're all alone in Sarah's old house, I thought you might get cold at night." She slowly lifted a white quilt with purple-and-blue panels. "It's my favorite design, Log Cabin. I thought you might like deep purples and blues."

"Oh, Naomi." Reaching across the table, he ran his fingers over the soft material and intricate stitching. Guilt nipped at his soul as he imagined her slaving over this beautiful blanket for him. "You shouldn't have done this for me."

"Don't be *gegisch*, Luke." Her eyes were trained on his—intent and purposeful. "I wanted to."

"*Danki*," he whispered. "I'm not worthy."

"But you are, Luke. You truly are." She gave him a hopeful smile. "I hope you'll stay here in Bird-in-Hand."

He nodded, overwhelmed by her frank admission of feelings and her generous nature. "I guess we'll see what God has in store for me."

"I can hardly wait," she whispered with a smile.

"Naomi," he began. "I appreciate your friendship. You're a lovely *maedel*, and you'll be a *wunderbaar fraa* someday."

He paused to gather his thoughts, and her smile fell in anticipation of his unspoken "but." Leaning over, he took her hands in his. "I'm not sure what my future holds or where I'll wind up living, so you shouldn't waste your time waiting to court me. You should find someone who is available for you now."

She shook her head and pulled her hands back. "No, no. I want to wait for you, Luke. I'm willing to wait as long as it takes you to move here. You're the one for me. I can feel it." She placed a hand over her heart. "I know in my heart God wants us together. I truly believe that."

Luke sighed, lamenting that he had to be more direct. "Naomi, I'm not ready to court anyone. Please don't wait for me." He nodded toward the quilt. "I can't accept that quilt from you."

She frowned, and her eyes glistened. "I'll wait as long as I need to. You are the one for me, and you must take the quilt. I insist."

"Naomi, please look into my eyes." He held her hands tight. "I want to be your friend."

Her lip trembled. "Are you breaking up with me?"

He paused, debating how to respond. "I want to be your friend. I enjoy spending time with you, and I enjoy our lunches. Right now, I'm trying to figure out where I belong. Please don't wait for me. You're a beautiful *maedel*, and I'd hate to see you wasting your time on me."

She sniffed and wiped her eyes. "You're not a waste."

He gave her a sad smile. "*Ya*, I am." He touched the quilt. "That's a beautiful quilt. I'm honored you made it for me, but I can't accept it."

Clearing her throat, Naomi forced a smile. "We're friends, *ya*?"

"*Ya*, we're friends."

She raised her eyebrows. "Friends give each other gifts, *ya*?"

A smile crept over his lips. "You're not going to let this go, are you?"

"Nope." She lifted her glass of iced tea.

"*Danki.*" He smiled. "I appreciate the gift."

They chatted about the weather and their weekend plans until it was time to head back to work. She packed up her basket and then stood.

"*Danki* for having lunch with me."

He folded the quilt into the bag and rose alongside her. "*Danki* for the *appeditlich* meals and fabulous cake. I will cherish the quilt."

"Can friends have lunch together sometimes?" she asked as they walked toward the front of the store.

"I don't see why not."

"*Gut.* Enjoy your afternoon." She gave him a quick hug.

Before he could respond, she trotted across the street toward the farmer's market.

❄

Sarah wrapped a quilt around her shoulders and stared off across the dark pasture toward her former home. She breathed in the fresh scent of wood burning in the fireplace, mixed with the newly harvested hay.

The past month had dragged by at a turtle's pace. At the doctor's orders, she'd spent most of her time on the sofa with her swollen feet and achy legs keeping her from baking the dishes she loved and sewing clothes for the children. Her sweet niece, Nancy, had waited on Sarah and worked around the house. While she loved spending time with Nancy, she missed the bakery.

Gazing across the fields, she thought about Luke. She had expected him to stop by to visit or for supper. However, she hadn't seen him once since Thanksgiving dinner last week. She wondered what had kept him away all week. They'd chatted briefly after Thanksgiving supper, and he'd asked how she was feeling. After that he was dragged outside to the barn for the usual men talk.

She'd found herself missing him all week. She longed for their previous conversations on the porch and hoped she hadn't scared him off by being too bold that Sunday when she had shared the twins' kicks with him. She had felt at the time their friendship allowed for that level of intimacy, but she must've been wrong. Letting him touch her may have been too much for him. She hoped he didn't think she was ... forward. Or, worse yet, loose.

She pushed that idea away and reflected on her week. Norman had dropped in for supper on Wednesday, and they'd spent the evening chatting about the children. She enjoyed their time together and appreciated his friendship. However, she sensed something more in his eyes lately. More than once, she'd found him staring at her with an intensity that made her uncomfortable.

Sighing, she cradled her belly and smiled when a baby kicked in response. Hearing her twins' heartbeats at the doctor's had deepened the excitement she already harbored for them. In a couple of weeks or so, she'd be holding them in her arms and gazing into their eyes

Cupping a hand over her mouth, she tried in vain to stifle a yawn. The screen door squeaked open and banged shut, and Timothy's boots scraped across the porch before he sank into a chair nearby.

"It's cold out here," he said, hugging his coat to his chest. "You should go inside."

"I will soon enough," she said through a second yawn. "I was just enjoying the cool air for a moment." She nodded toward her house. "I'm surprised Luke hasn't stopped by this week. Have you talked to him at all?"

"He's been real busy at work. Tonight he's working late helping Jake with a project that's due to a customer tomorrow."

"That's nice he's helping Jake," Sarah said, ignoring the disappointment flickering through her. She wondered if Luke and Naomi were still friends. She hesitated, since the question would sound like she was gossiping, which was a sin, but her curiosity won out. "Does Naomi come by the shop at all?"

"She brings Luke lunch sometimes," Timothy said. "She was by a couple of times this week."

"Oh?" Sarah pushed the rocker back and studied her dark house across the pitch-black pasture.

"I think she would like to court him," Timothy said. "But I have the feeling Luke isn't going to stay around here."

She looked at him. "You don't think so?"

Timothy shook his head. "He belongs in Ohio."

"He said that?"

Timothy shrugged. "In not so many words, but *ya*."

Sarah battled the disappointment bubbling up inside her. "I thought he might stay to be with the *kinner*."

"He'll probably be gone right after Christmas. He'll stay long enough to see them born and then head back home to live his own life." Yawning, Timothy stood and started down the stairs. "I reckon I should hit the hay. The alarm goes off early in the morning. *Gut nacht*."

"*Gut nacht*." Sarah heaved herself from the swing and started toward the door.

Climbing the stairs to her room, she wondered what would become of Luke Troyer. Somehow she couldn't imagine losing him. And yet, she couldn't figure out why she felt so attached to him.

13

"What do you think, *Aenti* Sarah?" Nancy nodded at the poinsettia she'd placed on the mantle in preparation of Christmas dinner tomorrow night. "Do you like the flower there?"

"Oh, it's love—" Sarah gasped and groaned, her words stolen by a unexpected sharp stab of pain, slicing through her lower back like a knife.

She sucked in a breath and rubbed her stomach as a cramp radiated through her abdomen. All week she'd endured pressure and occasional cramps. Today they felt more intense as she sat in her father's favorite easy chair.

"*Aenti* Sarah!" Nancy yelped, rushing over and dropping at Sarah's feet. She grasped Sarah's hand in hers. "Are you all right?"

Sarah could only manage a slight nod as the pain radiated again, more intense than ever.

"Katie!" Nancy yelled. "Katie, come quick! We need help!"

Her older sister trotted in from the kitchen. "What's wrong?"

"Something's wrong with *Aenti* Sarah." Fear shimmered in Nancy's big, blue eyes.

"I think it's time," Sarah whispered, her voice raspy and breathless. "I think I'm in labor. Please get help."

Katie pulled Nancy to her feet and pushed her toward the kitchen. "Go! Run! Get help!"

Katie then looked at Sarah. "I'll get you a glass of water and a compress for your head." Her expression was calm, her words steady and even—evidence she'd been present when her *mamm* delivered her younger siblings at home.

"*Danki*," Sarah whispered. She sucked in a breath when another cramp gripped her.

Katie returned with a cold washcloth and swiped it over Sarah's clammy forehead and cheeks. She then held a glass of water to Sarah's lips. Sarah held her breath through more cramps while Katie brushed Sarah's hair back from her face and chatted about their plans for Christmas dinner.

After what seemed like an eternity, the back door slammed open and *Mamm* entered, followed by Rebecca and Lindsay. Sarah only heard the echo of voices as another cramp hit, stronger and more intense this time. The pressure on her abdomen felt like fire and stole her breath.

"Sarah Rose!" Her mother's voice cut through her fog of pain. "I'm with you now. Everything's going to be just fine. We've called Nina, and she's on her way. We'll have you to the hospital soon, *mei liewe*. I promise."

Pulling up a chair, Rebecca sat next to Sarah and took her hand. "Squeeze when it hurts."

"I'll get your bag." *Mamm* hurried up the stairs.

Sarah stared into Rebecca's eyes and gripped her hand. "It's time."

"*Ya*." Rebecca smiled, pushing a wet wisp of hair that had escaped Sarah's prayer *Kapp* back from her face. "It's time. I'll stay with you the whole time. I promise."

"*Danki*." Sarah sucked in a breath as another cramp set in.

Rebecca quietly counted.

When it released, Sarah felt a dribble between her legs and gasped. "I think my water just broke."

Rebecca squealed and squeezed her hand.

Closing her eyes, Sarah said a silent prayer the labor would be smooth and the twins would be healthy. She couldn't help but wish Peter were with her.

❧

The following afternoon, Christmas Day, Sarah stared down at the beautiful baby girl in her arms. After twenty-four hours of labor, she had delivered two perfect babies, each weighing a little over six pounds.

"A boy and a girl," *Mamm* cooed while holding Sarah's son. "They are just precious, Sarah Rose, just precious."

"I'm so blessed," Sarah whispered. Her heart had been bursting with love and joy ever since she'd laid her eyes on her twins. "I had no idea being a *mamm* would be like this. There's no joy like it." She glanced over at *Mamm* and wiped a tear. "*Danki.*"

Mamm chuckled. "Why are you thanking me? You're the one who delivered them."

"No." She held her free hand out, and *Mamm* leaned over the hospital bed and took it. "*Danki* for being here. I couldn't have done it without you."

"You're welcome, Sarah Rose." *Mamm* squeezed her hand and then pulled back, staring down at her new grandson.

Sarah studied her daughter. The baby's chubby, pink face was accented with bright eyes. Her bald head was shielded by a pink stocking hat, and her little body was covered in a white blanket trimmed in pink and blue. "I've decided on names."

"Oh?"

"Rachel Elizabeth and Seth Peter." When *Mamm* didn't answer, she glanced over to find her wiping her eyes. "*Mamm?*"

"*Danki,*" her mother whispered. "I'm very touched."

Sarah looked down at her daughter just in time to see her yawn. Her little mouth opened wide, revealing bright pink gums and a matching little tongue. Sarah grinned.

If only Peter were here to see his beautiful twins.

No, she would not be sad now. He was in her heart and in the eyes of her babies.

Rachel fell asleep, and Sarah ran her finger over the baby's head. While she watched her daughter sleep, she opened her heart to God, silently thanking him for her two wonderful miracles, her children.

For the first time since Peter's death, she felt true happiness.

Turning to *Mamm*, Sarah found her humming softly to Seth, who slept in her arms. *Mamm* met her gaze and smiled.

They sat in silence for a few moments. Sarah stared down at her baby girl, thinking of Peter. He would've been elated.

"Merry Christmas, Peter," she whispered. "I wish you were here to hold your babies. They are a gift from God, the perfect Christmas gift to fill my heart."

"*Ya*," *Mamm* whispered, her voice trembling as she wiped again at her eyes.

A knock sounded from the door.

"Come in," Sarah called.

The door squeaked open, and a knot of Sarah's sisters and nieces paraded through into her room, oooing and ahhing with love. The littlest nieces pushed forward and stood on tiptoes to view the new babies.

Sarah smiled, scanning the crowd and finding her brothers standing near the door. She searched the sea of faces and a twinge of disappointment hit her when she didn't find Luke there.

Kathryn appeared from the crowd, her arms extended, and her face expectant. "May I?"

"Of course." Sarah handed over Rachel and sighed.

"Merry Christmas and Happy Birthday, little one," Kathryn cooed, rocking her niece to her chest.

❧

Luke paced outside Sarah's hospital room, gripping the brim of his hat. Laughter and voices rang through the door. Although he knew most of her family members were there celebrating the birth of the twins, he felt like an intruder. Or perhaps he felt more like a fraud, since he was posing as a cousin to the children when he was really an uncle. However, he was so knee-deep into the falsehood that there was no turning back for fear of being ostracized.

Nevertheless, it wasn't a lie. He'd never said he was a cousin; the family had assumed it. Just the same, he hadn't corrected them either ... which made him a liar.

Taking a deep breath, he marched to the door and knocked. Receiving no response, he pushed the door open to find a crowd of Kauffmans surrounding Sarah, who was propped up in the bed, smiling and laughing with her family.

She looked breathtakingly beautiful dressed in a blue hospital gown with her golden blonde hair hidden under her prayer *kapp*. He couldn't help but wonder if his brother had ever spent time staring at her and contemplating how something so perfect existed in nature. God had blessed Eli and Elizabeth when He created their youngest daughter.

Her eyes met his and lit up as if her heart swelled with joy. His smile broadened at the thought that he could bring her such happiness.

"Luke." She extended her hand in his direction. "I'm so glad you came. I was hoping you'd heard the news." She beckoned him over.

He weaved through the knot of visitors and stood next to her. "You didn't think I'd come?" He wished he'd brought her something—a bouquet of flowers or a small gift. However, the gift he had waiting for her at home would be special enough.

"I was afraid no one told you." She started to adjust herself in the bed and then winced in pain.

"Are you okay?" He reached for her hand but stopped himself from touching her.

"*Ya*." She forced a smile. "I'm a bit sore."

Elizabeth leaned over her daughter. "You want me to call the nurse for more medicine?"

Sarah shook her head and waved her mother off. "I'm fine. It passed." She then faced Luke. "Have you seen them? Aren't they exquisite?"

Luke nodded, staring at the baby in Beth Anne's arms.

"That's Seth Peter." Sarah beamed. "Doesn't he look like Peter? It's uncanny. His eyes are the same shade of hazel." She pointed to the baby in Kathryn's arms. "Rachel Elizabeth has blue eyes, like me."

Luke studied his nephew, and warmth washed over him. His eyes filled with tears as he was overwhelmed with a mixture of love and grief for his brother. He fought the urge to flee the room in order to deal with the confusing emotions in private.

A gentle hand encircled his arm.

"Luke? Are you okay?" Sarah asked.

The concern and affection in her eyes caused the emotions within him to churn. He cleared his throat and wiped his eyes, hoping to stop the tears.

"I'm fine. It's just warm in here." He hoped he sounded convincing.

Beth Anne angled the baby boy toward Luke. "Would you like to hold him?"

"No," Luke said, shaking his head in protest. "I don't want to—"

"You won't hurt him," Sarah said with a chuckle. "*Bopplin* are resilient."

"I couldn't," he said. "I don't know the first thing about them."

"Don't be silly." Sarah hoisted herself up from the bed, wincing slightly as she moved toward him.

His eyes raked over her, taking in how tiny she was.

She lifted the baby from her sister's arms and held him close to Luke. "Seth, meet your *onkel* Luke."

His eyes snapped to hers at the word *uncle*. Did she sense the truth? Did she know who he was?

"Oh, I'm sorry." Her pretty face flushed a bright crimson. "It's just automatic for me to say *onkel* since I have three brothers."

"It's okay," he whispered, his voice quavering. He cleared his throat, but emotion ruled his words. "They can call me *onkel*."

"I think the *zwillingbopplin* would be happy if you were their *onkel* Luke." Her smile was bright, and he feared he might shed a tear or two after all. She held Seth out to him, her arm resting against his, mixing their body heat. "Would you like to hold him?"

"I don't think I could," he whispered.

"It's not so hard, Luke," Daniel chimed in. "I've held my nieces and nephews plenty."

"It's good practice," Rebecca said with a grin.

"Just don't drop 'im," Timothy added, and the crowd laughed in response.

Luke succumbed to the request and took the tiny child in his arms. His heart felt as if it would overflow with love as his brother's tiny offspring opened his hazel eyes, yawned, and fell asleep again.

Lowering himself into the chair next to the bed, Luke held the baby. The rest of the world disappeared, and he was alone with the boy who would never know his father.

At that moment, Luke silently vowed to help raise his niece and nephew, in honor of his brother, whom he missed more than words could express. He was going to stay with the twins in Bird-in-Hand. There was no doubt in his mind or his heart; this was where he belonged.

14

Glad to be home from the hospital, Sarah climbed the stairs, taking each with care due to her lingering aches and pains. She followed *Mamm* toward her room.

The twins' cries echoed from downstairs where her sisters tended to them. She stopped and started toward the stairs.

"Sarah Rose!" *Mamm* chided. "Your sisters can handle the *kinner*. You need to get some rest."

"But they're crying ..." Sarah bit her lip.

Mamm gave a knowing smile. "Babies cry, *mei Liewe*. They will be fine. You need your rest. You just gave birth three days ago."

Sighing, Sarah hobbled to her room. Stepping in, she glanced around at the familiarity of the room that had become hers since Peter died and she moved out of her house. She stopped in her tracks when something out of place caught her eye.

On the floor next to the cradle her father had made was the most exquisite cradle she'd ever seen. It was simple yet elegant, with a pattern engraved in the sides. It was stained a deep cherry color and sparkled in the low light of the lamp. A large red bow hung over the side.

Sarah gasped and crossed the room. She bent and touched it, and it rocked back and forth, scraping the wooden floor with a quiet whooshing sound.

"You kept your promise, Luke," she whispered, running her finger over the slick wood and sniffing back tears. "*Danki.*"

"It's your Christmas gift from Luke," *Mamm* said. "Actually, he said it was for you and the *zwillingbopplin*. He had intended to give it to you himself on Christmas, but the *kinner* had other plans. Since he's at work today, he asked *Dat* to give it to you for him."

"It's perfect," Sarah said, meeting *Mamm's* gaze. "How *wunderbaar.*"

"I think he loves those *kinner*, you know." *Mamm* dropped Sarah's bag onto a chair by the bed. "He said he'd come by to visit when you were ready to have company."

"He can come any time." Sarah crossed to the bed and lowered herself onto the side.

"You get some rest. The babies will be fine with your sisters and me."

Sarah nodded. "Okay."

"Call me if you need anything." *Mamm* disappeared through the door, gently closing it behind her.

Rolling onto her side on the bed, Sarah closed her eyes and drifted off to sleep, dreaming of Peter, the babies, cradles ... and Luke.

❈

Sarah yawned as she lounged on the sofa with Rachel in her arms. She hadn't achieved much rest last night since the babies had their days and nights mixed up. Although *Mamm* had helped with the middle-of-the-night feedings, Sarah still found herself awake most of the night.

Sarah was thankful to have *Mamm's* help during the night. And since the bakery was only open part-time during the winter, she was also grateful to have *Mamm* home to help along with her nieces most days.

It was hard to believe she'd been home a week with the twins. She'd expected to have a house full of visitors; however, only her sisters and a few of her friends from the church district had stopped by and brought food and gifts for the children.

If Sarah were honest with herself, she'd admit she was disappointed one guest in particular hadn't stopped by at all, and that guest was Luke. She'd asked Timothy if he'd seen Luke, and her brother had explained Luke hadn't missed a day of work.

While she was rocking Rachel back to sleep early this morning, she'd pondered the question of why Luke had been staying away. She couldn't get the image of Luke at the hospital out of her mind—the way his brown eyes had filled with tears when he saw the children touched her deep in her soul. She wondered if his absence had anything to do with the emotion he'd displayed then. Was seeing the twins too difficult for him because they reminded him of his beloved cousin?

She hoped Luke wouldn't stay away. For some reason she craved Luke's presence even more now that the children were here. Was it because he was her only connection to Peter beyond the twins? Or did she miss his friendship? Her gut told her it was a combination of both. Sarah felt a connection to Luke that was unlike any other friendship she cherished.

A flurry of activity and a chorus of children's voices sounded from the kitchen, announcing the arrival of visitors.

Mamm entered the living room with a smile on her face. "You have a visitor. Or rather, you have visitors."

"Send them in." Sarah adjusted a sleeping Rachel on her shoulder and then ran her hand over her prayer *Kapp* to make sure she was presentable. She felt silly for fussing over her appearance. After all, she was a sleep-deprived woman who'd given birth less than two weeks ago.

She hoped Luke was among the visitors, but a quick glance at the clock on the mantle showed it was shortly after four and too early for Luke to arrive on a weekday.

Mamm disappeared into the kitchen and a few moments later, Norman appeared in the doorway followed by his daughters.

"Norman." Sarah smiled. "It's so good to see you."

He glanced down at Seth sleeping in the cradle and then back at Sarah, who turned slightly, angling Rachel toward them.

Norman smiled at the babies. "Beautiful," he whispered. "Congratulations. God is good."

"*Ya*," Sarah said, rubbing Rachel's back. "He is."

The girls stood over the cradle and cooed at the babies.

"Why don't you two go back in the kitchen and have cookies with Nancy and Katie?" Norman asked. "Sarah and I are going to visit, and the babies are sleeping."

The girls retreated to the kitchen.

"Please have a seat." She gestured toward the chair with her free hand.

"*Danki*." Norman folded his stocky body into the sofa across from her. "How are you feeling?"

"Exhausted but happy." She covered her mouth to shield a yawn. She then adjusted Rachel on her shoulder, which had started to ache.

"Are they sleeping well in the night?" he asked.

Sarah snorted with sarcasm. "No, not yet. *Mamm* says I slept through the night at three months. I'm hoping these two figure out their nights and days faster than that. If not, then I may pass out soon from exhaustion."

Norman's eyes trained on Seth, and a smile broke through his pleasant countenance. "How does it feel to be a *mamm*?"

"It's more *wunderbaar* than I ever imagined." She ran a finger over Rachel's soft cheek. "I stare down at my *kinner* and can't believe they're mine."

"Blessings from God," he whispered.

"Absolutely." She shifted to the edge of the chair and gently placed Rachel into the cradle next to Seth. Sitting back in the chair, she sighed and rubbed her shoulder. "Little ones weigh more than you think."

Norman smiled.

They fell into an easy conversation, discussing everything from the weather to the children.

After an hour, he stood. "I reckon I should get back home and feed my own *kinner* before they start grumbling."

Sarah walked with him to the kitchen. "I can whip up something to feed all of us."

"No, no." He touched her arm. "I wouldn't want to do that to you. You have your hands full."

"Don't be silly." She glanced at *Mamm*, who was sitting at the table talking with *Dat* and the children. "Do we have something we can throw together for supper for everyone?"

Mamm stood and went to the refrigerator. "Of course we do. Let me see. I can make this stew quickly. It's plenty for everyone."

"No, I couldn't impose." Norman snatched his coat from the rack by the door and glanced at his daughters. "Get your wraps on. We're heading back home."

"Norman, don't be silly." Sarah touched his arm. "I haven't seen you in a couple of weeks. I'd be happy if you and the girls stayed."

"Another night. I promise." He glanced at his girls, who were ready at the door. "Say good-bye to everyone. We'll see them very soon." He said his farewells to her parents and then steered his girls out the door.

Sarah followed close behind, hugging her arms to her chest as the January wind sliced through her caped dress. She inhaled the chilly air, breathing in the aroma of wood fireplaces.

Norman directed his girls to the waiting buggy and then turned to Sarah. "You best get inside before you catch a cold."

"*Danki* for visiting," she said through her chattering teeth.

"We'll have dinner together very soon," Norman said, his expression flickering with an intensity she'd never seen before. "I'd like to see you more often."

Unsure of the meaning behind his words, Sarah was rendered speechless for a moment.

"*Gut nacht.*" He paused for a moment and then touched her arm. "Take care of those *wunderbaar zwillingbopplin.*"

Norman clattered down the porch steps and loaded the girls into the buggy. Sarah waved as they drove off toward the road.

The crunch of stones drew her gaze toward the path. Spotting Luke heading for the porch, she rushed down the stairs toward him.

"Why don't you have a coat on, Sarah Rose?" he scolded, shaking his head in disapproval.

She stopped in her tracks and scowled. "And it's nice to see you too."

He gave a bark of laughter, and she grinned.

"How are you?" he asked.

"Angry with you."

He raised an eyebrow.

"Why haven't you been by to see me and the *zwillingbopplin*?" She folded her arms across her chest. "I feared you'd moved back to Ohio without any notice."

His smile disappeared. "You think I'd leave without telling you?"

She shivered.

He nodded toward the house. "How about we take this disagreement inside?"

They climbed the porch steps side by side.

"Did you hear the news?" she asked. "Daniel is a father. Rebecca gave birth to their son, Daniel Jr., last night."

"I did hear." Luke's smile was genuine. "Eli told me this morning."

"I can't wait to see my new nephew." Sarah's heart swelled with love. She knew Daniel and Rebecca were elated to welcome their first child into the world after fifteen years of marriage. It was a miracle.

Her thoughts turned to cradles, and she stopped short of the door.

Luke reached for the doorknob, and she blocked it. "Sarah Rose, you're going to catch a cold or, worse yet, pneumonia."

"That's not the first time I've heard that tonight," she quipped.

He reached for the knob again, and she stopped him by taking his hand in hers. The warmth of his skin took her by surprise, and she pulled back.

"I need to tell you something in private," she said, shivering again.

"Tell me quickly. I don't want to see you back in the hospital." His eyes were full of concern.

"The cradle you made is beautiful. It's the most *wunderbaar* gift I've ever received, and I love it. *Danki.*" She looked into his eyes and for the first time since she'd met Luke, her stomach fluttered. She tamped down the feeling and turned toward the door.

"Wait." He touched her shoulder, and she faced him. "I'm glad. I wanted to do something special for the *kinner* in memory of Peter. I'm very happy you like it."

"It's perfect. No, it's better than perfect. It's magnificent."

He nodded, his eyes intense.

They stared at each other for a long moment and then he broke away and turned the doorknob.

Sarah stepped into the kitchen and took in the delicious scent of *Mamm's* stew.

"Sarah Rose!" *Mamm* snapped. "What on earth were you doing out there without a coat? Did you forget it's January?"

Sarah sighed, and Luke snickered.

"Luke!" *Mamm* stepped toward him. "You're just in time for supper. Take off your coat and make yourself at home."

"*Danki.*" Luke hung his coat on a peg by the door and greeted *Dat* and Sarah's nieces.

Sarah touched his arm. "Would you like to see the babies?" she whispered, noticing his warm scent.

"Are you kidding? I really only came to see them, not you." His crooked grin was teasing.

She laughed and led him into the living room, where the babies were fast asleep in their cradles. She stood back while he squatted between the cradles and gazed between them. His smiled faded, and his expression turned to reverence.

For a moment, Sarah wondered if she should leave the room and give him privacy. When he reached for Seth and then pulled his hand back, she stepped over by him.

"You can touch them," she whispered. "I promise they won't break."

He glanced at her in disbelief.

"Go ahead. Don't be afraid. Touch them."

Leaning down next to Luke, she lifted his hand to place it on Seth's back. Liquid heat coursed through her veins at the touch, and for a split second, she couldn't breathe. She pulled her hand back as if to stop the fire burning within her.

Again his eyes bored into hers, and they studied each other for a brief moment.

Standing, she folded her arms as if to guard her confused heart.

Luke glanced back at the babies and, placing his free hand on Rachel's back, he caressed their backs simultaneously. His expression was filled with emotion, similar to the day in the hospital. His eyes glistened.

Feeling like a voyeur, she backed toward the door to the kitchen. "I'm going to go help *Mamm* with supper," she whispered, gesturing toward the kitchen.

"Don't go." His eyes locked with hers.

She stopped and wracked her brain for something to break the protracted silence between them. "Why haven't you visited until now?"

"I didn't know if it was proper to come see you when you first got home." His smile was back. "I'm new at this whole *boppli* thing."

"I was afraid it was too much for you at the hospital."

He stood, his eyebrows raised in question. "What do you mean?"

"You seemed so emotional at the hospital when you held Seth. I was afraid the *bopplin* scared you off."

"Are you joking?" He stepped toward her. "You couldn't beat me away with a two-by-four. I want to be a part of their lives."

"Supper's ready," *Mamm* said from the doorway. "Robert's here for the girls, and he's going to join us."

Sarah followed her *mamm* into the kitchen, where they served the meal to the guests. While they ate, Sarah was aware of Luke studying her, and she wondered if he'd always been so observant of her or if she'd only just noticed it.

After supper, Robert and the girls headed home. Sarah excused herself to her bedroom, and her parents helped her carry the babies and cradles upstairs, where she fed and rocked the babies until they fell asleep.

Returning to the living room, she found Luke chatting with her parents. She sat on the couch with *Mamm* and joined in the easy conversation. She again found Luke's eyes honed in on her. What surprised her the most was that she enjoyed the conversation and the attention from Luke.

What was wrong with her? She didn't feel this awareness or excitement when she was with Norman. What was different about Luke Troyer?

And why did she like it so much?

Sarah didn't know the answers to those questions, but she knew one thing for certain—she hoped Luke would visit again soon and often.

※

Luke said good night to Eli and Elizabeth and thanked them for supper before they disappeared upstairs.

Turning to Sarah, he found her standing by the kitchen doorway with a comfortable smile on her face, and his heart turned over in his chest. She was different tonight—more at ease and more intent on him. He wondered where the change came from. Had giving birth to the children released stress for her?

He wasn't sure what had made her different, but he knew that he couldn't take his eyes off her tonight. Although she'd been beautiful when she was pregnant, she was even more stunning now. Her body was petite, and her eyes seemed brighter.

And when their hands touched, something had ignited between them. Had she felt it too?

"I had a nice time tonight," she said.

"Me too." He rose and crossed the room. "I reckon I should get on home, and you should get to bed."

She sighed. "*Ya*. Those *bopplin* will have me up most of the night, so I might as well get some sleep while I can."

He studied her, wishing he could read her thoughts. "Your nieces are helping you during the day, *ya?*"

She nodded as they walked to the kitchen. "Robert brings Nancy and Katie by every morning, and they stay all day. *Mamm* is only opening the bakery every other day, so she's here too. It's nice to have help. I can nap a little during the day since I don't sleep much at night."

"That's *gut*." He glanced out the dark window and remembered a question he'd wanted to ask. "I saw a buggy leaving when I was walking over. Who visited here earlier?"

"Norman came by to see the babies." She yawned, cupping a hand to her pretty face. "Oh, excuse me. It's not the company making me yawn. It's lack of sleep that's tiring me out."

Jealousy twisted his gut at the mention of Norman's name. Why was he jealous of her friend? "I better let you get some sleep. I've taken enough of your time."

"You're welcome anytime," she said. "You're family."

"*Danki.*"

He felt an insatiable need to touch her. No, more than that, he found himself resisting the urge to kiss her forehead.

"*Gut nacht*, Sarah Rose." Snatching his coat from the peg by the door, he slipped his arms into it.

"*Gut nacht*. I hope you'll come back again soon." She opened the back door and handed him a lantern. "You best not stay away too long next time."

He smiled, stepping onto the porch and shivering in the whipping wind. "I promise I'll see you again before the week's out."

"I'm going to hold you to that." Glancing across the field, her eyes widened. "Is that snow?"

Luke held his hand out and smiled when large, fat flurries danced over his fingers. "*Ya*, it is. You better get inside before you catch a cold."

"You hurry home too."

"Stay warm." He hopped down the porch steps and rushed through the wind toward the house.

Glancing up, he smiled as the flurries kissed his face. The evening had been like a dream, spending time with Sarah, her parents, and her precious children—his niece and nephew, his only living link to his only brother.

For the first time since his *mamm* died, Luke felt like a part of a family, a real family. He understood why Peter had stayed in Bird-in-Hand—he had been surrounded by people who loved him. Luke wanted that too. Being with the Kauffmans was a dream come true.

Life was pretty close to perfect.

In his heart, he knew he longed to be more than a friend to Sarah, but those thoughts were inappropriate. His brother hadn't been gone a year, and it was disrespectful to even consider courting Sarah.

Aside from that, coveting his brother's widow was a sin in itself. However, even if he could never be more than a friend to Sarah, he would be satisfied. Just knowing her and the twins was a gift from God after losing his parents and brother.

What happens when she finds out you're her brother-in-law and not her husband's cousin? How will that knowledge change her feelings for you? Will she ever trust you again?

The questions came from deep within his heart and slammed him back to reality. He didn't know the answers, and he dreaded the day when she found out the truth.

Loping up the front steps of the house, he glanced over his shoulder and saw a light burning in Elizabeth's kitchen. He wondered if Sarah was watching him walk home. He hoped she would remember this evening with as much happiness as he did.

The wind shifted, and his teeth chattered as the air sent a frosty shudder through him. The snowflakes picked up, and he glanced up at the sky, feeling the very air around him changing, as if a big storm was coming to Bird-in-Hand.

15

Sarah awoke with a start after a night of jumbled dreams and nightmares. She'd dreamed she was sitting on a stool in the kitchen of the bakery and telling Peter about the twins. Then she was in a strange house in Ohio, and Luke was telling her about Peter's past. Next she was in the nursery of her former home rocking one of the twins to sleep while Luke stood at the window overlooking the pasture, holding the other baby.

When she sat up in bed, she felt a burning desire to go to her other home and sort through Peter's clothes. She couldn't explain why, but she needed to hold one of his shirts and inhale his scent—if any remained on his clothes. Perhaps his scent would make her feel close to him again.

Nancy and Katie had planned to come by today to help Sarah while her parents kept to their Saturday routine of running errands and visiting the market. Sarah fed the babies and then dressed. She was gathering up the babies' supplies when the girls appeared in the doorway, eager to help. Together, they brought the twins and their things downstairs and then ate breakfast while the children rested in their cradles.

Once the girls were settled with the children, Sarah asked them if they were comfortable staying alone with them while she ran to her house to get a few things. They both told Sarah to take her time and not worry about the children.

Slipping on her cloak, Sarah hurried down the gravel lane to her former home. The dream was still vivid in her mind, and her heart thumped in her rib cage as she climbed the front steps to the porch. The brisk February wind soaked through her shawl, and she shuddered.

Taking a deep breath, she wrenched open the front door, wondering if she'd find Luke at home. She'd seen him nearly every day for the past three weeks when he'd stopped by after work to hold the twins and visit.

"Hello?" she called, her voice echoing throughout the downstairs. "Luke? Are you home?" The floorboards creaked beneath her shoes as she wandered through the living room, laundry room, pantry, kitchen, and bathroom. Finding them all empty, she gripped the banister and headed to the second floor.

"Luke?" she called. "Are you here? Hello?" Sarah stuck her head into her former bedroom, sewing room, and nursery. Again, each was empty.

Standing before the closed spare bedroom door, her pulse skipped at the idea of finding Luke asleep in bed. What would she say to explain an awkward situation such as that? Lifting a trembling hand, she gingerly knocked on the door.

"Luke?" Her voice quavered with embarrassment. "Luke? Are you here?" After waiting a brief moment, she turned the knob and the door creaked open. The room was quiet, and the bed was made. No sign of Luke.

"I guess you got an early start this morning too," she muttered.

She crossed the room and peered down at a pile of his clothes. The dark-colored trousers and shirts lay neatly folded and piled on the hope chest by the window. A spare pair of boots sat in the corner, lined up symmetrically like corn in *Dat's* field.

Looking at Luke's clothing brought back thoughts of how Peter kept his personal belongings. Sarah's lips curled in a melancholy smile. A love for the neat and orderly ran in the Troyer family. Peter used to get frustrated if the cans weren't lined up perfectly in the pantry—labels all facing the same way.

She smiled at the memory before padding back down the hallway to her former bedroom. Her stomach flip-flopped with anticipation when she opened the doors to Peter's armoire. Although a part of her had hoped to see Luke, she was also relieved to have privacy while delving into Peter's things for the first time since his death. Shaking her head, she tried to fathom the nine-month period since he'd died. Where had the time gone?

Her hands shaking like dandelions in a spring breeze, she pulled out Peter's favorite dark-blue shirt. She closed her eyes and buried her face in the fabric as if it were the oxygen her lungs needed to sustain her life. A faint whiff of his scent filled her soul. He'd always smelled like wood, stain, and a hint of earth.

Tears of mourning began to sting her eyes, and she was dragged back in time to their last conversation on the morning of his death. He'd kissed her lips on the porch and told her to have a good day. She'd held onto him and asked him to wait a few more minutes since she'd wanted to clear the air between them. He'd been cool and withdrawn toward her for a week, and she couldn't take it any longer. She'd needed to know what was on his mind.

Her hopes of a meaningful talk were derailed when his ride pulled into the driveway. Before trotting off to the car, he promised they'd talk later.

However, later never came.

Looking back on that time, she wondered again if Peter's cold behavior had something to do with the lies he'd told her. She dug deep into her memories, searching for other signs of his deception. When they'd first met, she'd ask him about his family, and he'd give quick, evasive answers and then change the subject. Perhaps the signs had been there all along, and she'd chosen to ignore them because she was so consumed with love.

She pushed her thoughts away, leaving them in the past where they belonged. Wiping her eyes, she set the shirt down on the end of her bed and ran her fingers over the sleeve while studying the garment. It served no purpose keeping the clothing in the armoire. She wondered if Luke would want to pick out a few pieces to keep and then she could give the rest to her nephew Samuel. He was growing up so quickly and would wear them soon enough. She would also hold a few shirts back for Seth, who would want to know about his father when he was older.

With memories raining down on her, Sarah sorted through the remaining shirts in the top of the armoire. Finally she stood before the armoire, ready to conquer the drawers of socks, underwear, and suspenders. When she leaned down to open the drawer, she spotted what looked like a long, flat wooden box stuck in the back of the emptied shelf. She fetched it and sank down onto the chair next to the bed.

The box was stained a deep cherry, and the hinges were simple but elegant—no doubt Peter's work. She flipped the tiny latch on the front and lifted the top, revealing stacks of letters, all addressed to Peter in beautiful handwriting accented with flourishes—obviously written by a woman. The return address on each letter was "D. Maloney" in Middlefield, Ohio.

Sarah bit her lip, and her stomach tightened as questions swirled through her mind. She'd never heard of a person named D. Maloney, and she had never known of Peter keeping in touch with someone in Middlefield, Ohio. Who from Ohio had been writing to Peter, and why would he keep this secret from Sarah?

Her stomach roiled, and she groaned. *Oh no! More lies!*

Sucking in a deep breath, Sarah examined the top envelope. The postmark was from ten months ago, a month before he died. Pulling out the letter, guilt nipped at her. She felt as if she were invading his privacy, but the question rang through her mind: why had he kept this from her?

Holding her breath, she read the letter.

Dear Peter,

I hope you and Sarah are doing well. Congratulations on your news! You must be so excited to be expecting a baby. Cody is doing well and is excited to be finishing up first grade. In fact, he's counting the days until summer break. I'm enclosing a snapshot of him in his soccer uniform. Thank you for the check. It will help pay his summer camp tuition.

Take care,

DeLana

Sarah's brow furrowed while she reread the letter, wondering who Cody was. From the letter, she deduced he was English. She'd never heard of an Amish boy named Cody, and Amish children didn't go to summer camp. Why would Peter secretly send money to a strange English child?

Sarah fished the photo from the envelope and studied it. A boy with light-brown hair and bright hazel eyes, clad in a blue shirt and matching shorts, grinned while holding a soccer ball. The shape of his face, his smile, his eyes, and the color of his hair were all very familiar.

Then it hit her.

She gasped.

No, it couldn't be.

But it was.

He looked like Peter.

"No, no, no." Her voice croaked with worry and hurt. This child couldn't be Peter's son. There was no way! Peter would've told her.

Would he have?

Could her husband have been so deceitful?

Yes, he could have. He lied about his childhood.

One by one Sarah pulled out the letters and read them; each was similar to the previous. This mysterious DeLana wrote short, one-page notes, telling Peter how Cody was doing in school, including that he excelled in math but abhorred reading and that he loved to play sports, especially soccer. She would always wish Peter and Sarah well and end with thanking him for the check.

The checks.

Money Peter and Sarah had earned for their own family.

Sarah blinked back tears, and a lump swelled in her throat. How could Peter send their money to another family every month and not tell her?

How could he have a child and not tell Sarah!

The realization of the growing web of his deceit drowned her in a deluge, and she couldn't fight the hurt anymore. Hugging the letters to her chest, Sarah dissolved into tears as sobs wracked her body and soul.

As she succumbed to the emotion rioting within her, one question echoed through her mind:

Had she known her husband at all?

❄

Luke's boots scraped the porch steps to Peter's home, a counterpoint to the conversation from the morning that replayed in his mind. He tried in vain to suppress the excitement coursing through his veins. It seemed too good to be true, but he had asked the farmer to repeat the offer to him twice, and the price for the house and twenty acres was only half of what the developer had offered Luke for his farm in Ohio seven months ago.

If the offer still stood, he could sell his farm in Ohio and move to Bird-in-Hand with money in his pocket to start a cabinet-making business in town. The farm was about a mile up the road; therefore, Luke would be close to Sarah and the twins.

Entering the living room, Luke tossed his hat onto the peg by the door and then shucked his coat and hung it next to the hat. He ambled toward the kitchen, but stopped dead in his tracks, thinking he'd heard a voice coming from upstairs. He listened, and again he heard the sound of a moan, or perhaps a sob.

"Hello?" he called. He waited for an answer and then ascended the stairs, his boots clomping up the hardwood. The sound of the voice grew louder when he reached the hall. It was a woman crying.

"Hello? Are you all right?" Luke called. "Who's there?"

He stepped into the master bedroom and sucked in a breath at the sight of Sarah slouched in a chair and crying while holding a stack of crumpled envelopes. A pile of men's shirts littered the bed.

He shook his head. Memories of Peter must have shattered her.

"Sarah!" Crossing quickly, he crouched before her and took her hands in his. "Are you all right?"

Meeting his gaze, she threw herself into his arms, sobbing on his shoulder. He leaned forward to balance his weight on the chair while he rubbed her back. The warm, sweet scent of her hair reminded him of vanilla mixed with hyacinth, and his pulse quickened. Holding her was almost too much for him; it felt like a sin. But she needed him. How could he push her away?

"Sarah Rose," he whispered. "It's okay. The hurt will get better. I promise. I know he's gone, but your heart will heal. You have to be strong for your *zwillingbopplin*. You can show them all of the love that Peter gave you."

Her body trembled against his, and his throat tightened. Despite the exhilaration of holding her close, he concentrated on consoling her.

Suddenly, she pulled back, and fire flashed in her blue eyes. "He has a son. How could he not tell me?" Fresh tears pooled in her eyes. "Why didn't you tell me, Luke? Why did *you* lie to me?" She smacked his arm, and he jumped back with a start. "You're just as bad as he is!"

Shaking his head with shock, he stood. "Cody," he whispered.

"Yes, Cody! I was going through Peter's clothes, and I was going to offer you some of his shirts as a memory of him. I found a box hidden behind the clothes, and it contained these letters." She shook the envelopes in front of his face for emphasis.

Standing, she marched across the room, pacing. "I guess the Troyer family is full of liars! He was sending her money without telling me."

She threw the letters onto the bed. "I trusted you, Luke. I trusted you to tell me everything. I knew all along you were holding something back. But I thought you were my friend." Her voice trembled. "I really trusted you." The tears overtook her again, and she wilted against the wall, sobbing, her hand at her mouth.

"Sarah Rose." He gathered her into his arms, and she wrapped herself around him. "I'm so sorry. I thought it would hurt you if I told you, but finding out this way was much worse than I ever imagined."

"Oh, Luke," she whispered, her voice quavering along with her body. "I don't know who my husband was. I'm so confused. How could he keep this from me?"

"I think he was afraid of losing you." Stepping back, he placed his finger under her chin, lifting her eyes to meet his. He wiped a stray tear from her soft cheek and suppressed the urge to kiss the sadness away. "Why don't I make you some tea and we'll talk? I'll tell you anything you want to know."

She nodded, her expression softening. "I'd like that."

❈

Sarah sat across from Luke at the kitchen table and cradled the warm teacup in her hand. Biting her bottom lip, she tried to mentally sort through the letters she'd read, but she couldn't grasp the idea that Peter had withheld from her the fact he had a son he was supporting in Ohio.

Her eyes fell on the small wooden box full of letters and her mouth trembled. "I just don't understand," she whispered, her voice thick with emotion. "Peter has a child?"

Luke studied the wood grain on the table. Why was he avoiding her gaze? Was he filtering what to share?

"Please, Luke. Tell me everything. I can handle it." Reaching over, she touched his hand.

"Peter met DeLana when he was seventeen," Luke began. "We both were working in our uncle's cabinet store, and her father owned the local wood supply shop. Peter made a supply run one day with the English driver, and DeLana was working in the office. From what he told me, it was love at first sight."

Sarah's stomach tightened. As ridiculous as it seemed, the idea of Peter falling in love with another woman caused her stomach to sour. How silly was it to be jealous of a person from Peter's past?

She knew the answer—the woman meant so much to Peter that he'd never told Sarah about her. The thought made Sarah's stomach churn with a mixture of jealousy, anger, and betrayal.

"They courted in secret for a long time, probably close to a year." Luke ran his fingers over the grain in the table, his mocha eyes lost in the past. "He would sneak out his window late at night and meet her in the barn behind her father's house. Sometimes he would say he was at a singing but drive out to a field near her house instead."

Sarah sipped her tea, wondering if she was going to wake up from this nightmare of deceit. Peter meeting an English girl in a field or in a barn late at night . . . She gripped the mug.

"Then one day—" Luke stopped and cleared his throat. "Then one day," he began again, "his father found out and was furious." He sighed, shaking his head. "They argued, and his father forbade Peter from seeing her. Peter stormed off, saying his father had no right to run his life."

He raked his fingers through his hair, a gesture she'd seen Peter do a thousand times when he was anxious. "From what my uncle told me, DeLana's father found out and came to the shop one day, ranting about how the Amish had no right to mingle with the English girls. His father agreed, and they made a pact to keep the two of them apart. So he told Peter he would with-hold all of the money Peter had made working in the shop for the past two years unless Peter joined the church and stopped seeing DeLana."

Sarah tilted her head in question. "How could he do that?"

"He had control of the money." He slouched in the chair and folded his arms. "The accounts were in his name at the local bank. So Peter's dad laid the law down, and Peter went crazy. And that's when he revealed DeLana was pregnant."

Groaning, Sarah shook her head.

"His dad muttered something about how disappointed his *mamm* would be, and Peter went to pieces. He left on foot and walked for miles."

Tears spilled from Sarah's eyes. "He must've felt so alone."

Luke laid his hands on hers. "Before he ran off, I tried to talk to him, but he locked himself in his room. He told me he tried to see DeLana, but her parents kept her prisoner in her house. They took her car and drove her to and from school. She was in her senior year of high school. They had dreams of her going to college and marrying a rich *Englisher*, so they were determined to keep her away from any Amish man. They wanted her to give the *boppli* up for adoption."

Sarah swallowed, hoping to wet her dry throat. "What happened?"

"Peter joined the church the following spring and he kept working at the shop. He and his father barely spoke. Then one day, months later, he ran into DeLana at the market. She was married to an *Englisher* and had kept the *boppli*, Peter's son. The child's name was Cody Alexander Maloney. Her husband adopted him without Peter's consent." Luke frowned. "When he looked into his child's face, he crumbled. He came home that night and had it out with his father. It nearly came to blows. That was when he left and never came back."

Sarah shook her head with disbelief. "Why didn't he tell me the truth?"

Luke squeezed her hand. "He probably didn't want to tell you because he was afraid you would think lowly of him."

Sarah stood, grabbed the two mugs, and walked to the sink. With tears streaming down her hot face, she washed the mugs and placed them on the counter. Questions surged through her. The story seemed so surreal.

How could Peter keep this secret for so long? How could he walk away from his son in Ohio and act like it never happened? It just didn't make sense.

She obviously had never known her husband at all.

Grief, anger, and betrayal drenched her soul. She felt as if he'd died all over again, the grief was so raw, so penetrating, so new.

"Sarah Rose." Luke's voice was millimeters from her ear. "Talk to me. Don't hold your feelings inside."

Sucking in a deep breath, she turned, finding his chest inches from her.

"I feel so betrayed," she whispered, her voice quavering again. Why couldn't she stop crying? She wished she could rein in her emotions. "I don't understand why he would keep something like this from me. I was his wife."

She pointed to her chest. "I shared everything with him— my heart, my soul, and my love. I lived our wedding vows, but he lied to me. He sent out our money every month to his son without telling me. How could he not tell me he had a son? I don't understand. Why, Luke?" Her voice broke on the last words, and then she was sobbing again. She closed her eyes and covered her face with her hands.

Strong arms pulled her to his hard chest, and his voice was comforting in her ear. "It's okay to cry, Sarah," he said gently. "But I'm sure he loved you. He was the luckiest man on earth to have you as his *fraa*."

"You're so different from him," she whispered with her head on his shoulder. She contemplated the story Luke told and wondered about a detail he'd missed. She stood and faced him. "What happened to Peter's parents?"

"They're gone. Both have passed away."

"When?"

"*Mamm* died when Peter was little." He blew out a sigh and raked his hand through his hair. "Pop blamed himself after Peter left. He tried to find Peter, but couldn't. The guilt was too much for him. He suffered a massive stroke and died about a year ago."

The story clicked together in Sarah's mind. "Oh, my goodness." She gasped, cupping her hand to her mouth.

"What?" Luke's eyes fill with concern. "What's wrong?"

"You nursed him." She pointed at him. "You nursed him because he was *your* father too."

Something resembling fear flashed in Luke's eyes. "Wait. I can explain—" He reached for her, and she backed up.

"Don't touch me!" She held her hands out, blocking his. "You're a liar, Luke Troyer! You're not Peter's cousin. You're his brother!"

"Sarah, give me a moment to explain. I never lied." Luke stepped toward her. "I never said I was his cousin either. Everyone assumed it."

"But you never told me the truth." She leaned back on the counter and shook her head. "It all makes sense now. How could I have been so stupid?"

He frowned. "You're not stupid."

"How could I have missed the obvious? It was right before my face just like Peter's deception." She gestured toward Luke. "You look like him. You sound like him. When I first saw you in the bakery that day, for a split second, I thought you were him."

He raised his eyebrows in surprise. "You did?"

She ticked off a list of similarities in her mind. "You hold onto your suspenders and then smooth your hair when you're trying to remember something, just like Peter. You run your hands through your hair when you're nervous, just like Peter. And you separate your food on your plate so that it doesn't touch, like Peter did."

She ignored his shocked expression and continued her rant. "And you know the intimate details of his life. A cousin wouldn't know the details of every conversation that goes on in inside a home. You said you tried to talk to Peter, and he locked himself in his bedroom. A cousin wouldn't know those things. My nieces and nephews don't live with me."

"Sarah Rose," he began, reaching for her. "I wanted to tell you, but every time I shared a story about his past, it seemed to hurt you. The last thing I wanted to do was hurt you even more than Peter did."

"So you thought lying was the answer?" She gestured widely. "Don't you realize you did exactly what Peter did to me? You omitted the truth, Luke. That's the same as lying!"

"But I wanted to tell you, Sarah Rose. I really did." His eyes pleaded with her, tugging at her heartstrings.

"You could've told me at any time," she snapped. "We spent plenty of time talking and sharing." She groaned, contemplating how much she'd shared with him. "I feel like such a fool for trusting you, Luke."

"No, no." He placed his hands on her arms. "Don't feel like a fool. You know me. You know the real me." Taking her hand, he held it to his chest. "You know my heart."

She pulled her hand back to her side. "Don't touch me! I don't know you at all. You're a liar just like your brother!"

Stomping over to the table, she grabbed the box of letters and held it up. "See these letters? That's what Peter did to me for years. He never told me he had another child, a son, in Ohio. That's the same as not telling me who you really are. You're my brother-in-law, the uncle of my *zwillingbopplin*. No wonder you gave me a surprised look in the hospital when I called you *onkel*. You were afraid you were caught."

Luke gave her a pained expression. "That's not true, Sarah Rose. I was afraid of hurting you. Timothy warned me not to tell you who I was or share more about Peter's past for fear it would break your spirit even more."

Her eyes widened. "Timothy knew too? My own brother kept the truth from me?"

"He didn't know about DeLana, but he knew about me."

Sarah sniffed, fighting tears at the realization she'd been betrayed by Peter, Luke, and Timothy. "You and Timothy have managed to break my heart once again."

She started for the door. Then she stopped short of it and faced him. "Tell me one thing, Luke, and I want to know the truth."

He nodded. "Anything. I'll tell you anything you want to know, and I promise to tell the whole truth this time, not leaving one detail out."

"How many siblings did Peter have?" She ignored the quaver in her voice and held her head high, giving the pretense that nothing more would hurt her.

"Only one—me." He pointed to his chest.

"*Danki.*" She turned her back to him and started for the door.

"Sarah Rose, please wait."

Ignoring his pleas, she slipped on her cloak and stalked out the front door, nearly walking into *Mamm*, who was coming toward the door.

COCONUT CHEWS

½ cup butter
2 cups brown sugar
Melt butter in saucepan, then stir in sugar until dissolved. Cool.

Slightly beat in:
2 eggs
1 tsp. vanilla
1 cup flour
1-1/2 tsp. baking powder
½ tsp. salt
1-1/2 cups coconut

Pour batter into a greased 9x13 pan lined with wax paper. Cut in squares. Bake for 35 minutes at 350 degrees.

16

Sarah Rose?" *Mamm's* eyes filled with worry. "I was concerned when I got home from the market and the girls told me you'd been here for a couple of hours. Are you all right?"

"No, I'm not. Follow me home." Sarah marched down the stairs.

"Sarah Rose!" Luke rushed out onto the porch. "Wait!"

Ignoring him and the pain surging through her soul, Sarah continued on, her head held high. The betrayal would not steal her confidence. She had to think of the twins and be strong for them.

"What's going on?" *Mamm* asked.

"He's a liar, just like his brother," Sarah snapped through gritted teeth.

"What?" *Mamm* yanked Sarah to a stop. "Like his brother?"

"*Ya*, like his brother—Peter." She sucked in a breath, willing her body to stop quaking.

"His brother?" *Mamm* gasped, her hand at her mouth. "Oh, my word. I had no idea. Why didn't he tell us?"

"Because he didn't want to hurt me. Instead he lied and hurt me even more."

Sarah hugged the wooden box to her chest. Her husband had been supporting a child she never knew existed, and now the man she'd considered a dear friend wasn't who she thought he was. He'd turned out to be deceitful, just like her husband.

Her heart ached with renewed grief.

Whom could she trust?

Her eyes filled with fresh tears.

"What's that?" *Mamm* pointed to the box.

"I found it in Peter's armoire," Sarah said, her voice hoarse. "It has letters from his English girlfriend."

"An English girlfriend?" *Mamm's* eyes widened with shock.

Sarah wiped her eyes, trying in vain to stop the tears. "He was with her before he abandoned his father and Luke and came here to start a new life."

Mamm's voice clouded. "What do the letters say?"

"He was sending her money."

"Why would he do that?"

Opening the box, Sarah fished out a photo of the boy and handed it to her. "This is why," she whispered.

Mamm studied the photo, then glanced at Sarah. Brows furrowed in confusion, she shook her head. "Sarah Rose, I don't understand."

"That's his son," she said, her voice trembling as much as her body.

Mamm's eyes rounded as she inhaled.

Sarah sobbed, and *Mamm* pulled her into her arms. "There, there, Sarah Rose." She patted her back. "We'll get through this. *Kumm.* Let's go home."

❀

Sarah fingered the crumbs left from her homemade bread while sitting across from *Mamm* at the kitchen table. She'd just finished telling her *mamm* the details of the letters and the story Luke had relayed regarding Peter's past.

Mamm had listened with wide eyes. Taking a bite of bread, she shook her head with disbelief. "I don't know what to say. I never imagined Peter had such a troubled past."

"I don't understand why he didn't tell me," Sarah said, pushing back a strand of hair that had escaped from her *Kapp*. "It was bad enough he lied about his family, but now I found out he lied about a child he was supporting. I don't know who my husband really was, *Mamm*. I never imagined he was a liar."

Mamm took Sarah's hand in hers. "I know this is difficult, but you must forgive him. I'm sure he had his reasons. Maybe he worried that you wouldn't love him if you knew he'd made mistakes in the past."

"That's what Luke said." Wiping more tears with her free hand, Sarah shook her head. "But I would've loved him anyway, *Mamm*. It doesn't make sense. There should be no secrets between a husband and wife. I was never dishonest with him."

"Never?" *Mamm* raised her eyebrows in disbelief. "Not even when you bought extra material for a new dress without checking with Peter first? Or when you bought a little gift for one of your nieces without telling Peter? Or how about when you bought a few extra books to read without checking your weekly budget?"

"That's different." Sarah yanked her hands back and folded them on the table. "Buying a few extra things at the market is not the same as hiding information about your past—especially information about a child you're supporting."

She pictured Luke, and her anger simmered. "I'm so upset with Luke for not revealing his identity. He said every time he shared more of Peter's past, I seemed more and more hurt and upset. But not telling the whole truth is lying too." Her eyes narrowed. "And to make it even more hurtful, he said Timothy has known all along that Peter had family in Ohio. My own brother kept the truth from me. Why did they all lie? I could've handled the truth, *Mamm*. I'm a strong woman."

"You just gave the answer, Sarah Rose." *Mamm* patted her hand. "They didn't want to hurt you. Luke and Timothy could see how much you were hurting after Peter died and then you found out that he wasn't an orphan as he'd said."

"It's wrong to be deceitful. It's a sin." She swabbed a napkin across her cheeks and then her nose.

"Sarah Rose, you must remember the words of the Bible. In Luke 6:37 we read, 'Do not judge, and you will not be judged. Do not condemn, and you will not be condemned. Forgive, and you will be forgiven.'" *Mamm* covered Sarah's hands again with her own. "Peter was wrong; he never should've kept those secrets from you. But he was human just like you and me. You must forgive him. He's not here to defend himself. We can only assume he did it to protect you."

"Protect me from what?" Sarah snapped.

"He loved you and didn't want to hurt you."

"How can you be so sure he loved me?" Sarah tried to clear the knot in her throat. "Love means you're open and honest. Love means you trust your spouse completely."

Mamm sighed. "You're hurt, but you can't deny he loved you. I saw it in his eyes every time he looked at you and every time he held your hand or hugged you. He wore a smile on his face for weeks after the day you were married. He walked around with a glow on his face when he found out you were expecting a *boppli*."

Sarah blew out a quivering breath as she thought back to those days. Then it clicked, like the latch on the back gate. Everything suddenly made sense. "That could be why he stopped talking to me. Maybe he felt guilty for not telling me he had a son in Ohio when he found out we were having a child of our own."

Mamm gave a sad smile and a slow nod. "That could very well be it, Sarah Rose. And you must forgive him. And you also must forgive your brother and Luke. They care about you too."

Sarah nodded, even though it was easier said than done. But forgiveness was the Amish way, and she knew she had to let go. Somehow.

"I'll forgive them, but I won't trust them again, especially Luke. He took advantage of me. I thought we were friends." She shook her head. "He'll be a part of the *bopplin's* lives because they're family, but that's it."

"Don't be so hard on him, Sarah Rose. Now that you know he's Peter's brother, you must remember he's grieving too."

"That's all the more reason why he should've told me the truth. I thought we were close. I shared so much with him, and now I feel betrayed and used."

Mamm squeezed her hand. "He cares for you. I can see it in his eyes. I'm sure he felt he was justified in not telling you the whole truth."

Sarah glanced down at the remaining crumbs on her plate. "And I'm going to have a word with Timothy."

"Go easy on your brother. He's been hurt too."

The sound of infant cries rang from the living room, and Sarah jumped up. After warming two bottles, she and *Mamm* headed for the cradles.

She lifted Seth and snuggled him close while feeding him. *Mamm* sat next to her and hummed a lullaby as she fed Rachel.

Sarah traced a finger along Seth's soft chin and contemplated the news of Peter's older son. The photograph of Cody was burned into her memory, and she could see a resemblance between Seth and Cody—they both looked like Peter and Luke.

She wondered how DeLana had felt raising Cody without his biological father and how Cody would feel if he knew Peter had been his father. The three children—Cody, Seth, and Rachel—would never know what their father looked like or hear the sound of his voice or see the color of his eyes.

Sarah sighed. The children would want to know each other. She would have to contact DeLana and see if she would feel comfortable getting the children together.

Her thoughts moved to Luke, and she frowned. She would allow him to be a part of the twins' lives, but that was as far as her relationship with him would go. She could no longer trust him with her heart. She'd believed their friendship was special, and she'd even felt a teensy hint of affection for him, but those feelings had dissipated today. The children had a right to know their uncle, but Sarah would no longer allow him into her heart.

And her last issue was with her brother Timothy. She would address his lies the next time she saw him.

Pushing her hostility away, Sarah concentrated on the beautiful baby boy in her arms. Closing her eyes, she thanked God for her healthy twins. Even though her heart was broken by the deception she'd received from those she cared about, her heart swelled with love for her children, a true miracle and gift from the Lord.

❀

Luke trudged up the gravel driveway to Eli's house, hoping to see Sarah sitting on the porch. The memory of the anger in her eyes had haunted him all day. Her sadness and her devastation at finding out about Cody and then finding out about his own identity had broken his heart. He wished he could take away the pain he and his brother had caused. He worried he had lost her friendship forever. He couldn't stand the thought of not being her friend, and he longed to make things right between them.

His hope deflated when he found Eli and Elizabeth sitting on the porch without their youngest child.

"*Wie geht's*," Eli called with a bright smile.

"*Gut*," Luke said, climbing the stairs. "How are you both tonight?"

"*Gut*," Eli responded, looping his arm across the back of the swing and behind his wife. "Right, *mei fraa?*"

Elizabeth gave a sad smile. "*Ya*," she said.

"I wanted to check on Sarah," Luke said, leaning against the porch railing. "She was a mite bit upset earlier."

"*Ya*, she was," Elizabeth said. "She's fine now. She's resting since the *zwillingbopplin* are sleeping. She has to get her sleep whenever she can."

Luke nodded, wondering if Elizabeth was telling the truth. Was Sarah truly resting well or was she still distraught, crying alone in her room or sitting alone, contemplating how much he, Peter, and Timothy had hurt her. "I'm sorry that my brother hurt her so much. And I'm sorry I wasn't upfront with all of you about being Peter's brother. I should've told you the first time I met you. I only did it because I was afraid of hurting her more. I wish I could make it better. I was wrong, and I regret it with my whole heart."

"She'll be just fine." Elizabeth's expression softened. "She's stubborn like the rest of the Kauffmans." She elbowed her husband, who shrugged. "She'll be angry for a few days, but I'm sure she'll get through it. We just need to give her time."

Eli glanced at his wife, his eyebrows careening with feigned anger toward his hairline. They exchanged a private conversation without words, and she smiled.

Luke longed to have a loving relationship like theirs. He'd thought he and Sarah had that kind of friendship, where they could poke fun of each other and almost read each other's minds; however, he'd ruined it by not telling her the truth from the beginning. Now it was all lost, and he was alone — again.

Elizabeth eyed Luke. "Have you eaten? We have leftover meatloaf and chocolate cake."

Luke considered the offer for a moment and then shook his head. It was obvious he'd worn out his welcome with Sarah Rose. In order to regain her trust, Luke knew he should keep his distance and give her time to heal, as much as it would hurt his heart to stay away from her and the twins.

"*Danki*, but I ate a little bit earlier." He stood up straight. "I just wanted to make sure she was okay. Please give her my regards."

"Will do, son." Eli smiled. "You have a *gut* night."

"You too." After a quick nod, Luke descended the stairs and walked slowly back toward the house.

Climbing into bed that night, he prayed for Sarah, asking God to comfort and bless her and her twins and to find room for Luke in their lives. He prayed giving Sarah space would help him win a place in her family.

❈

Sarah hugged Rachel closer to her body and swung gently back and forth on the porch the following afternoon, enjoying an unusual break in the normally bitter-cold February weather. *Mamm* sat beside her with Seth while Rebecca held Junior on the chair beside the swing.

Gazing out over the yard, Sarah spotted her nieces and nephews racing to and fro, screeching and laughing during a competitive game of tag. Her sisters sat nearby chatting while her brothers leaned on the fence by the pasture. The sights and sounds were all fitting for an off Sunday without church service, and normally it would be a comfort.

However, today it was anything but comfortable. Instead, Sarah glanced around the scenery and gave a shuddering sigh.

After crying most of the night, her tears had dried up. Numbness had settled in her soul around four this morning. Betrayal and disappointment filled the hole in her heart that had been left after Peter died. She felt like an empty shell of the woman she once was.

Her gaze trained on Timothy, and her stomach soured. She planned to give him a piece of her mind the first chance she had to speak to him in private.

Junior fussed, and Rebecca stood. "I'm going to go in and feed him."

Sarah and *Mamm* nodded as Rebecca disappeared through the door with her infant.

"How are you?" *Mamm* asked.

"*Gut,*" Sarah said, but her voice was flat and devoid of the emotion she'd hoped to convey.

Mamm patted her arm. "It will get better. Have faith, Sarah Rose."

Sarah let the words soak into her as she stared across the pasture toward the house where Luke was staying. Bitterness and disappointment rolled through her.

The clip-clop of a horse and the crunch of wheels on gravel yanked Sarah back to the present. She glanced toward the barn as Norman and his family emerged from their buggy. Timothy greeted Norman. The children joined her nieces and nephews in their game of tag, the eldest girls caring for the younger children.

Sarah plastered a smile on her face as Norman and Timothy sauntered toward the house, talking. Norman met her stare and gave her a sincere smile. She was thankful for his friendship.

Something she'd thought she shared with Luke.

The men climbed the stairs, and Norman greeted her mother and sisters before turning to Sarah. "*Wie geht's*," he said, his eyes warm.

"*Gut*," she said.

"How are the *zwillingbopplin*?"

"They're sleeping better at night. I'm getting almost four solid hours of sleep." Sarah angled a sleeping Rachel toward him.

"*Ack*, she looks just like you." Norman's face beamed. "She's beautiful."

Sarah felt her face heat at the compliment.

Mamm stood with Seth asleep in her arms. "Would you like me to take the *zwillingbopplin* in so you can talk?"

"You can't handle them both." Sarah stood. "I can take Rachel in."

"Don't be silly." Her *mamm* turned toward the older girls sitting on the other side of the porch. "Katie, would you please help me put the *zwillingbopplin* to bed?"

Katie hurried over and took Rachel from Sarah's arms.

"*Danki*," Sarah said as *Mamm* and Katie disappeared through the door with the sleeping children.

"Would you like to go for a walk?" Norman offered.

"That sounds nice."

Sarah followed him down the steps, and they walked side by side on the path toward her former home. Her heart fluttered at the idea of seeing Luke, considering how hurt she was by his actions.

"What's on your mind?" Norman asked. "You seem preoccupied."

She silently marveled how well Norman could read her emotions. He seemed to have a gift. "I found out some more disturbing things about Peter's past yesterday."

"Would you like to talk about it?"

Sarah frowned. "I feel bad for dragging you into my problems."

Norman stopped and stared into her eyes. His expression was serious. "Sarah Rose, I want to help you. You forget I also suffered a loss, and I know how difficult it can be to wade through the grief, bitterness, and anger after someone you love leaves you. I want to help you through this."

"*Danki*," she whispered. "I appreciate your friendship more than you know."

Something flickered in his eyes, but she wasn't sure what it meant.

"While I was going through some of Peter's things yesterday, I found some letters written to Peter from a woman in Ohio." Sarah paused, choosing her words. "I discovered he was sending the woman money to support his son—a son they'd had together."

Norman's mouth gaped.

"The woman is English, and they had an affair when Peter was seventeen. His father broke them up, and the girl married someone else. Peter left his family after he found out she'd married someone else. While he and I were together, he was writing her and sending her money every month to help care for the boy." Sarah shook her head. "There was a photograph of the boy. He's handsome and looks just like Peter and Luke."

"He looks like Luke?" Norman's eyebrows knitted in confusion. "Why do you say that?"

"Because it's true. That's the other detail I uncovered. Luke is Peter's brother, not his cousin." She glared toward Timothy across the pasture. "I found out Peter, Luke, and Timothy have all lied to me."

"What do you mean?" Norman asked.

She met his confused expression. "You already know about Peter's deception about his past. Luke also omitted the truth that he's Peter's brother, and Timothy has known about Peter's past for some time. I'm going to have a few words with my brother when I can get him alone."

"Timothy never said anything to me about it, but I know he and Peter were close when Peter was alive."

Sarah wrung her hands together. "I've been trying to sort through it all and figure out how to get past the hurt."

Norman took her hands in his. "Give your burdens up to the Lord, and He will see you through. Have faith that He is leading you down the path toward happiness."

She gazed into his brown eyes, astounded by his strong faith. "You are so calm and faithful."

He smiled. "It took me a long time to get here after losing Leah, but I'd like to help you find your strength." His expression became serious. "I would like to spend more time with you, Sarah, and help you through this."

"I appreciate you so much, Norman. *Danki*." She led him back toward the path to her parents' house. "Let's go see if there's any chocolate cake left."

❀

Later that evening, Sarah tiptoed down the stairs after rocking the twins to sleep. Heading toward the kitchen, she heard soft masculine voices. She stepped into the doorway and found her *dat* and Timothy sitting at the table. Her expression hardened as Timothy saw her.

"Sarah Rose," *Dat* said. "I thought you were asleep."

"I was just coming down to get a drink before heading to bed." She crossed the kitchen and poured a glass of water. Standing at the counter, she sipped it while her *dat* and brother discussed the weather. Anger swirled in her while she studied her brother. Sensing her observation, he raised a brow in question, and she scowled in response.

"I reckon I better head to bed," Timothy said, standing and stretching. "Work comes early in the morning."

"*Ya*, it does." *Dat* also rose. "It was *gut* talking to you, son."

"You, too, *Dat*." Timothy headed for the door. "*Gut nacht*."

Dat said good night and disappeared through the doorway toward the stairs.

"What was that look for, Sarah Rose?" Timothy said, crossing his arms and leaning on the door.

"I found out some interesting information yesterday." Placing her glass on the counter, she stood before him, hoping her eyes resembled the daggers she felt in her heart.

"Oh?" His expression was one of teasing, despite her harsh words. "Please, enlighten me."

She ignored his attempt at a joke and got to the point. "First of all, I found out Peter was sending money to an English girl in Ohio."

Timothy's eyebrows careened toward his hairline. "What are you talking about?" he questioned, shocked.

"*Ya*." She gave him a smug smile. "Your best friend was sending money to support his son in Ohio. His *Englisher* son."

Timothy gasped. "Peter had an English son? Are you certain?"

"Absolutely. I found the evidence: a box full of letters from DeLana Maloney." She studied his dumfounded appearance. "I can show it to you if you'd like."

"I believe you, but I had no idea."

"I also found out Luke is his brother, and you knew *that* all along, Timothy." Her voice was thick. "That brings the total number of men whom I trusted and who have lied to me to three." She counted them off on her fingers. "Peter, Luke, and you, my brother."

"Whoa, now, Sarah Rose." He held his hands up in protest. "I didn't know about DeLana and this boy you're talking about."

"But you knew Peter had family in Ohio, and you knew Luke was his brother." Her voice shook. "How could you do that to me, Timothy? You're my brother. I trusted you! You've been hurt before, and you know what it's like to lose someone you love."

His expression softened. "I only meant to protect you."

"Your big plan to protect me wound up hurting me even more!" Disgusted, Sarah started toward the stairs.

"Wait!" Timothy caught her arm and pulled her back. "Hear me out."

She yanked her arm out of his grasp and glared at him.

"Peter was my best friend, and I miss him every day." Timothy pursed his lips. "You have to know he loved you, and he hated lying to you. He told me the truth about a year before he died. I saw him coming out of the post office one day, and I think he felt he had to explain why he was there. I didn't know about the letters to the girl in Ohio, but I knew he had family back there. He told me he had an older brother he looked up to because he was so loyal to their family and faithful to God. He said Luke was everything he wanted to be but knew he couldn't."

Sarah sniffed. "Why didn't he tell me, Timothy?"

"He wanted to, Sarah. He wanted to tell you the truth. He said he knew he had to be honest with you since you were expecting a child. He was planning to find the right words, but he ran out of time. He wanted to make things up to his family too—his *dat* and his brother."

She wiped her tearing eyes and shook her head. "I would've forgiven him. I loved him."

Timothy touched her arm. "He loved you too."

She wished she could speak to Peter herself and hear those words from him one more time.

"Can you forgive me?" Timothy's eyes were hopeful.

She frowned. "I don't have a choice. You're my brother."

He shrugged. "I'll take that as a yes."

She nodded toward the door. "Go home. The *zwillingbopplin* will have me up soon enough for a feeding."

"How are things with Norman?"

She faced him. "What?"

"You and Norman, you're close, *ya*?"

"*Ya*," she said with a nod. "We're *gut* friends. What's wrong with that?"

He waved off the question and started toward the door. "See you tomorrow."

"No." She rushed after him. "What are you implying, Timothy?"

"I'm not implying anything at all. Talk to you later." He patted her head. "Stop worrying so much."

She rolled her eyes. "I'm so tired of being treated like a child." She headed for the stairs. "Good night, Timothy."

Climbing the stairs, Sarah let Timothy's words sink in. Peter had truly loved her, and he'd wanted to tell her the truth. He'd planned to tell her the truth before he'd died. The words warmed her and settled her heart. And, yet, she still felt betrayed by Timothy and Luke. They'd known the truth and kept it from her.

She yawned as she entered her room. It was too late to figure out her feelings. However, she knew one thing for certain: her brother's question about Norman had her stumped. Why would he ask about their friendship? Why did he care?

17

Luke dried his hands and stepped from the restroom into the shop hallway. Deep in thought regarding Sarah and her well-being, he jumped when a strong hand on his shoulder stopped him mid stride. Turning, he found Eli frowning at him.

"Eli," he said. "You startled me."

"Sorry. Can we talk?" The older man nodded toward the door leading to the parking lot.

"Of course." Luke followed him outside, his stomach in knots of anticipation.

They walked to the far end of the lot, where Eli leaned against the fence and sighed.

"Is everything all right?" Luke asked. "Are you feeling okay?"

"I wanted to ask you why you haven't been by the house since Saturday," Eli said. "You left abruptly, and we haven't seen you since. Did something offend you?"

Luke stuffed his hands in his pockets and kicked a stone while contemplating how to respond. He couldn't tell Eli that he had strong feelings of affection for Sarah and was giving her space in hopes of her forgiving him.

"Luke?" Eli asked. "What is it?"

Glancing up, Luke gave a tentative smile. "I was afraid I'd worn out my welcome after Sarah found out about my brother's past and found out I'm her brother-in-law. I thought I should give her a few days to come to terms with the news and figure out how she felt about the rest of the Troyer family."

Technically, he wasn't lying. He was worried about how she felt about the rest of the Troyers—especially him, since he hadn't been upfront with her about Cody from the beginning.

Eli nodded and looked at something past Luke's shoulder. "Don't stay away too long. Elizabeth was right when she said Sarah was stubborn, but she'll get over her hurt. I know you've been a good friend to her, and I'm sure she misses you."

Luke nodded. He missed her too . . . a lot.

"I was surprised you didn't have lunch with Naomi today," Eli said.

"What?" Luke asked, surprised by Eli's quick change of the subject. "Naomi?"

"*Ya*, Naomi." Eli grinned. "You know, the *maedel* who brings you lunch a few times a week." His smile clouded. "Did you two have a disagreement?"

Luke shook his head. "No. I think everyone got the wrong idea about us. We're just friends."

Eli gave him a look of disbelief. "Does Naomi know that?"

"I told her that back in December before Christmas."

"Oh. How'd she take it?"

Luke kicked another stone, trying to suppress the guilt. "She wasn't happy. She had her heart set on courting me. But we decided to stay friends, and she insists on bringing me lunch. I guess she has other plans today."

"It's *gut* that you're friends. Maybe your friendship will develop into something more as you get to know each other. She's a sweet *maedel*." The older man smacked Luke's shoulder. "I just wanted to tell you not to be a stranger. Come by the house and see us." He started for the door. "I reckon I better get back to work. I have quite a few impatient customers."

"I'll be there in a minute." Luke leaned on the fence, staring out over the field behind the shop while he pondered Eli's words. Maybe Sarah only needed a few days to mull things over, and he'd have a chance to win back her friendship … hoping it would turn into more.

Luke made up his mind that he would visit the Kauffman house tonight. He missed the twins. He'd made a promise to be a good uncle to the twins in honor of his brother's memory, and he intended to keep that promise. And of course he also missed Sarah. He needed to show Sarah he cared for her and had only lied about his identity to save her more heartache.

❀

Luke climbed the steps of Eli's porch later that evening. The warm glow of a kerosene lamp illuminated the kitchen. After taking a deep breath, he rapped on the back door. Elizabeth peered through the glass and frowned at him before opening the door.

"*Ya?*" she asked. "Oh, hello, Luke. How are you? We haven't seen you in a few days."

"Hello, Elizabeth," he said. "I hope you're doing well this evening. May I speak with Sarah?"

"I think she's putting the *zwillingbopplin* to bed."

"Oh." He frowned. "I'm sorry I missed seeing them."

"I'll check for you. Just a moment."

"*Danki.*" While she disappeared into the house, he paced, his heart pounding and his mind searching for the right words to express how he felt about Sarah's friendship and how special the children were to him. He prayed for the right words. He didn't want to cause her more pain; as Eli said, she'd been through so much already. His soul would shatter if he continued to be another source of sorrow for her.

The door squeaked open, revealing Sarah clad in a black cloak with a white gown peeking out at the bottom.

"What do you need, Luke?" she asked, her voice flat and her expression tired, as if the life had been sucked from her. His heart broke as he remembered the life dancing in her blue eyes the night they had spent visiting with the children and her parents.

"Have a seat." He gestured toward the swing.

"I'll stand, *danki.*" She hugged her arms to her chest. "Why are you here?"

While her tone cut him to the bone, he kept his expression even, hoping to shield the hurt she caused him. "I'm here to apologize again." He leaned back against the railing. "I'm sorry for not being forthright about my identity. You and the *zwillingbopplin* mean more to me than you know. I want to be a part of their lives since they're my only link to my brother. I'm very sorry, and I hope you can let me back into your life, Sarah Rose. I care for you."

Sarah paused, her eyes flashing with emotion before returning to their flat blue. She angled her chin in defiance of his comment. "You'll always be a part of my *kinner's* family. You're welcome to visit them any time. However, our friendship will never be the same. I've lost all trust in you."

He flinched. Where was the sweet, suffering Sarah who had sobbed in his arms on Saturday? How had she transformed into this cement statue, devoid of warmth?

"Is that why you came here?" She gestured as if to dismiss him. "To try to prove to me that you're a trustworthy man after you deliberately posed as my husband's cousin instead of his brother?"

Frustrated, he shook his head. *Why are we beating this subject to death?*

"Sarah Rose, I never posed as a cousin. I just didn't tell you I was his brother. There's a difference between pretending to be something you're not and omitting information."

She blinked and then frowned. "Your standards of truthfulness astound me. I guess lying runs in the Troyer family. I can only hope my *kinner* take after the Kauffmans."

"And lie like Timothy?" He couldn't stop his smug expression.

Her mouth gaped with shock.

Elizabeth appeared in the doorway. "Sarah Rose," she said. "Seth is screaming again."

"*Ack*." Groaning, she shook her head. "I'll be right in." She glanced back at him and nodded curtly. "I have to go. I think Seth is getting his first ear infection. We've had a long day."

"Oh, no." Panic gripped him. "Is he going to be okay?"

"*Ya*." She waved off his worry. "*Bopplin* go through this. He'll be just fine. It's more exhausting than anything else." She started for the door.

"Can I come see them?"

Hesitating, she nodded. "You can visit them anytime. I'll give you some time alone with them when you're here. That way you can really bond." She squeaked open the door.

He couldn't let her go. Not like this. "Sarah."

She faced him, her eyes exhausted, no doubt due to the sick baby. However, her beauty glowed in the low light of the lanterns.

He knew at that moment he loved her, truly loved her, but he couldn't form the words to tell her so.

"I care about you," he whispered, stepping toward her and hoping she understood. "I mean that."

She blanched. "I don't understand."

Their eyes locked, and his heart skipped.

"I'm not sure how you can't understand. I care about you, Sarah Rose."

"And how would Naomi King feel if she heard you tell me that?" she whispered, her voice quavering. "I've heard that you and Naomi have lunch together frequently."

"What does Naomi King have to do with my feelings for you?" he asked.

"I have to go," she whispered. "*Gut nacht*."

Before he could respond, she slipped through the door, which slammed behind her.

Strolling back to the house, Luke felt his heart splintering into a million pieces, like a thin piece of wood shattered with a hammer. He wanted to tell Sarah he loved her and wished he could care for her and the twins; however, her cold stare had prevented the words from forming on his lips. His feelings for Sarah had taken him by surprise. He'd never felt love like this before. It was overwhelming and all-consuming. He was truly in love for the first time in his life.

Stepping into the house, he wondered if he should remain in Bird-in-Hand. While he had found a farm to purchase and had a possible buyer for his home in Ohio, he couldn't bear the thought of Sarah avoiding him when he visited the twins.

Luke shook his head as he climbed the stairs to the bedroom. While dressing for bed, he contemplated why Sarah had mentioned Naomi King. Were rumors floating around the community about his relationship with her?

Climbing into bed, he turned his cares over to the Lord. He prayed God would lead Sarah toward a life of love and laughter, not one of misery and regrets. He also prayed he would find his own way in the world and figure out where he truly belonged—in Ohio or in Pennsylvania.

❧

Sarah snuggled down under the quilt and closed her eyes. She felt as if the world were crashing in around her. In just a matter of days, she'd discovered her late husband was supporting a child she never knew existed in another state. Then she'd found out her own brother had lied to her about her husband's past to "protect" her. To make matters worse, Luke had stopped by this evening to try to apologize for his deceit and then told her he cared for her.

She frowned. *How dare he!*

Sarah pulled herself up to a sitting position, then swung her legs over the edge of the bed. She crossed the room and snatched Peter's wooden box from her bureau. Sinking into a chair, she opened the box and stared at the letters in the low light of the kerosene lamp.

She fished a stack of photos of Cody from the box and stared at the child's face. He was the spitting image of Peter with his bright hazel eyes and light-brown hair. Even his dimpled smile reflected his late father. She also saw Luke's features in the boy's delicate face. He was a Troyer, through and through. Seth would probably resemble him as well.

Sarah closed her eyes and tried to conjure Peter's face in her mind's eye. She searched her memory, concentrating on the week before she lost him. She tried to remember the details of his face, his eyes, his nose, his lips.

But only one face kept coming to mind ... *Luke.*

Huffing out her frustration, she stood, dropped the box onto the chair, and padded to the window. She lifted the dark-green shade and stared across the jet-black pasture toward her former home. A soft light glowed from the living room, leading her to wonder what Luke was doing up so late.

Tears filled her eyes as she remembered their conversation earlier. He'd had a lot of gall coming over and trying to apologize after what he'd done.

She sat on the edge of the bed as his voice echoed in her mind. She could still see the genuine warmth in his eyes when he'd said he cared about her. Why had he said that? He didn't mean it. He was seeing Naomi King. It was the talk of the community. She'd heard from more than one person at church service that Naomi brought him lunch a few times each week. He'd probably marry Naomi, and they would live together happily, having babies of their own.

Sarah believed Luke cared for the twins because they were his only living link to Peter. He didn't truly care for Sarah as more than a friend or a family member. And she didn't care for him either.

At that, she gave a sarcastic laugh. Her inner voice challenged her: *If you don't care for him, then why are you crying? And why does Luke's voice and face fill your dreams at night?*

Why did all of her thoughts of Peter end with visions of Luke? Why had her hands trembled and her heart skipped a beat when Luke pulled her into his arms and consoled her?

She grimaced with disgust. She needed to put Luke Troyer out of her mind and concentrate on her future with her twins. They were all that mattered.

Standing, she crossed the room and lifted the box from the chair, then slipped the photographs back inside. As she placed it on the bureau, she heard something metal clink against the side of the box. She opened it again and removed the letters and photographs, stacking them on the bureau until the box was empty. A small brass key lay on the bottom.

Picking up the key, she examined it. It was inscribed with "U.S.P.S. Do Not Duplicate" followed by a series of numbers.

"Post office box," she whispered, closing her fingers around the cool key. Her stomach tightened. "Another secret."

After dropping the letters and photographs back into the box, Sarah lay the key down on the bureau, snuffed out the lamp, and climbed back into bed. She closed her eyes and silently recited her evening prayers.

God, please lead me down the right path for my and my zwillingbopplin's future.

18

"Thank you for coming with me," Sarah said, stepping into the post office with Kathryn the following afternoon. "I convinced Nancy and Katie I needed to run to the market, but *Mamm* knew the truth when she left for the bakery this morning."

"Did you really think I would let you come here alone?" Kathryn looped her arm around Sarah.

"I'm just glad *Mamm* let me come without her. She's been so worried about me. I know she thinks I should just let Peter's memory go and concentrate on the future. But how can I when I have so many unresolved questions?" Her chin wobbled.

Kathryn gave her a sad smile and touched her shoulder. "Sarah, it's okay to cry. And it's okay to ask questions. You need to understand the past before you can concentrate on Rachel and Seth's future."

"*Danki.*" Sarah hugged her sister. "You're the only one who understands."

They took their place in line, and Sarah studied the key, wondering what secrets that little brass clue held about her late husband's past. When they reached the counter, Sarah pulled the key and a stack of letters from the concealed pocket in the back of her apron.

"May I help you?" a young man in a postal uniform asked.

"Yes," Sarah said. She placed the key and letters on the counter, trembling with anxiety about the secrets the key would reveal to her. "My husband passed away in the fire at the Kauffman & Yoder furniture store almost ten months ago."

He frowned. "I'm sorry to hear that, ma'am. I'm very sorry for your loss."

"Thank you." She cleared her throat, and Kathryn placed a hand on her shoulder, silently encouraging her to continue. "I found a box with this key and these letters. I would like to clear out his box and close it."

"Is your name on the box, ma'am?" he asked.

Sarah shook her head. "I had no knowledge of the box until I found the letters and key."

The man grimaced, tapping the counter. "What's your name, ma'am?" he asked.

"Sarah Troyer." She twirled her finger around the tie to her cloak. "My husband was Peter Troyer."

The man took the key, studied it, and then examined the letter. "Excuse me for a moment while I get my supervisor. I'll need permission since your name isn't on the box." Taking the keys and letters, he disappeared into an area behind the counter.

"Don't worry," Kathryn whispered. "They'll understand. This can't be the first time a spouse has found a post office box."

Glancing to her left, Sarah spotted a young English woman mailing a package while a toddler boy sat in a stroller and whined. Sarah smiled.

She was still thinking of her twins when the young man returned to the counter, accompanied by a middle-aged man holding the key and letters.

"Mrs. Troyer," the older man said. "I'm so sorry for your loss. I was so saddened to hear about the fire. I bought a hope chest for my daughter at Kauffman & Yoder, and I've known Eli Kauffman for years." He handed her the letters.

"Thank you." Sarah nodded and slipped the letters into the

pocket of her apron. "Eli is my father. This is my sister, Kathryn Beiler."

The man smiled at Kathryn. "It's a pleasure to meet you." He glanced back at Sarah. "I understand Mr. Troyer didn't have your name on the box. It's not our policy to allow other folks access to the box. However, under these circumstances, I can make an exception. Mr. Troyer had paid for the box a year in advance. I'll get a form for you, and you can close the box and receive any remaining mail."

"Thank you," Sarah said.

With the key in his hand, he disappeared behind the counter.

Kathryn rested a hand on Sarah's shoulder while they waited for the man to return. Sarah's mind swirled with questions. Would the box reveal only letters from DeLana Maloney or would there be more secrets? Could Sarah stomach the lies the letters would share with her? Her heart ached with worry. She prayed the letters would only confirm what she already knew—that Peter had a son named Cody Alexander Maloney whom he was supporting. Sarah didn't want to know any more than that.

A few minutes later, the postal worker returned with a stack of three letters and a form. Sarah filled out the form, closing the box and forwarding any remaining mail to her parents' home. Thanking the man, she and Kathryn headed out to the parking lot where Nina Janitz waited to drive them back to the bakery.

After they climbed into the car, Sarah examined the three unopened letters. Each one included DeLana's return address. Her hands trembling, she slipped them into her apron, deciding to open them later when she was alone.

Leaning over, she touched Kathryn's arm. "*Danki.*"

"*Gern gschehne*, sweet Sarah Rose." Kathryn patted her hand. "Give yourself time to heal and figure things out. Don't feel rushed to accept Peter's past. Remember the verse from the service last week? It was 2 Corinthians 1:3: 'Praise be to the God and Father of our Lord Jesus Christ, the Father of compassion and the God of all comfort.'"

"*Ya.*" Leaning back in the seat, Sarah closed her eyes and thanked God for the support from her wonderful family members, especially Kathryn.

❋

Luke wiped his brow and retrieved his can of Coke from the workbench. He glanced down at the entertainment center he was sanding and heaved a sigh that seemed to carry the weight of the world.

The entertainment center wasn't his best work, and he owed it all to one distraction—Sarah. Their disagreement and the sadness in her eyes had haunted him since they spoke last night. He couldn't sleep. He couldn't eat. He couldn't concentrate. It was shattering his soul.

Glancing across the shop, he spotted Eli weaving through the projects and carpenters toward Luke's workbench. Taking a long gulp of Coke, he imagined what Eli would say about the entertainment center. "Try again" was the most likely comment. Luke set the can on the workbench and hopped up on a stool.

"Great work, Luke," Eli said, studying the furniture piece. "I think Mitch Harrison will love it."

With a brow arched in disbelief, Luke glanced at Eli. "You've got to be kidding me. Those corners aren't perfectly square. I figured you'd tell me to start over."

Eli chuckled, patting Luke on the shoulder. "You're way too hard on yourself. You remind me of myself at your age." His expression softened, becoming serious. "You know, losing your brother was a huge blow to our family. He was like a son to me, and he meant the world to my Sarah Rose. He also did great work, just like you."

Luke lifted the can and took another long drink, willing the emotions within him to settle. Hearing about his brother this way caused his stomach to tighten and a lump to swell in his throat.

"What I want to say, Luke, is I'd be honored to have you as

a part of our family here at Kauffman & Yoder. I've spoken to Elmer about it, and we want you to stay here and work for us." Eli gave him a hopeful smile. "Please, son, say you will. We need you."

Luke took another swig and then set the can down again. "*Danki* for asking me. It means a lot." He took a deep breath, searching for the correct words. "But I can't accept."

Eli frowned. "Why not? Don't you like working here?"

"*Ya*, I do." Luke slowly rose from the stool. "But I'm thinking it's time I head back home."

"Home?"

"Back to Ohio. I'm just not sure I belong here." Luke studied the piece of furniture, staring at the corners he should've squared better. *Pop would turn over in his grave if he saw this poor excuse for an entertainment center.*

"You're talking nonsense." Eli smiled and patted Luke's shoulder. "You think about it and get back to me on Monday." He looked back at the entertainment center and shook his head. "You did a great job on that. I don't know what you're bellyaching about."

Luke rubbed his bottom lip, considering Eli's offer of a permanent job. It was tempting to stay, but it would torture him to see Sarah with anger in her eyes, silently accusing him of being a liar, time after time, when he visited the Kauffmans or went to church services.

But how could he walk away from his brother's children? He supposed he could always visit periodically, and he could call and write letters to keep in touch. Perhaps he could keep in touch through Eli.

He lifted the can to his lips again and glanced at the piece of furniture. Maybe leaving was the best choice. He could sand and stain the entertainment center this evening and ask Jake to finish it for him next week. He had forged a great friendship with the young man, and Luke imagined Jake would be happy to help him complete the project.

Gazing across the shop, his eyes settled on Jake walking to his workbench, a wide grin splitting his young face. Luke tossed the empty can of Coke into the trashcan and then weaved through the shop to Jake's workbench, giving him a friendly smack on the back. "Hey, there, Jake. Do you have a minute to talk?"

"Sure thing." Jake nodded toward the door. "Outside?"

"*Ya.*" Luke followed him out to the parking lot, where they sat on the concrete step. "What are you grinning about?"

"I just talked to Jessica." Jake folded a piece of gum into his mouth and held the pack out to Luke, who took a piece. "She's coming to visit soon. She said she's doing real well in school, and she misses me." His grin was back. "She's planning to come to visit her sister, and she can't wait to see Sarah's twins."

"That's *wunderbaar*," Luke said, slipping the cinnamon gum into his mouth and the wrapper into his pocket. "You're pretty crazy about her, *ya?*"

"Oh, yeah." Jake's face became serious. "You know when it just feels right? It's like everything clicks between you and your girl, and you just know in your gut that it's right?"

Luke nodded. He knew exactly what Jake meant. He only wished Sarah felt it in her gut too.

"I hope I can convince her to go to college here. I can't imagine having her so far away for four more years. Just waiting for her to finish school is going to be next to impossible." Jake chewed his gum and sighed. "I guess only time will tell, though. She's a stubborn one."

Luke snorted, thinking he again knew just what the young man meant. *Stubborn* was the perfect word to describe Sarah Rose Troyer.

Jake bent his legs and rested his elbows on his knees. "You didn't invite me out here to discuss how nuts I am about Jessica. What's up?"

"I was wondering if you would finish that entertainment center for me next week," Luke said. "I'll stay late tonight and get it stained and all. I was just wondering if you would put the clear coat on and then the hardware."

Jake nodded, chewing the gum. "Sure thing. Are you starting something else?"

Luke shook his head. "I'm leaving, heading back to Ohio."

"Oh?" Jake looked surprised. "For good?"

Luke nodded. "*Ya*, but I'll visit."

"It's none of my business, but why?"

Luke chewed his gum, debating what to tell him. He hated to lie, but the truth was too personal. "I need to get back to my old job and my house. It's just time."

"I hate to see you go, but I guess you gotta do what you gotta do." Jake slapped Luke's arm. "You better keep in touch or I'll come find ya."

Luke gave him a sad smile. "You know I will."

Jake stood and headed into the shop while Luke remained and stared across the parking lot. The sound of boots crunching on the gravel drew his attention to Timothy walking from the supply truck toward the back door.

"Sitting down on the job again, huh, Troyer?" Timothy quipped as he approached.

"Yup, that's what I do—goof off all day long." Luke stood and shook his head. "You don't need to worry about me anymore. I'm heading back to Ohio."

Timothy's face mirrored his surprise. "And what made you change your mind about staying here?"

"I don't belong." Luke said, deciding to tell Timothy the truth since Timothy already knew the whole story about Luke's identity. "Sarah has decided I'm a liar like my brother, and I can't bear to stay under those circumstances. I'll keep in touch with my niece and nephew and maybe visit a couple of times a year."

"I can't say I'll regret seeing you go since you already ratted me out." Timothy rubbed his chin.

"What do you mean?"

"Sarah thinks I'm a liar, too, thanks to you. I thought you were going to keep our little secret to yourself, but you've blown it for both of us."

Luke shook his head with regret. "I'm sorry. I never meant to get you into trouble with her too. It just slipped."

"Right." Timothy shrugged. "I guess I'll see you when you visit the *kinner.*"

Luke studied Timothy. "Why do you hate me so much?"

"I don't hate you." Timothy's expression softened. "You just remind me of all I lost when we lost Peter."

"Why can't we be friends, since you and Peter were? I didn't come here with a chip on my shoulder, but you've certainly had one from day one."

"You did just what I worried you'd do—made me look like a liar in front of my family. That's what I've always feared."

"You're her brother, Timothy. She'll forgive you. I'm nothing to her now. What I thought we had was ruined when she realized I wasn't a cousin. I lost everything, but you have her love as a brother."

"She'll eventually forgive you." Timothy smiled. "Things are about to get better in her life. Pretty soon it will be a year since Peter died and she can court again. I'm fairly sure she'll be getting married here shortly. Maybe she'll get married this spring, since it'll be the second marriage for both, and they won't have to wait until fall."

Luke's stomach roiled. "She's getting married?"

Timothy folded his arms. "She and Norman are becoming really close, and I have a feeling he's going to ask her soon. He's had feelings for her for a long time, but he's kept it to himself so as not to pressure her."

"Norman?" Luke asked, his stomach churning with jealousy.

"It makes sense for them to get together, don't you think? They've both lost their spouse, and they have *kinner* to raise. It's the perfect partnership."

Luke swallowed his disgust.

"It's not public knowledge, so don't get me in trouble with this one, okay? Norman's told me he's going to propose, but he hasn't even asked Sarah yet." Timothy pointed to Luke's chest. "Promise me, all right?"

"Your secret is safe with me." Luke couldn't fathom saying those words aloud.

"And for the record, I don't hate you. I'm sorry I came off that way." Timothy held his hand out and Luke shook it. "Friends?"

"*Ya.*" Luke stared after Timothy in disbelief as he disappeared into the shop.

Bile rose in his throat at the thought of Sarah marrying Norman. He was sure that was a sign for him to leave Bird-in-Hand. He couldn't stand to watch her marry another man. Luke's decision was made for him—he was going home to Ohio.

❊

Later that evening, Sarah stared at the letters in her hands, re-reading the words for what felt like the hundredth time. Each of the three letters had the same overall message from DeLana to Peter. She asked if he was okay and if he had forgotten to send the child support. DeLana requested that Peter call her to let her know everything was okay, and her cellular phone number was scrawled at the end of each note. Sarah had committed the number to memory.

She couldn't stop the overwhelming urge to call DeLana.

She wanted to hear DeLana's voice and ask her several questions, such as how she and Peter had met, how long they courted, why they broke up, if they truly loved each other, and why Peter had walked away from his son.

Sarah closed her eyes and hugged the letters to her chest. She had to know exactly what had happened between Peter and DeLana and verify that Luke's version of the story was accurate. The questions would haunt her until they were answered.

A knock on the door startled her. Sarah slipped the letters into the pocket of her apron.

"Sarah Rose?" *Mamm's* anxious voice sounded outside the door. "Are you all right?"

"*Ya.*" Sarah rose from the chair. She wiped her eyes, and adjusted her prayer *Kapp* on her hair. She then forced a smile and opened the door. "I was just resting. Is *Dat* ready for devotions?"

"No." *Mamm's* eyes studied Sarah's. "Norman's here for a visit. Are you well enough to come see him?"

"*Ya.*" Sarah straightened her dress. "The *zwillingbopplin* are fast asleep in the nursery." She stepped past *Mamm*, but a strong hand on her shoulder stopped her.

Mamm didn't look convinced. "You've been quiet all day. What did you find out at the post office?"

Sarah paused, debating what to say. "I closed out his box and I got a few more letters. All from DeLana."

"Did the letters upset you?" *Mamm* touched her hand. "You must let go of all of this hurt. Please do it for your heart and for the *kinner.* They can sense when you're sad, *mei liewe.*"

"I'm fine." Sarah took *Mamm's* hands in hers. "I promise you I am. Let's go see our guests, *ya?*"

Sarah and *Mamm* met Norman and his family in the kitchen, where they ate dessert and talked late into the evening. While the children played games in the living room, Sarah and Norman retreated to the porch and sank onto the swing.

Wrapped in a blanket, Sarah breathed in the chilly air and stared toward her dark house, wondering where Luke was. Was he working late? Had he not made it home safely? Was he still angry with her? Did he feel the same ache in his heart for her as she did for him?

Against her will, Sarah heaved a heavy sigh that carried the weight of her regret for snapping at him.

"Sarah?" Norman asked with a chuckle. "I'm boring you to tears, no?"

"*Ack,* I'm so sorry." Sarah sat up and smoothed the blanket. "You're not boring me at all. I'm just tired. It was a long day."

"*Mei freind,*" Norman said, squeezing her hand. "You don't

have to explain yourself to me. I know this is all overwhelming for you. You lost Peter not even a year ago. Please don't make excuses for yourself. You're permitted to be a bundle of emotions."

Sarah forced a smile. Norman continued his conversation about his extended family that had visited today from Gordonville, and Sarah tried to concentrate on it.

The clip-clop of a horse and crunch of tires rolling up the lane stole Sarah's attention from Norman's voice. Her heart flip-flopped in her chest when the buggy stopped in front of *Dat's* barn and Luke emerged from the driver's seat.

While Luke unhitched Molly, Sarah clasped her hands together and sucked in a deep breath. He stowed the buggy and Molly and then emerged from the barn.

Part of Sarah hoped Luke would just disappear down the lane to the house without so much as a greeting for her, while another part prayed he would stop by and say hello.

His tall, slender silhouette sauntered toward the porch, and Sarah's pulse quickened. When the light of the lamp kissed his chiseled countenance, her breath caught in her throat.

"*Wie geht's,*" Norman said. "It's good to see you, Luke."

"You too." Luke nodded at Norman. He then turned to Sarah, and his brown eyes sizzled with hot emotion. Was it anger? Or was it passion?

Sarah cleared her throat.

"Sarah Rose," Luke said, his voice cool.

She nodded in response, her voice still lost in her throat.

He tapped the railing. "I'll leave you to visit. Have a nice evening." He then turned and started down the gravel toward her former house.

"You too," Norman called after him. "*Gut nacht.*" After a few beats, he rubbed Sarah's arm. "He's a *gut* guy."

Sarah nodded and cleared her throat, hoping to stop the tears that threatened. She couldn't stop the foreboding feeling that Luke was walking out of her life.

❀

Luke threw his bag on the bed and tossed his shirts into it. His heart pounded in his chest while anger, resentment, and regret rioted in his gut. Seeing Sarah sitting on the porch with Norman's arm around her had sent his blood pressure soaring. To make matters worse, she never spoke to him, never even acknowledged him beyond a slight nod. It was as though he meant nothing to her now that she had her future husband, Norman.

Timothy's words stung his ears—it made sense for her to marry Norman since he was a widower and had children to raise. Perhaps Timothy was right. However, he couldn't shake one question: did Sarah even love Norman? If so, she'd never expressed it to Luke.

Sarah had made her choice, proving Luke didn't belong here. The Lord was telling him he was wrong to covet his brother's widow, and it was time he faced up to that fact. By going home, he could find a way to heal his heart and move on without any reminder of what Peter had left behind.

He packed up his clothes and then moved to the master bedroom where the pile of Peter's shirts still sat patiently waiting for a new home. Tears stung Luke's eyes as he sifted through the clothing.

Memories of his brother crashed down on him—holidays with their parents before their *mamm* died, playing volleyball in the back pasture with friends, walking to school together, and sitting in the loft of the barn late at night and talking about everything from girls to their deep faith in God.

He allowed the memories to carry him back to a less complicated time, and the mourning he'd held at bay since he learned of his brother's death assaulted his emotions. The release was cleansing, but it left Luke feeling like a cold, empty shell of who he'd once been.

After choosing four shirts, Luke tossed them into his bag. His thoughts then turned to the twins. His heart ached at the realization of leaving them, but he couldn't bear to watch their mother, the woman he loved, marry someone else.

The pain was too much for him. He felt as if he was breaking a promise to Peter by leaving, but it was the best choice for Luke. He would visit the children and keep in touch with them. They would know their uncle Luke; he'd make certain of it.

Needing to exit the house in an attempt to clear his head and quell his emotions, Luke grabbed his coat and stalked out the front door. The cold air kissed his face and filled his lungs with the heavy aroma of wood fireplaces.

He lowered himself onto the porch steps and reflected on the events of his four-month stay in Bird-in-Hand. The reality of leaving filled him with regret. He'd enjoyed being a surrogate member of the Kauffman clan, and he would miss their closeness. Yet he had good friends in Mel and Sally. It wasn't as if he would be alone back in Ohio. He also had a few cousins, aunts, and uncles.

He had to get out of Lancaster County while he still had some of his heart and soul intact. Tomorrow would be the day. He needed to be on that first train.

Something flashed in his peripheral vision, and Luke turned toward Eli's home. A Coleman lamp held by a tall figure floated near the large barn. Judging from the height of the silhouette, Luke deduced it to be Eli—just the man he needed to arrange for a ride to the station.

Luke hopped up and jogged toward the barn, reaching it just as Eli finished locking the large doors. "Eli," he called. "Do you have a moment?"

"Luke." The older man gave a surprised expression. "What are you doing out this late?"

"I couldn't sleep." Luke jammed his hands into the pockets of his coat. "Do you have a minute to talk?"

"Of course." He nodded toward the porch. "Would you like to have a seat?"

Luke hesitated. Scanning the property, he found Norman's

buggy was gone; however, he feared Sarah might be awake. Luke didn't want her to overhear his conversation with Eli and find out he was leaving.

"Something wrong?" Eli asked.

"How about we walk along the fence?" Luke asked. "It's a beautiful night."

Eli eyed him with suspicion. "It's a bit cold for a leisurely walk. Let's go back into my woodshop. We'll have privacy there."

"*Danki*," Luke said, wondering if his apprehension was more transparent than he feared.

He followed Eli around the back of the barn and into a shed converted into a carpentry shop, complete with several workbenches, stools, and a sea of tools. An unfinished bookshelf and an end table sat in the corner awaiting stain. The scent of wood and paint filled Luke's nostrils as he hopped up onto a stool.

Eli set the lantern down, leaned against the bench, and studied Luke. "What's bothering you, son? You seem preoccupied, like you're wrestling with the meaning of life."

Luke hugged his arms to his chest; however, the cold seeping into his bones seemed to be more than the temperature in the shed. "I was wondering if you'd arrange for me to get a ride to the train station early tomorrow morning."

A frown clouded Eli's face, and he fingered his beard, deep in thought. "I guess my suggestion for you to wait before making a decision didn't help, no?"

"I appreciate all you and your family have done for me, but I feel like the Lord is telling me that it's time to go home." Luke leaned back against the workbench and ran his fingers over the grain of the wooden top. "I'll be back to visit the *zwillingbopplin*."

Eli was silent for a moment, still rubbing his beard and studying Luke. His expression softened. "This is about Sarah Rose, isn't it?"

"No," Luke said, shaking his head. "I just feel it's time to go home. That's all."

"Don't deny it." Eli gave a knowing smile, folding his arms across his muscular frame. "You love my Sarah Rose."

"No, I don't," Luke said with a shrug, hoping he appeared nonchalant.

Eli rested a foot on the rung of a stool. "Why are you retreating to Ohio when your heart will remain here?"

Luke blew out a sigh and glanced around the shop in an attempt to avoid Eli's knowing expression. The question left Luke's lips before he could squelch it: "How do you know where you truly belong?" He glanced down at his lap and then met Eli's warm gaze.

"You know in here." Eli pointed to his heart. "God fills our heart with clues for what He wants us to have in life. If something seems to fit, then we know it's what God wants for us."

"But I feel like I should go home." Luke crossed his arms and shivered. "I don't feel like I belong here."

"Are you sure?" Eli raised his eyebrows in anticipation. "Is that really what your heart is telling you? Is that what you came to tell Sarah Rose the other night when you found out she was still angry with you?"

Luke blanched. "How did you know—"

"Elizabeth told me. She overheard some of the conversation." Eli's eyes probed Luke's. "Are you sure you want to leave?"

"*Ya*. I think it's best." Luke nodded with emphasis.

"Then you best give me your contact information. I'd like to keep in touch." Eli fetched a notepad and pencil from the bench behind him and passed it to Luke.

"I'll be in touch and visit. I want the *zwillingbopplin* to know me. I'm their only connection to Peter." Luke recorded his address and the phone number to the shop where he worked. He then handed the notepad back to Eli, who slipped it into his coat pocket.

"You don't have to run." Eli touched Luke's shoulder.

"I'm not running. I'm doing what's best for me and also for Sarah. She's my brother's widow." He shook his head. "It's just not right for me to even think of her that way, and I would guess she knows it. I'm sure my being here brings back memories she needs to forget."

Luke sighed. "I messed things up for her by telling her the truth about Peter's past and who I was. I did nothing but hurt her. The best thing I can do for her now is to leave and let her live a new life. She deserves happiness, not bad memories and lies Peter selfishly left for her to sort through."

"There's a verse I read during our devotion time the other night that reminds me of this situation. It was 1 John 4:18." Eli squeezed his shoulder. "'There is no fear in love. But perfect love drives out fear, because fear has to do with punishment. The one who fears is not made perfect in love.' Don't fear your love for Sarah Rose. See where it takes you."

Luke shook his head despite the warmth the verse gave his soul. "No. I need to go before I cause her more pain. Will you help me get a ride to the train station tomorrow?"

Dropping his hand to his side, Eli frowned and blew out a defeated sigh. "If that's what you want, then yes. But think about what I said."

"*Danki.*" Luke walked back to the porch with Eli.

The door opened revealing Sarah standing in a white robe tied tightly over a white nightgown. Her golden hair hung in waves touching her waist. He'd never seen her with her hair down before, and thought she resembled an angel. Her flawless beauty was so striking that his heart pounded in his chest. He'd give anything to hold her in his arms, kiss her, and tell her that he loved her.

But she was marrying another man who would hold her in his arms and love her.

He frowned, and his stomach twisted at the thought of Norman touching her.

All the more reason to go home to Ohio.

❀

Sarah shivered as she ambled onto the porch. She looked at her father standing at the bottom of the porch stairs with Luke, and her throat dried.

"*Dat?*" she asked, ignoring Luke's stare. "What are you doing out here so late?"

Dat turned to her, his eyes wide. "Sarah Rose! Get inside before you catch pneumonia!"

"Are you coming in?" Sarah asked. "You don't need to be out here either."

Dat trotted up the stairs and opened the door. Turning back to Luke, his expression softened. "Think about what I said. Don't make any hasty decisions."

Luke nodded and started down the gravel drive to her former home.

"Sarah Rose?" *Dat* asked, holding the door open. "Are you coming inside?"

Her eyes darted toward Luke. She couldn't squelch the urge to talk to him, even though she didn't know what she wanted to say.

Dat pulled off his coat and handed it to her. "Here. You'll need this if you stay out here and chat." He then placed the lantern on the small table next to the swing.

"*Danki.*" She put on the coat and then stepped to the edge of the porch as the door shut behind her. She spotted Luke's tall, slim silhouette stalking through the dark to her former home. "Luke!" she called. "Luke! Wait!"

Luke stopped and faced her, and she wished she could read his expression through the dark. For a moment he hesitated, and she was certain he was going to go back to the house without talking to her.

Holding her breath, she prayed he'd come back and talk to her. However, considering the way she'd treated him the last two times she'd seen him, she couldn't blame him if he decided to continue back to the house.

When he started back toward the porch, her heart turned

over in her chest. He came to the bottom step of the porch. His dark eyes shimmered in the low light of the kerosene lamp as they studied hers.

"*Ya?*" he asked, his voice soft but intense.

She cleared her throat and wracked her brain, trying to think of something to say. She'd called him back to her, but now she was dumbstruck, unsure of how to open a conversation with him. The sight of his chiseled features rendered her speechless.

He folded his arms. "What is it, Sarah Rose?"

"What were you discussing with my *dat?*" she asked, twirling a strand of hair around her finger. She realized she was clad in her father's coat over her robe and nightgown, and she suddenly felt exposed. Only a woman's husband should see her hair, and she wished for her prayer *kapp* or a shawl to cover her head. Yet there she stood exposed in the late February night with her brother-in-law's intense eyes probing her.

He frowned. "It was nothing you need to worry about. *Gut nacht*, Sarah Rose." He started for the house again.

"Wait!" She hurried down the porch stairs, holding onto the banister for balance. She couldn't let him go, but she had no idea why she was so panicked at the thought of his leaving.

He stopped. Facing her, he sighed with frustration. "It's late, and it's cold. Your pop's right, and you should go inside before you catch pneumonia. There's nothing left for us to discuss. *Gut nacht.*" He gestured toward the door. "Go in where it's warm."

"Don't dismiss me like some child!" She frowned with her hands on her hips. "I wasn't finished talking to you."

"What on earth could you possibly have to say to me? You already told me our friendship is over and I'm a liar like my brother." His eyes flashed with anger. "I know where I stand in your life."

"Do you?" She held her breath in anticipation of his answer.

"*Ya.* I'm somewhere around that annoying gum that gets stuck on the bottom of your shoe."

She gasped at his biting tone. "How could you say that?"

"How could I say that?" He gave a sarcastic laugh. "You didn't even have the decency to speak to me earlier tonight when I saw you on the porch with Norman. That told me how important I was to you. I'm not worth your breath. Our friendship means nothing to you anymore."

"Luke, that's not true." Her voice quavered, betraying her attempt to appear cool and collected.

He shook his head and grimaced. "Don't worry, Sarah Rose. I won't butt into your business anymore."

"What do you mean?" She wiped at the tears that had appeared without her knowledge.

"I'm leaving tomorrow." He jammed his hands into the pockets of his coat. "I'm going home to Ohio. That's where I belong."

"What?" She stepped toward him, feeling as if she'd been punched in the stomach. "You're leaving?"

"I am. I'll be in touch." His expression softened. "I'll want to see the *zwillingbopplin.*"

"If you cared so much about them you'd stay." She glared at him.

He shook his head. "You just don't get it, do you?"

"What don't I get?" She sniffed. "I don't understand what you mean."

"Forget it, Sarah Rose." He nodded toward the house. "Go inside before you get sick."

"Fine." She slapped her hands to her sides. "Just walk out of my life. Walk out of the *zwillingbopplin*'s life. That's what you Troyers do best, right? Peter walked away from his son, and you're walking away from Peter's *kinner.*"

His eyes flashed with fury. "Don't compare me to my brother," he said, seething. "I never would've lied to you, and I never would've walked away from you. But you wouldn't give me the chance."

She gasped as more tears streamed down her cheeks.

"Good-bye, Sarah Rose. May God bless you and your *zwillingbopplin*." He turned and stomped toward the house.

Hugging her arms to her chest, she sobbed while he left her standing in the bitter cold.

19

Luke sank back in the seat and closed his eyes in an attempt to shut off his brain and sleep to the monotonous clickclack of the train. He'd spent a restless night tossing and turning in bed and then pacing around the room.

His heart ached when he thought of Sarah. He wished he could take back the words he'd said to her, but the hurt had boiled over from his soul after carrying it for so long. She was wrong, so wrong, to run after him and act like she cared for him after the way she'd treated him. Perhaps she was the liar instead of Luke.

To make matters worse, no matter how hard he tried, he couldn't shut off the echo of Eli's words in his head. He kept pondering what Eli meant when he said Luke was running. Was Luke running back to Ohio out of fear of his love for Sarah?

Was going back to Ohio a mistake?

But Luke kept coming to the same conclusion: if Sarah loved Luke, then she wouldn't marry Norman. It was a simple assessment. Being with her felt so right, yet it was so wrong. It was a sin, and she was marrying another man. It made more sense for Luke to forget her.

Luke imagined Sarah's beautiful face—her ivory skin, skyblue eyes, and pink lips. She would be a beautiful bride. Norman was the luckiest man on the planet.

Yet he couldn't deny the affection for her that surged through his heart and his soul.

And then there were the twins. When they were born, Luke had made a vow to be the uncle they needed and deserved. Yet here he was retreating to Ohio with his tail between his legs because he couldn't face Sarah marrying another man. He was breaking his promise to Peter's children, but he couldn't stand the idea of seeing Sarah with Norman.

How on earth would Luke be able to let the twins and Sarah go and move on with his life?

Staring out the window at a wide-open field rushing by, Luke opened his heart to prayer, asking God to lead him down the right path. He hoped he could arrive back in Ohio thankful for his days in Bird-in-Hand and, somehow, through a miracle only God could provide, with his heart and soul glued back together.

❄

After getting the twins settled in their cradles, Sarah joined *Mamm* at the breakfast table and lowered her head in silent prayer. Lifting her gaze, she scooped scrambled eggs from a bowl onto her plate and then handed the bowl to *Mamm*. "Where's *Dat*?" she asked.

"He had to run an errand. He should be back shortly." *Mamm* passed the plate of rolls to Sarah. "How did you sleep last night?"

Sarah shrugged, studying the contents of her plate. "*Gut*. The *zwillingbopplin* only had me up twice."

It was a bold-faced lie, but she couldn't bring herself to tell the truth. *Mamm* would worry if she knew Sarah had been up praying and crying between feedings. She'd spent the night drowning in guilt for yelling at Luke. She'd deserved the cruel words he'd spat at her.

She remembered how he'd stalked off. The anger in his eyes had split her heart in two, and she had to face the fact that he hated her.

She'd prayed most of the night, begging God to convince Luke to stay. Yet she feared the inevitable—that he would go back home to Ohio to forget her and the twins forever.

Sarah tried to smile but worried her lips formed a grimace instead. She buttered her roll while *Mamm* yammered on about her plans for the day. Sarah nodded at the appropriate times.

The door opened and slammed, and *Dat* slipped into the chair next to *Mamm*. "Smells *appeditlich!*" He reached across the table aiming for a roll.

"Eli Kauffman," *Mamm* scolded, slapping his hand. "Wash your hands!"

"*Ack,* my hands are clean." He rolled his eyes and schlepped to the sink. After scrubbing, rinsing, and drying his hands, he returned to the table and then bowed his head in silent prayer.

Finishing, he looked up and smiled. "How are you this morning?" he asked Sarah while loading his plate.

"*Gut.*" She forked some egg from her plate. "Where did you have to run to so early?"

"I had to meet Mike Gray to get someone to the train station." He buttered a roll. "What do you ladies have planned for today?"

"Train station?" Sarah's stomach plummeted. "Mike Gray gave someone a ride there? Who had to take a train?" She knew the answer before he reported it.

"Luke went home." He said the words as if they were mundane, but something in his eyes revealed more. It was as if he knew how she felt. How could he know? Had Luke told him about their argument last night?

Speechless, Sarah stopped chewing and studied her father. Out of the corner of her eye, she spotted *Mamm* watching her, a curious expression clouding her face.

"He asked me to arrange for a ride, so I took him to Mike's early this morning." *Dat* shrugged, but his eyes were more honest—they were filled with hurt. "He said he felt like it was time to go." He brightened. "But he'll keep in touch and wants to come visit the *zwillingbopplin.*"

Sarah's stomach twisted.

Luke was gone. Gone for good.

And she had pushed him away.

And he hated her.

Her throat dried and her eyes stung. Setting her fork next to her plate, she pushed back her chair.

"Sarah Rose," *Mamm* said. "You must finish eating and keep your strength up so you can care for the *zwillingbopplin*."

"I'm not as hungry as I thought." Standing, she took her dishes to the sink. "I need to go lie down for a bit. I'll finish the dishes later."

Mamm rose and took Sarah's arm. "Please sit. You must eat."

"Maybe later." Sarah gently pulled her arm back. "I need to go rest." She headed for the stairs, avoiding her parents' stares.

"I thought you wanted to go to the market with me," *Mamm* called after her. "Your *dat* can watch the *kinner*."

"Later," Sarah called back, her voice thick. She hurried up the stairs, reaching her room just as the tears began to splatter.

Flopping onto her back on the bed, she sobbed, silently scolding herself for pushing Luke away. Would she ever see him again? Did she even deserve to see him again?

No, she didn't, after the way she'd treated him.

Covering her face with her hands, Sarah wished she could turn back time to the day of the fire. If only she'd convinced Peter to stay home with her that day and talk, then maybe, just maybe, he'd still be alive. If she hadn't lost him, she'd never have wound up in the mess she was in now—alone and confused, raising two babies without a husband.

She never would've met Luke.

And she never would've loved Luke either.

Applesauce Cake

1 cup granulated sugar
1/2 cup shortening
2 tsp baking soda
3 cups flour
1 cup raisins
1–1/4 cups nuts
1–1/2 cups sweetened applesauce
Pinch of cream of tartar
1 Tbsp cooking sherry
1/4 tsp salt
1–1/2 tsp cinnamon
1/2 tsp cloves
1/2 tsp allspice
1/2 tsp ginger

Cream sugar and shortening. Sift in baking soda and flour. Add raisins and nuts, then add remaining ingredients. Bake in a greased 9-inch square pan at 350 degrees for 35 to 40 minutes.

20

Sarah stared down at the ledger and frowned. At *Mamm's* request, she was balancing the bakery books in preparation for the start of the tourist season at the end of the month.

Although she tried to concentrate on the numbers, her mind repeatedly wandered to Luke—how he'd chatted in the den with the family after meals, how he'd looked every time he gazed down at the twins with love in his eyes ... how he'd smiled at her during their conversations on the swing ...

Leaning back in the chair, she covered her face with her hands. Why was Luke still haunting her nearly two months after he'd left? She'd attempted to engross herself in the *zwillingbopplin*. However, time and time again, her thoughts meandered back to Luke. She could see the pain in his eyes the night before he left. She could still feel his anger, hear it in the tone of his voice.

She'd hurt him. How could she have hurt the one man who made her feel safe? Why did she push away the one man she could possibly love?

But how could she court her late husband's brother? It was wrong to covet him. Nevertheless, she couldn't stop her mind from constantly concentrating on him and dreaming of him every night.

Sarah closed the ledger and stared out the window at the

light rain cascading down from heaven and soaking the field behind the bakery. Spring was on its way to Lancaster County. She wondered if the temperature was warming in Ohio yet.

Was Luke working late tonight at the cabinet shop? Was he thinking of her and the twins? Why hadn't he contacted her since he'd gotten home?

Her mind turned to Peter, and she stood and moved from the office into the kitchen. She wondered when Peter had planned to tell her the truth about his past. Would he have taken her to Ohio to meet Luke or Cody?

Pulling a letter from the pocket inside her apron, Sarah stared down at DeLana's cellular phone number for what felt like the hundredth time.

Sarah had considered calling DeLana several times over the past two months since the woman had a right to know why the checks from Peter had stopped coming. Sarah wondered if Luke planned to tell DeLana what had happened to Peter, although she knew it wasn't his responsibility. This was something Sarah should do.

She walked out to the front counter and stared at the phone hanging on the wall. She was alone in the bakery and had the perfect opportunity to make the call. She just needed the strength.

A knock on the glass door sounded through the silence of the empty bakery. Sarah looked up and found Kathryn grinning at her and hugging her cloak to her chest. Sarah unlocked and held open the door.

"Hi," Kathryn said, stepping in and shaking the raindrops from her arms. "Spring is coming to Bird-in-Hand."

"What are you doing here?" Sarah asked. "Don't you have to cook for your family?"

"*Ya.*" Kathryn rolled her eyes. "I forgot to grab my change purse." She padded back to the kitchen. "I took it out to give Lindsay some money earlier and forgot it," she called from around the corner. "Here it is." She reappeared and pulled her cloak closer to her body. "The *kinner* are waiting for me at *Mamm's* house. I told them I'd be right back."

Sarah forced a smile, only half listening to her sister's chatting.

Kathryn shook her head. "I'm so scatterbrained lately. David says I need to slow down, but there are only so many hours in the day and so much to do. Running a farm and taking care of *kinner* is a full-time job. And then I have to work in the bakery. I mean, just yesterday I had a difficult time—"

Her sister stopped mid-sentence, her expression clouding. "Sarah Rose, what's wrong?" She touched the ties to Sarah's prayer *kapp*. "You look as if you're carrying the burden of us all on your little shoulders."

Sarah leaned against the counter and shook her head. "You need to get home to your family. Don't worry about me."

"Don't be *gegisch*." Kathryn led her to two chairs in the back of the kitchen and motioned for her to sit. "I always have time for you. What's wrong?"

Sarah pulled out the letter and handed it to Kathryn. "I feel like I should call DeLana and tell her why Peter's checks stopped."

Kathryn shrugged. "So call her. Want me to dial?"

"That's not it." Sarah shook her head. "I want to go to Ohio. I want to see DeLana and talk to her, face-to-face, about Peter. I need to know more. I need to know the details. I have to understand it all before I can move on."

Kathryn nodded, taking in her words. "That makes sense. I understand."

"I know you do." Sarah sighed. "But *Mamm* never will. She'd never let me go. But I can't leave the *zwillingbopplin* without telling her."

Her sister took Sarah's hands in hers. "Do you want me to go to Ohio with you?"

"You're sweet and so thoughtful." Sarah dabbed away the sudden moisture in her eyes. "But I need to do this alone."

"So, do it," her sister said. "Call DeLana and then go ahead and plan a trip to Ohio. Find out what you need to know and let your heart mend, Sarah Rose."

Kathryn stood and steered Sarah to the phone. "Call Nina and ask her to take you to the train station early in the morning. I'll come over and care for the *zwillingbopplin*. I'll tell *Mamm* you had to take care of some business. If she's angry, she'll just have to forgive us. You need to listen to your heart, Sarah, not everyone else." She lifted the receiver and dialed the number. She then handed Sarah the phone. "I'll wait in the office so you can have privacy."

Sarah put the receiver up to her ear and held Kathryn's arm. "Stay." She leaned against the counter and stared at the numbers on the cash register.

The phone rang several times and then a voice spoke. "Hello?"

"Hello," Sarah said, her voice shaky. "Is this DeLana Maloney?"

"Yes. Who is this?"

"My name is Sarah Troyer."

DeLana paused as if contemplating the name. The voice of a child rang out in the background, and Sarah imagined it was Cody. The noise softened, and Sarah assumed DeLana had moved to a quieter area.

"Sarah," DeLana said. "Sarah Troyer?" Her voice rang with recognition. "Peter's wife?"

"*Ya*," Sarah said. "I mean, yes." She nervously drew circles on the counter with her fingertip. "I hope it's okay I'm calling you. I wanted to tell you some news, and it didn't seem appropriate to write you a letter due to the lag time of the mail system."

"Of course it's okay that you called," DeLana's voice was gentle. "What's going on?"

"You're probably wondering why your child support money has stopped." Sarah took a deep breath. A hand on her shoulder gave her the support she needed to trudge on. "I'm sorry to tell you that Peter … Well …" Her voice quavered. "Peter died in a fire almost a year ago."

"Oh, Sarah, I already knew." DeLana's voice was full of concern and sympathy. "Luke, Peter's brother, called me about two months ago and told me. I'm so, so sorry."

"Luke told you?" Her heart fluttered as she said his name. Sarah glanced at Kathryn, who gave her a sad smile.

"Yes, he did," DeLana said. "I'm so very sorry for your loss."

"Thank you."

"How are you coping?" DeLana asked.

"God is seeing me through it. My family has been my strength." Sarah wiped her cheeks. "I'm sorry I didn't contact you sooner, but I found your letters when I was going through Peter's things. I didn't know about you or Cody until fairly recently and then I had to find the strength to call you. It was a shock to find out about Cody. I had no idea."

DeLana sighed. "I'm sorry about that. Peter said he wanted to keep it a secret because he didn't want to hurt you."

Sarah bit her bottom lip. It seemed now was the time to ask. "I was wondering if I could come meet you. I have some questions I would like answered."

There was a pause, and a few awkward moments of dead air on the line. "You want to come visit me?" DeLana's voice was full of surprise.

"If it's okay with you …" Sarah cut her eyes to Kathryn, who squeezed her hand.

"Well, sure. Why not? When would you like to come?"

"Would Thursday be too soon? I can catch a train tomorrow and meet you Thursday afternoon." Sarah held her breath, expecting a lame excuse for her not to come.

"That sounds perfect."

Sarah grabbed a notepad and pen and wrote down the particulars of where to meet DeLana. Then she thanked her and hung up.

Turning, she pulled Kathryn into a warm hug. "Thank you

for giving me the strength to do it," she whispered. "I'm meeting her at a restaurant in Middlefield on Thursday."

"You're welcome." Kathryn rubbed her back. "Now you need to call Nina to arrange for a ride early tomorrow morning. I'll plan to be there and care for the *zwillingbopplin* for you."

❀

Later that evening, Sarah climbed the stairs of her former home and entered the master bedroom. Tomorrow morning she would head to Ohio, and she wanted to bring a gift for Cody. Someday he might want to have something from his biological father, if DeLana ever told him who his biological father was.

She found the pile of shirts arranged neatly by color. Not at all resembling the way she'd left it. Luke must've gone through the pile and picked a couple for himself.

Considering, she lifted a shirt, inhaling a faint scent of Peter still clinging for dear life to the fibers. She chose two for Cody and draped them over her arm. She then headed down the hallway and stepped into the spare bedroom where Luke had slept.

Standing in the middle of the room, her mind flooded with memories of the night she'd given him a tour. She sank onto the bed and lifted the pillow to her nose. The faint aroma of Luke, stain and wood mixed with earth, washed over, and her pulse skipped. Again she wondered if he'd thought of her since he'd gone back home. Did he miss her?

Glancing at the ticking clock on the wall, Sarah realized it was time for devotionals. Her parents would suspect she was up to something if she missed the nightly Kauffman ritual.

She rushed back to the house, making it just in time. But while her father read from the Bible, her mind kept wandering to her trip to Ohio and how it would feel to meet DeLana.

When her father finished his reading, they bowed their heads in silent prayer. Sarah then excused herself for the evening and rushed to her room. She packed a small bag of clothes and then wrote her parents a note she would leave in the kitchen on her way out the next morning.

During the night, Sarah tossed and turned in between feedings, unable to sleep due to the anxiety of her trip.

❀

Elizabeth rushed down the stairs the following morning, her heart beating like a racing horse. She bounded into the kitchen where Eli sat drinking his coffee. "Eli, I can't find Sarah Rose. Her bed is made, but she's not in it. And the *zwillingbopplin* are gone too."

"She's gone," he said.

"What?" Elizabeth stared at her husband in disbelief. "What are you saying?"

"She's gone and Kathryn is in the living room with the *zwillingbopplin*. They're sleeping in their cradles, and she's fast asleep in my chair alongside them. You must've rushed right past them in your haste." He passed her a note. "I found this by the coffee machine. It will explain everything."

Elizabeth held up the note, and her eyes rounded with shock as she read it.

Dear Mamm and Dat,

I left early this morning to go to Ohio to meet with DeLana Maloney. Forgive me for not telling you ahead of time, but I knew you would try to talk me out of it. I have some questions I need answered about Peter's past before I can move on with my life. Nina is going to take me to the train station this morning, and I'll arrive in Ohio tomorrow. Kathryn will be here to help with the zwillingbopplin until I return. I'll get the first train back and be home late Friday night. Please don't worry about me. I'll be just fine.

I love you,
Sarah Rose

Elizabeth's eyes filled with tears. "My *boppli* is traveling all alone." She glared at Eli. "How can you sit there like everything is okay?"

"Because it is, Elizabeth." He sipped the coffee and set down the mug. "She's a grown woman, and she'll be just fine. Just have faith."

She threw her hands up in frustration. "Why would I expect you to understand? You're a man!" Muttering under her breath, she headed for the peg by the door and slipped on her cloak.

"Elizabeth!" Eli bellowed after her.

She glowered at him.

"Sarah Rose is a capable young woman, just like the rest of our girls. She's confident, like you." Moving toward her, he took her hands in his as a smile softened his countenance. "Elizabeth, I married you because you're beautiful, intelligent, confident, and a smart business woman. I see you reflected in our girls' eyes. That's why I trust that our Sarah Rose will come back to us in one piece, and she'll have settled some things that are preventing her from moving forward. Trust her."

Elizabeth sniffed. "I worry about her every night. I pray for her for hours, begging the Lord to guide her and take care of her and her *zwillingbopplin*."

"The Lord will provide. The Lord will bless her and her *zwillingbopplin*. Trust Him." Leaning down, he brushed his lips against hers. "*Ich liebe dich, mei fraa*."

A sad smile curled her lips. "I love you, too, Eli." Closing her eyes, she wrapped her arms around his neck and sent up a silent prayer to the Lord to protect their youngest daughter.

21

Luke straddled a chair in the break room, popped open a can of Coke, and opened the latest copy of *The Budget*. While scanning the articles, he tried in vain to concentrate on the words, yet his mind wandered to Sarah—again.

Ever since he'd arrived back in Ohio, it seemed he couldn't make it through five minutes on any given day without falling into memories of her—her face, her smell, her gorgeous blue eyes, the sweet lilt of her laughter, the way the sun highlighted the wisps of hair cascading from under her prayer *kapp*, and the way she—

"So, how long are you going to mope, Troyer?" Mel's voice wrenched him back to the present.

Luke frowned as Mel sat down across from him and fished a snack-sized bag of pretzels from his pocket.

"Who's moping?" Luke asked.

Mel snorted with sarcasm. "Please. You've done nothing but work and mutter since you got back from Bird-in-Hand. Sally keeps accusing me of not inviting you for supper, but the truth is I can't get you to come."

"I don't mutter." Luke trained his eyes on the paper, still not comprehending the words in the articles, or even the headlines.

"*Ya*, you mutter. A lot." Mel munched the pretzels. "What happened in Bird-in-Hand? It's been two months, and you still haven't told me anything except that you found out about Peter."

Luke sighed and folded the paper. "I met his family. They were *wunderbaar*. They were warm. They made me feel as if I were a part of their family too."

Mel raised an eyebrow. "That doesn't sound so bad."

"It wasn't." Luke ran his thumb over the cool can. "I met Peter's *fraa*."

"Oh?"

"She's ... incredible." Luke lifted the can and took a swig.

"Oh?" Mel's eyebrows rose.

"I can't believe Peter snatched her up." Luke studied the can to avoid Mel's probing stare. "She had *zwillingbopplin* on Christmas Day. A boy and a girl, and they're beautiful. Perfect."

His gaze collided with Mel's, and he found his friend grinning like the cat that ate the canary.

"You're in love with her." Mel pointed at him, wagging an accusing finger. "I haven't seen you light up about a *maedel* since you were with what's-her-name."

"My former girlfriend's name was Millie." Luke glowered. "Peter's *fraa* is Sarah Rose, but don't plan my wedding. Her year of mourning is up next month, and she's marrying someone else, a man I don't think she even loves."

"Why aren't you stopping her?"

"Because I'm here in Ohio, and she's in Bird-in-Hand, Pennsylvania."

Mel drew an imaginary map on the table with his fingers and pointed out the spots. "We're here. She's there." He connected the two areas by running his finger in a straight line between them. "You get on a train and go back to Bird-in-Hand." He shrugged. "Simple answer. Now tell me—What are ya doing here?"

Shaking his head, Luke sighed. "Are you listening to me? She's marrying someone else. That's why I'm here. I'll visit my niece and nephew, but it would be too painful to live there and watch her with another man. I can't do it."

"So, you're just going to give up, *ya?*" Mel clicked his tongue. "That's a shame."

Luke glared at him. "I didn't give up. She didn't give me a chance."

"I guess she wasn't worth fighting for." Mel crunched another pretzel.

Luke opened the paper again. "The night before I left, we argued. I said some pretty awful things to her. I wouldn't be surprised if she hated me now."

"So go tell her you didn't mean it."

Luke looked up. "It's not that simple."

Mel grimaced. "Why isn't it? Life is short. You lost your parents and your brother, so you know how short life is. Go to her before you wind up an aging single guy without a *fraa* or a family. Before you know it, you'll be a bitter old man."

"Like my pop, right?" Luke scowled at him.

His best friend shrugged. "I didn't say it. You did."

"I didn't expect you to understand." Luke pushed back his chair and stood. "You have Sally. You don't remember what it's like to court. You never knew what it was like to live alone. I'm almost thirty, so it's not like I can go to a singing and find a group of girls to pick from. It's not easy when you're older."

"You have to decide how important she is to you. If you can just walk away from her like you never met her, then it's not meant to be." Mel lifted another pretzel to his lips. "End of story."

"Right. End of story." Luke tossed the empty can into the trash. "I better get back to work." He headed for the door.

Sauntering to his workbench, he wondered what Sarah was doing and if she'd thought of him since he left. Did she miss him as much as he missed her?

❦

Sarah fingered the ties of her prayer *kapp* and glanced around the diner. The large dining area was full, evidence of the lunchtime rush. Outside the wide front windows, large, sloppy raindrops danced through the air on their way down from heaven.

The aroma of hamburgers and fries filled Sarah's nose, and the grumblings of conversations swirled around her. Dishes and utensils clanged, and waitresses weaved through the sea of tables taking and delivering orders.

Glancing through the menu again, Sarah's stomach tightened. She wondered if she'd made a mistake traveling this far just to ask DeLana a few questions. Perhaps it would've been more intelligent and economical to have interviewed her over the phone.

Sarah didn't know DeLana, and she may have been naïve to trust a stranger. She also wished she'd remembered to ask DeLana what she looked like. Or maybe she should've asked Luke for a description of the woman she was going to meet.

Luke.

She bit her lip. Ever since the taxi had pulled into town, she'd wondered where he was. Where was his shop located? Had he thought of Sarah since he'd left Bird-in-Hand?

Scanning the dining area, Sarah's eyes found an Amish family seated in a corner. The young couple looked to be in their late twenties. A toddler sat at the table eating a dinner roll while the parents chatted and enjoyed their lunch. The woman's belly was round.

Sarah sighed. If Peter were still alive, they might've resembled that family now. Perhaps they would've been blessed with a large family in the making too.

Sarah tried to imagine sitting at a restaurant table with another Amish man, maybe a friend from her community such as Norman, but the image didn't come into focus. Instead, she saw herself sitting with Luke while her *zwillingbopplin* smiled from their highchairs ...

Why did her musings always lead her back to Luke? Was God trying to tell her something?

She frowned at her silly thought.

How ridiculous ... Luke hates me.

"Sarah?" A voice beside her asked. "Sarah Troyer?"

Turning, Sarah found a tall, thin woman with a long dark ponytail and brown eyes smiling down at her. "DeLana?" She stood from the seat.

DeLana gave her hand a firm shake. "It's so nice to meet you." She shrugged out of her heavy gray parka, dotted with fresh raindrops, and hung it on the back of the chair across from Sarah.

"I'm sorry I'm a few minutes late. This rain has everyone driving like crazy. There were a few fender benders near my house. You'd think we never get rain here." She set a small tote bag on the floor next to her chair and then sat down. "So, how was your trip?"

"*Gut.*" Sarah nodded, trying to imagine Peter with DeLana. The woman sitting across from her was very attractive. She wore a tinge of makeup to accentuate her bright eyes and rosy lips.

Sarah couldn't help but wonder if Peter had yearned to be English. How much was there that she'd never learned about her husband? Regret nipped at her soul.

A waitress appeared and took their drink order.

When the girl disappeared, DeLana gave Sarah a sad smile. "I'm so sorry for your loss. I know Peter loved you very much. He spoke very highly of you in his letters."

Sarah swallowed the lump forming in her throat. "Thank you."

"May I ask what happened? Where was the fire?"

Praying for strength, Sarah explained the events that had taken place the day of the fire.

When she finished, DeLana shook her head. "I'm so sorry. I had no idea. I was surprised when the letters and checks stopped. He'd been so faithful sending them over the past several years. I could count on receiving a short letter with a check on or about the fifteenth, no matter what."

"How long had he been sending them?" Sarah fiddled with a napkin on the table.

DeLana's eyes took on a faraway look as she tried to remember. "I got the first letter and check when he got his first steady job in Lancaster County. Cody was about two, so I guess that was seven years ago. I was really surprised. He sent this short note saying he wanted to help provide for his son. I was pleasantly surprised."

Sarah nodded, letting the words soak in.

"I'm sorry he never told you." DeLana hesitated, then reached over and took Sarah's hand. "He never wanted to hurt you. That's why he kept it a secret. I think he was afraid you'd leave him if you knew he'd fathered a child outside of wedlock."

"That never would've happened," Sarah whispered, her voice ragged. "We don't believe in divorce."

Pulling her hand back, DeLana nodded. "True, but I think he was afraid for your happiness. He didn't want to lose you emotionally. It really bothered him that you didn't know—especially since you were expecting a child. In his last letter, he told me he was contemplating telling you the truth. He just didn't know how." She touched Sarah's hand again. "I want you to know he felt terrible not telling you the truth. Peter loved you more than life itself."

Sarah blinked back tears, hoping she wouldn't dissolve into sobs in front of DeLana and the whole restaurant.

She was relieved when the waitress arrived with their drinks and took their lunch order. Since she hadn't taken the time to read the menu, Sarah chose what DeLana ordered, hoping the soup-and-sandwich special would warm her freezing heart.

Sarah took a long drink of iced tea and then cleared her throat. "Would you tell me about how you met Peter?"

DeLana explained the story, similar to how Luke had told it. DeLana had worked for her father at a large wood wholesaler, and she'd met Peter when he accompanied his English driver on a supply run one hot summer day.

According to DeLana, it was love at first sight. Peter had invented excuses to handle the supply runs once a week during the next month, and he eventually worked up the courage to ask DeLana to meet him after work one day. That first meeting led to frequent secret dates and then a secret courtship that ended when their parents discovered the relationship.

"According to Luke, your parents didn't want you to see someone who was Amish, and Peter's *dat* didn't want him to see an English girl." Sarah ran her fingers down the cool glass of tea.

"That's right." DeLana smiled. "I'm glad you got to meet Luke. I knew Peter had cut off his family when he moved to Pennsylvania. It's good you connected."

Sarah nodded. "I had no idea Peter had any family until Luke showed up in October."

"Interesting." DeLana tapped her glass, deep in thought.

The waitress dropped off their food, and Sarah took a bite of the ham sandwich despite her dissolving appetite.

"I heard their father died last year, and I felt bad," DeLana said. "Despite all that happened, I think he was an okay guy. He was just really controlling and overbearing." She grinned, lifting her sandwich. "He was just like my dad."

"When did you find out you were expecting your son?" Sarah asked.

"After we broke up. I managed to meet him in secret one night," she began, "and I told him the news. He begged me to run off and marry him, but I knew it would lead to disaster. We had no money and nowhere to go. My parents had convinced me to go to college and give the baby up for adoption."

Between bites of her sandwich, DeLana explained how furious her parents were when they found out she was going to have Peter's baby. They forbade her from leaving the house except to go to school. Peter's father did the same and also took away money Peter had saved up to pay for his first home.

"And that was the night he had the fight with his father and ran off?" Sarah asked.

"No." DeLana shook her head while wiping her mouth with a napkin. "That was later on. I decided to keep the baby, against my parents' wishes, and I met Alex soon after."

"Alex?" Sarah asked.

"My husband. We met while I was pregnant. I had gone out shopping with a friend one day, and he was at the mall. I was able to hide my stomach with a large shirt. When I told him I was pregnant, I figured he wouldn't have anything to do with me, but he saw past that." DeLana smirked. "I upset my parents when I told them I was going to scratch their college idea, keep Cody, and get married. But they got over it. Alex is a good guy and a great father. He wanted to marry me and raise Cody as his own. Since I had lost Peter, I felt lucky to meet someone who loved me despite my past."

Sarah nodded, wondering how all of this had affected Peter. "So you ran into Peter after Cody was born."

"That's right. I was at the market one day with Cody, and Peter was there with Luke. He saw me and Cody, saw my wedding ring, and went nuts. That night he had it out with his dad and then left town." DeLana frowned. "I hate that I hurt him, but we just weren't meant to be. He tracked me down through the phone book in the library and sent a letter with a check about a year later. We've appreciated the money. Alex owns his own garage, and some months are rough. It seems like folks want their cars fixed in spurts. The child-support checks helped pay for extras, like Cody's soccer fees and summer camp—things like that."

"Had you kept in touch with Luke?" Sarah asked, her breath held in anticipation of the answer.

DeLana shook her head while chewing. "Not since the night Peter ran off. My dad had run into him a few times, but I never saw him."

Sarah stared down at her soup, taking in all that DeLana had said. The stories overwhelmed and confused her. Peter had truly loved DeLana and wanted to provide for his child. Why hadn't he ever told Sarah the truth? She would've found a way to understand it all. He had a right to love his child.

Was the problem that his heart had still belonged to Cody

and DeLana even when he was with Sarah? The thought caused her heart to sink.

"How are the twins?" DeLana asked, snapping Sarah back to the present.

Glancing up, Sarah found DeLana smiling. "*Wunderbaar.*"

"Luke told me that they were just exquisite. He was very excited about them. Congratulations."

"Thank you." Sarah was overwhelmed Luke had been excited enough about her children to mention them to DeLana. Perhaps he truly cared—although it meant he cared for the children, not for Sarah.

"That's so cool you have a boy and a girl," DeLana said. "I want to have another one, but the time never seems right. My mom says we should just go for it, but I don't know. Kids take so much time and money."

"They're a gift from God," Sarah said, lifting a spoonful of soup.

"Yeah. They are." DeLana pulled an envelope from the bag below her chair. She set it down in front of Sarah. "I know the Amish don't believe in photographs because of the whole 'do not make a graven image of yourself' verse from the Bible, but I thought you might like these. They're photos of Peter and also some of Cody."

Sarah's mouth gaped. "Photos of Peter?"

"Yeah." DeLana opened the envelope and out slid a stack of photographs. "They were taken while we were dating." She handed Sarah the pile. "I found them when I was looking through some old albums last night. I took a little trip down memory lane."

Sarah gasped as she stared at a photograph of Peter with his arm around DeLana while they stood in front of a large oak tree. His smile was wide, almost electric, and he was clad in jeans and a dark T-shirt. His hat was also missing. DeLana's smile was equally bright. Their love was obvious in their eyes.

Sarah glanced up, meeting DeLana's gaze. "Peter dressed English?"

DeLana smiled sheepishly. "We did a lot of things our parents would never have approved of."

Sarah flipped through a half dozen photos of Peter, some with him hugging DeLana, others with them sitting on a pier near a lake, and a few of him alone, just smiling while posing on stairs or in a hay loft.

She then sifted through photos of Cody, stopping when she came to one at the bottom of the pile. She studied his eyes, his nose, his mouth. The child resembled Peter, but he also looked like Luke.

She couldn't get Luke out of her mind's eye. She again wondered if she should visit him. Would he be happy to see her or would he tell her to go home?

"Is Luke's shop far from here?" Sarah asked, placing the photos on the table.

DeLana shook her head and finished chewing. "No. It's just on the other side of town." She sipped her iced tea. "I was surprised he never married that girl he was dating. I can't remember her name now. Was it Maddie? Maggie?" She snapped her fingers. "Millie! That's it. I wonder why they didn't get hitched."

Sarah stared at her half-eaten sandwich. "He took care of his ill father, and his girlfriend broke up with him. She didn't want to have to nurse him too." She explained how Luke and Peter's father had had a stroke after Peter left and died eight years later. "It's a shame he never married," Sarah whispered, her voice thick. "He's a *gut* man. He'd be a *gut* husband and father."

"I bet it was hard for him to find out about his brother by showing up at the shop where he died." Frowning with sympathy, DeLana shook her head. "I can't imagine how that felt."

"He was stunned. He didn't know about me, and I didn't know about him. It must've been hard on him to face losing his brother when he moved away, losing his *dat* to the illness, and losing Peter all over again when he found out he had died." Sarah stared down at the napkin she had folded by her plate. "Luke deserved better than that. He's such a kind, sweet, gentle man. He deserves a loving family. He has so much to give. He shouldn't be alone."

Glancing up, she found DeLana studying her with a wide grin and round, laughing eyes.

Sarah's face warmed. Could DeLana sense her feelings for Luke?

"How long did Luke visit?" DeLana asked, still smiling.

"Four months."

DeLana leaned forward on the table as if Sarah were going to share a juicy secret. "You guys got pretty close, huh?"

"Well, no. We visited and then he had to go home to get back to work."

"Have you two kept in touch?" DeLana asked.

"I haven't heard from him, and I haven't contacted him either."

DeLana's eyebrows rose in question. "How come? It sounds like you became close friends."

Sarah thought her cheeks might catch on fire as she searched for the answer to explain why Luke probably wouldn't contact her. DeLana was more outspoken than the English customers she'd encountered in the bakery.

"I don't think he would—" Sarah began.

The waitress appeared and cleared their dishes. "Did either of you save room for dessert?"

Sarah resisted the urge to kiss the waitress for interrupting her stammering. She glanced at DeLana, who shrugged. "Feel like some awesome chocolate cake?" she offered.

"Why not?" Sarah rubbed her flat middle. "It's not like I have to watch my figure. I lost quite a bit of weight after having those twins."

They both laughed, and Sarah realized she felt strangely at ease with this English woman from her husband's secret past. They drank coffee and enjoyed large slabs of rich, moist chocolate cake while discussing their lives. DeLana bragged about how well Cody was doing in school while Sarah told her about the twins, the bakery, and her father's carpentry shop.

An hour later, the coffee and cake were gone, and DeLana paid the check, refusing to take any of Sarah's money. They walked outside together. The rain had slowed a bit, and small drops tickled Sarah's nose and soaked her cloak as they maneuvered through the parking lot.

"I have an hour before Cody gets out of school," DeLana said, hitting the Unlock button on the keyless remote for her SUV. "Would you like a quick tour before I take you to the train station?"

Sarah shook her head. "Thank you, but I better get back and buy my ticket." She opened the door and climbed in. "My family is expecting me home tomorrow night."

"You sure?" DeLana folded herself in the driver's seat. "I can take you by Luke's shop."

"No, thank you." Sarah buckled her belt.

DeLana turned over the ignition. "We have time. I could even take you by his house so you can see where he and Peter grew up. Then we can drop by his work. Don't you want to see him? You came all this way, Sarah."

"No, thank you. I'd better get to the station and buy my ticket." Sarah kept her eyes focused on the passenger window. "The rain is beautiful, yes? I always loved running through puddles when I was a girl. My brothers, and sisters, and I would run through the mud in the back pasture, and—"

"Sarah." DeLana touched her arm. "You don't have to hide it from me. I know you want to see Luke."

Sarah met her gaze, hoping her voice wouldn't defy her. "I really don't want to. I need to get home to my babies."

DeLana nodded. "Fine. Suit yourself." She chatted about the scenery as she steered through the town.

When a sign for "Amish Custom Cabinets" came into view, Sarah's heart pounded. She glanced at DeLana, who kept droning on about the weather and her hopes for a warm spring as she steered into the parking lot of the cabinet shop.

"This is where Luke works," DeLana said, pulling the SUV

into a spot in front of the building. "This is your last chance to go see him."

Sarah gaped at her, wide eyed. Who did this woman think she was? Sarah had said no more than once.

DeLana folded her arms and grinned. "You don't have to lie to me, Sarah. I can see it in your eyes."

"You can see what?"

"Love."

"Love?" Sarah shook her head. "I don't understand what you mean."

"Sarah, I hear regret in your voice when you talk about Luke."

Sarah gasped. "You do?"

"Yes, you do," DeLana said. "Luke makes you happy, and you deserve happiness. I know it's none of my business, but you've been through so much. I'd hate to see you lose someone who can make you happy."

Sarah stared at the front door of the shop and took a deep breath. She absently wondered if DeLana could read her mind.

"Alex makes me happy," DeLana whispered, "but a tiny part of me regretted not running off with Peter that night he begged me to. We had a terrible fight, and we both said some horrible things and threw around nasty accusations. We didn't speak again until that time I saw him at the market. I saw remorse and hurt in his eyes, but it was too late to try to rebuild what he and I once had. I don't want you to live with that kind of sorrow, Sarah. You've lost Peter too. You know how short and precious life is."

"I can't face Luke," Sarah said, her voice trembling. "I said some terrible things to him."

"Sure you can face him. Just apologize and tell him you love him."

"You don't understand. I can't take back the hurt I caused him. I saw it in his eyes." Sarah stared straight ahead at the shop.

"He'll forgive you. They were only words." DeLana touched her hand. "Think about your life."

Sarah faced DeLana, tears filling her eyes. "We had an argument the night before he left Bird-in-Hand. He said some horrible things to me too, and I deserved them all." She sniffed and swiped a hand across her wet cheeks. "I was awful to him. I lost any chance with him."

DeLana gave her a sad smile. "If he loves you, he'll forgive you, and you can work it out. Don't make a mistake you'll regret the rest of your life, Sarah. You deserve some happiness."

Sarah turned back to the shop and stared at the sign above the door. "I can't see him. Please just take me to the train station."

"Suit yourself." DeLana put the truck in gear, and they drove to the train station in silence. The rain increased, and drops pelted the windshield, sounding like a chorus of hammers banging in unison.

When the windshield fogged, DeLana punched a series of buttons on the dashboard, sending air hissing through the vents to fill the thick silence between them.

The train station came into view, and DeLana maneuvered the SUV through the lot, parking one row from the entrance.

Sarah hefted her small tote onto her lap and fished Peter's shirts from the bottom of the bag. "I wanted to give these to you for Cody. They're not much, but they were Peter's. If you ever tell Cody about his biological father, then please give these to him as a memento."

DeLana's face lit up as if Sarah had just handed her a treasure. "Thank you. They're beautiful." Her lips turned up. "Actually, I do want to tell Cody about Peter soon. I wanted to ask you if we could keep in touch. You have Cody's only siblings, and I'd love for them to meet and foster a friendship."

Sarah smiled. "That would be *wunderbaar gut*. After all, they're family."

DeLana pulled a card from her purse, snatched a pen from the console, and jotted some numbers on the back. "Here's my number at work. I do the books for Alex's shop. You can reach me during the day if you'd like. Let me know how you and the twins are. We can meet up sometime in the summer if you'd like. I'd be happy to come see you next time."

"I'd like that. Thank you for everything." Leaning over, she gave DeLana a quick hug.

"Thank you too." Pulling back, DeLana gave her a stern look. "Don't give up on Luke. He's a good guy." She tapped her own chest. "Listen to your heart."

Sarah nodded even though she disagreed. Her heart told her that she'd lost him forever.

"Promise me, Sarah." DeLana wagged a finger at her.

"I promise. Good-bye." Sarah wrenched the door open.

"Call me!" DeLana said.

Rushing through the rain, Sarah entered the train station and purchased a ticket to go home, leaving behind Peter's past and Luke too.

Her heart swelled with a mixture of regret and hope as she headed toward her departure gate. She contemplated Cody, her twins, and their future relationship. She knew one thing for certain—Peter would live on through his three children.

22

The following evening Sarah thanked Nina, hoisted her bag on her shoulder, and trekked up the gravel driveway toward the porch stairs.

During the long trip home, she'd analyzed all that DeLana had told her and stared at the photographs. Although the man in the photos resembled her late husband, he felt like a stranger. She'd never imagined Peter had had a love affair with an English woman and considered running away with her. The Peter Troyer she'd married wasn't who he'd seemed to be, and she still wasn't sure how to open her heart to accept the past.

And yet, she'd felt a new sense of hope when she'd heard DeLana explain Peter had planned to tell Sarah the truth. According to her, Peter had lived with worry and regret for not being truthful with Sarah from the beginning, and he planned to make things right before the twins were born. DeLana's words had mirrored Timothy's, which only proved they were true.

Sarah smiled at that realization. Peter truly had loved her, and he'd planned to make things right.

Just knowing that settled her heart; she felt as though a weight had been lifted from her shoulders. Perhaps her anger and betrayal toward Peter could be put to rest.

Was this the faith her mother had suggested Sarah find? With prayer, Sarah had found the answers to the riddle of Peter's past—it was a past he regretted and had wanted to share with Sarah, his true love.

Sarah hurried up the porch steps. She longed to see the twins and had missed them every moment she'd been away.

As she approached the back door, she stopped when she heard a chorus of voices sounding from within the kitchen. She had only expected to come home to her parents, Kathryn, and the children, yet it sounded like the entire Kauffman clan awaited her arrival.

Taking a deep breath, she pushed the door open, and a sea of eyes focused on her. Scanning the group, she spotted her parents, Timothy, her sisters, her brothers-in-law, nieces, nephews, Norman, and his children. Then everyone began speaking at once—yelling questions, wanting details of her visit, asking if she'd seen Luke.

Sarah held her hand up. "Please. Everyone."

A hush hovered over the crowd.

"I'm home. I'm safe. I had a nice trip." She gestured toward the stairs. "Now, if you don't mind, I'd like to see my *zwillingbopplin*. I've missed them. *Gut nacht.*" Sarah ambled toward the stairs.

"Sarah Rose!" *Mamm* scurried after her. "You can't go to bed without telling me about your trip."

"I promise I'll tell you tomorrow," Sarah said, squeezing her hand. "I'm just wiped out. It was a long and bumpy ride home, and I couldn't sleep." She started up the stairs, ignoring voices calling her name.

Reaching her room, Sarah pulled off her cloak, tossed it onto the end of the bed, and let her bag fall to the floor with a *thwap*. She then hurried next door to the nursery and leaned down over her sleeping babies. She rubbed their backs and whispered her love for them before returning to her room.

Boots scraping in the hallway announced an approaching man. Sarah hoped it wasn't one of her brothers coming to lecture her about leaving without warning and worrying *Mamm*. Exhaustion filled her.

Glancing toward the hallway, her eyes widened when Norman appeared to stand frowning in her doorway. "Norman," she whispered.

"Hello, Sarah. I know it isn't appropriate for me to be up here alone, but I told your *mamm* I needed to talk to you. I'll keep our conversation short." He leaned against the door frame, folding his arms across his wide chest. "You gave your family and me a real scare running off like that."

"I didn't run off." She sat up straight and gestured toward a chair. "Have a seat."

"*Danki.*" His expression softened. Stepping into the room, he lowered himself into the chair next to her. "Your *mamm* was a bundle of nerves. Timothy came and told me you'd gone to Ohio, and I was really surprised."

"I know it was wrong not to tell her I was going, but I didn't want her to talk me out of it." Sarah fingered the hem of her apron. "It was something I had to do. I wanted to do it alone without any suggestions or advice."

"I care about you. Had I known you were going, I would've offered to accompany you to Ohio. I could've helped you through this ordeal."

"*Danki*," she said. "I appreciate the offer, but this was something I had to do on my own. Kathryn offered, and I told her I preferred she help with the *kinner* instead of going with me."

Leaning forward, his warm hands covered hers. "I'm not sure you know how much you mean to me."

Sarah studied the fire in his dark eyes, and her heart fluttered with panic, wondering what he was going to say.

"I think of you all the time, Sarah Rose," he said. "You're very important to me. I hope you can learn to trust me with your worries and your burdens in your heart. We're going to be lifelong partners."

"What did you say?" she asked, sitting up straight. "Lifelong partners?"

"*Ya.*" His eyebrows rose in question. "I want to marry you, Sarah Rose. Your year of mourning will be over next month, and I hope I can court you. We can be married in the spring, or we can wait until fall and do a traditional wedding."

"Wait a minute." Sarah popped up from the edge of the bed and stared at him. "What are you saying?"

He shook his head with confusion and stood before her. "I love you. I've always loved you. I thought you knew that."

"No." She shook her head as guilt rained down on her. How could she have missed his feelings? "I thought we were friends. Good friends."

"We are." He smiled. "And I love you. I want you to be my *fraa.* We both have *kinner,* and we can provide a good, strong, Christian home for them together." Again he took her hands in his.

She shook her head, and the warmth of his eyes burned her soul. He was such a good man. Marrying him was tempting. But Sarah didn't love him.

She knew in her heart she loved Luke.

Norman deserved someone who loved him with her whole heart; not someone like Sarah who couldn't fathom sharing his marriage bed.

"I never meant to hurt you or lead you on," she whispered, her voice quavering with guilt. "I want to be your friend, Norman, but I can't marry you."

His smile faded. "Oh. I had assumed our friendship was leading to a wedding date. I thought, from the long talks we've had, you loved me. Those conversations have meant so much to me."

"They've meant the world to me, too, but I'm not ready to get married."

He shrugged. "I can wait."

She smiled. "No, Norman, don't wait for me. I want to be your friend, but that's all I want. Just your *wunderbaar* friendship."

He paused. Then he opened his mouth to speak and then paused again, his expression falling to a deep frown.

"I see." He stepped toward the door. "If you ever need someone to talk to, please let me know. I'm here whenever you need me."

"*Danki.*" She smiled.

"*Gut nacht.*" He opened the door. "I'm glad you're home safe."

She swallowed her guilt. "*Gut nacht. Danki* for checking on me."

He exited the room, gingerly closing the door behind him. Sarah collapsed on the bed. She cried herself to sleep, praying that she could find a way to forget her love for Luke and let go of her guilt for not loving Norman Zook, the one who loved her in return.

❋

Sarah lounged on her bed the following afternoon and skimmed her Bible while the twins slept.

During breakfast this morning, Sarah had filled her parents in on her trip to Ohio, telling them the highlights of her conversation with DeLana. They listened with wide eyes when she explained how Peter had met and courted DeLana and detailed the events that led to their breakup.

Sarah shared the photographs, and her parents gasped at the shots showing DeLana frolicking with Peter clad in English clothing. She did not share the conversations about Luke, but she did explain she and DeLana wanted to keep in touch for the sake of the children since they were family.

Mamm and *Dat* were supportive, and elated to hear she had forgiven Peter. Sarah also noticed that her father seemed more attentive than usual. There was something in his eyes telling her he understood more than she knew.

As she lay in bed reading from her Bible, she wondered exactly what *Dat* was trying to tell her with his wordless expressions.

Sarah had considered telling *Mamm* and *Dat* about Norman's proposal, but she couldn't form the words. The guilt over turning him down still haunted her, and she couldn't admit to them she'd told him no. Logically, she and Norman would make the perfect couple with their blended family.

However, Sarah knew her heart belonged to Luke, a man who hated her after the way she'd treated him.

Sarah was reading from the book of John and trying to ban Norman and Luke from her thoughts when a knock sounded on her door.

"Come in," she called.

The door squeaked open, and Kathryn stuck her head in. "Hi. Can I come in?"

"*Ya.*" Sarah sat up and patted the edge of the bed next to her. "Please."

"How are you?" Kathryn closed the door, crossed the room, and lowered herself onto the edge of the bed.

"*Gut.* Tired. How are you?" Sarah closed the Bible and placed it on the end table.

"*Gut.*" Kathryn touched Sarah's hand. "I'm worried about you. Tell me how things went."

Sarah opened her heart and shared everything with Kathryn. With her eyes brimming with tears, she pulled out the photographs and explained all the stories about Peter's past. She even shared the conversation she and DeLana had had while sitting outside the cabinet shop. She ended with telling Kathryn that she and DeLana would keep in touch so that the children could meet someday.

Kathryn wiped her eyes and shook her head. "DeLana sounds like a *gut* person."

"She is." Sarah cleared her throat. "I can see why Peter loved her."

"You love Luke, don't you?" Kathryn took Sarah's hands in hers.

"*Ya,*" Sarah whispered, admitting it aloud for the first time. "I do. I can't stop thinking about him. I miss him so much that my heart aches."

Kathryn gave a sad smile. "You need to call him and tell him."

"No." Sarah shook her head. "I never could. It's not right. We don't belong together."

"Why not?"

"Because he only wants to be with me for the sake of the *zwillingbopplin*. He doesn't want to be with me because of his feelings for me."

Kathryn raised an eyebrow in disbelief. "How do you know that?"

"He feels a responsibility to take care of his brother's *kinner*. That's the only reason he wanted to be here."

"That's ridiculous." Kathryn waved off the thought. "When I saw him with you, he was attentive to you. I don't believe for a second he would only want to be with the *zwillingbopplin*."

Sarah shook her head. "We also argued the night before he left, and he said some nasty things. I'm convinced he hates me."

Kathryn scoffed. "Please. I don't believe that man could ever hate you, Sarah Rose."

Sarah told Kathryn the details of the argument.

"I think he said those things out of frustration." Kathryn squeezed Sarah's hands. "He was hurt and angry, but I don't think he hates you."

"You didn't see his eyes, Kathryn." More tears spilled down her cheeks. "I've never seen him that angry."

"I've made David that angry before, and he still loves me." Her sister frowned. "You should call Luke and give him another chance."

"There's more," Sarah said. "Last night Norman came up to see me after I got back. He asked me to marry him."

"What!" Kathryn gasped. "You're kidding!"

"Shh," Sarah warned her. "If you wake the *kinner* our visiting will be over."

"Sorry." Her sister giggled. "I'm stunned. I had no idea he was interested in you."

"I didn't know either," Sarah said, crossing her legs under herself. "I thought we were just friends."

"What did you say when he asked?"

"I told him no. I said I cherish his friendship, but I could never be his wife. I think I broke his heart." Sarah sighed. "I wonder if I made a mistake. Luke doesn't love me, and I may spend my life alone. Maybe it makes sense for me to marry Norman since we both lost our spouses and have *kinner* who need two parents. It's logical, really. We're *gut* friends already. Maybe I could learn to love him."

"*Ack*, don't say that." Kathryn squeezed her hands. "You did the right thing. You shouldn't marry the wrong person. Marriage is for life, and you should be happy, Sarah Rose. You've lost Peter. Don't marry for the sake of having a husband. Marry for love."

"But Norman is so *gut* and kind. He's a *wunderbaar dat*. He'll love me and my *zwillingbopplin* for life."

"But do you love him?"

Sarah shook her head.

"There's your answer." Kathryn nodded. "You made the right choice by telling him no. You need to listen to your heart and not make a mistake you'll regret the rest of your life. He'll still be your friend. He's a loyal man."

"But I don't think God's plan is for me to marry Luke."

"How do you know that?" Kathryn's smile was smug. "What is your heart saying?"

"I'm not sure." Sarah brushed away a tear. "I'm so mixed up. All I know is that I can't stop thinking about Luke, and it feels like a lost cause, a silly fantasy."

"Listen to your heart," Kathryn said again. "Close your eyes, open your heart, and pray for hope. Then listen to what God tells you. You'll get your answer, Sarah Rose. I promise the Lord will guide you to the right path."

Sarah pulled Kathryn into a hug. "I thank God for my wonderful family, especially you."

23

Elizabeth rolled the finished whoopie pies in individual pieces of plastic wrap. She hummed her favorite hymn to herself while the swirl of Pennsylvania *Dietsch* from her daughters filled the bakery kitchen around her. She smiled to herself. This bakery had been her dream when she was a young wife. Sharing it with her daughters, granddaughters, and daughter-in-law was more than a dream come true—it was a gift from the Lord.

"How's Sarah?" Kathryn asked. She hoisted herself up onto a stool beside Elizabeth.

"She seemed fine when I left this morning. Nancy and Katie were helping her with the *zwillingbopplin*." Elizabeth stacked the wrapped whoopie pies in a basket in preparation for taking them out front to the counter. She then faced her daughter and wiped her hands on a rag. "I'm worried about her. I think something is bothering her. She's been different ever since she got back from Ohio last month." She frowned. "I think that English girl said or did something to her. I'm not happy."

Kathryn bit her bottom lip and averted her eyes.

"What is it, Kathryn?" Elizabeth touched her shoulder. "You know something you're not telling me."

Her oldest daughter frowned. "I'm sorry, but I can't betray her confidence. I couldn't bear it if she didn't trust me."

"Please, Kathryn." Elizabeth pleaded with her eyes. "Of course I have to know what's wrong with my *dochder*."

Kathryn glanced around the kitchen.

"No one can hear you," Elizabeth said. "They're all baking and chatting. They have no idea what we're discussing over here."

"Sarah's miserable." Kathryn held Elizabeth's hand as if to convince her. "Norman proposed to her, but she doesn't love him. She feels horrible about telling him no, but it doesn't feel right."

Elizabeth gasped. "Norman proposed?"

"You can't tell anyone, *Mamm*." Kathryn's eyes were serious.

"When did he ask?"

"The night she got home from Ohio. She was caught off guard."

Elizabeth shook her head. "I had no idea. I wish she'd told me."

"She feels horrible about it because he said he loved her, but she doesn't love him." Kathryn shook her head, frowning. "She feels like she broke his heart because it may seem logical for them to marry. She said he's a *gut* friend."

"Why does she feel bad if she doesn't love him? No one is forcing her to get married. She can stay with your *dat* and me for as long as she wants."

Kathryn gave a knowing smile. "That's not it. She loves someone else."

"What did you say?" Elizabeth raised an eyebrow. "Who does she love?"

Kathryn nodded. "She loves Luke."

Elizabeth tilted her head in surprise. "Are you sure?"

Kathryn nodded again. "She's miserable over it. She said she can't stop thinking about him, and she feels horrible about the argument they had the night before he left."

Cupping a hand to her mouth, Elizabeth lowered herself onto a stool. "I feel wretched for not knowing this about my own *dochder*. How could I not know she's been suffering?"

"It's not your fault, *Mamm*." Kathryn placed a hand on her shoulder. "I'm just telling you so you can help her. She listens to you and looks up to you. I'm worried she's going to sink into a deep black hole in her heart. She's finally accepted Peter's past, which is *wunderbaar* and healthy for her. She can move on with her life now, but she's stuck because she thinks Luke hates her."

Elizabeth shook her head. "I hope I can help her."

"Just listen to her." Kathryn put her hand on Elizabeth's arm. "Please listen and really hear what she has to say."

Elizabeth nodded. She would do anything to help her youngest daughter find happiness again.

❄

Later that evening, Elizabeth found Sarah propped up in bed reading her Bible. Glancing up, Sarah smiled, and Elizabeth's heart warmed with hope. Maybe Kathryn was wrong, and Sarah was okay.

"Hi, *Mamm*." Sarah set her Bible down. "How are things at the bakery?"

"*Gut*." Elizabeth lowered herself onto the edge of the bed, which creaked under her weight. "The question is how are you?" She patted Sarah's hand.

Sarah shrugged. "All right. Just tired." She covered her mouth and yawned. Nodding in the direction of the nursery, she grinned. "They've been active today. They're wearing me, Nancy, and Katie out. I'm thankful they're sleeping now so I can spend some time with the Scriptures."

"I'm glad you had a *gut* day. The girls seem to like coming here to help you."

"We have a *gut* time together." Sarah glanced toward the window with a faraway expression. She looked as if she were a million miles away.

"What's on your mind, Sarah Rose?" Elizabeth asked. "You seem to be preoccupied."

Blinking, her youngest daughter met her gaze. "How do you

know what God wants for you? How do you know if you're on the right path?"

Elizabeth squeezed her hand. "You follow your heart and listen to what it tells you. Sarah Rose, what's really bothering you? You've been different since you came home from Ohio."

Sarah hesitated.

"Is something wrong?" Elizabeth searched her eyes, wondering if Kathryn's assessment was correct. "Is there something you're not telling me?"

Sarah took a deep breath and then shook her head.

Elizabeth studied her daughter's eyes. Was she lying? Did she really love Luke?

"Sarah Rose," Elizabeth said, holding her hands. "You can talk to me. I'm here to listen. Kathryn told me today she's worried about you too."

Sarah's eyes flashed with something resembling fear and worry at the mention of Kathryn's name.

"If something is worrying you, you can tell me," Elizabeth said. "If you don't want to talk about it with me, then you can always open your heart to God. You know what I always say."

"Yes, *Mamm*." Sarah's voice croaked with emotion. "You always tell us your favorite verse, 'Be joyful in hope, patient in affliction, faithful in prayer.'"

"That's right." Elizabeth smiled. "You can always pray about it."

Sarah wiped her eyes. "*Danki*. I'll do that."

Elizabeth nodded, hoping Sarah would open up to her. However, Sarah settled against the pillows and didn't speak. Elizabeth patted her daughter's hands and stood. "You call me if you need anything."

"*Danki, Mamm*." Sarah picked up her Bible from the end table and opened it.

❀

Elizabeth climbed into bed later that evening and watched Eli change into his nightclothes. She'd spent all evening worrying about Sarah and contemplating Kathryn's words. She wondered if Kathryn had been telling the truth. If so, then why hadn't Sarah confessed her feelings for Luke?

"Sarah Rose was quiet during devotions," Eli said, crawling into bed next to her.

She wondered if he'd read her mind. "I'm worried about her," Elizabeth blurted before she could stop the words.

"She seems unhappy," he said. "I've noticed it." Angling himself onto his side, he fluffed the pillow before lying down facing the wall.

"Kathryn has a theory." Elizabeth snuggled under the quilt and rubbed his back.

"Oh?"

"She insists Sarah Rose is in love with Luke. Do you think that's possible?"

Moving onto his back, he faced her and nodded. "I watched a beautiful friendship bloom between her and Luke, and I tried to encourage him to stay."

"What?" She gasped. "He was courting Naomi King, but you encouraged him to pursue Sarah Rose?"

"No, no, no." He blew out a sigh. "Elizabeth, I never said that." He reached over and patted her hands.

"First of all," he began, "Naomi King was trying desperately to court *him*, and he was just being nice. At first I thought there might be a romance. But I could see the frustration in his eyes every time Naomi showed up—uninvited, mind you—for lunch. And yes, when he came to me and said he wanted to go home, I encouraged him to stay. I told him I could see the love in his eyes for Sarah Rose. He didn't confirm my theory, but he also didn't deny it. He said Sarah Rose had made her choice by harboring her anger for not telling her he was Peter's brother when he first came, and he felt he had to leave because she didn't love him in return."

"Do you think they belong together?" she asked.

"If that's what God has planned for them, *ya*."

"Norman asked Sarah to marry him."

"He did?" In the dark Eli sounded surprised.

"She turned him down. Kathryn thinks it's because Sarah loves Luke."

"That could be," Eli said.

"I just want Sarah to be happy," Elizabeth whispered. "I want to see her smile again. It seems like she hasn't smiled since Luke left."

Eli's breathing became deep and rhythmic, and she knew he'd fallen asleep. It was typical that he would nod off when she felt the urge to talk to him.

Staring up at the ceiling through the darkness, she closed her eyes and considered what Eli had said. She agreed Sarah and Luke had formed a special friendship. She had thought it was merely the bond they'd shared through their love for Peter and the twins. Were they meant to be more than relatives?

She blew out a sigh and then began to silently pray, asking God to guide Sarah's heart to the right path.

POUND CAKE

1 cup shortening
1−1/4 cups sugar
5 eggs
2 cups flour
1/4 tsp salt
1/8 tsp nutmeg
1 tsp vanilla

Cream shortening and sugar together. Add eggs, beating well after each egg. Add flour, salt, and nutmeg. Add vanilla and beat thoroughly. Bake in greased loaf pan at 350 degrees for 50 minutes or until done.

24

Eli's conversation with Elizabeth the night before rang through his head all morning as he tried to concentrate on running the front desk, answering the phone, and taking customer orders. When Jake offered to take over, he was happy for the break. He weaved through the shop and stepped out the door to the back lot hoping to clear his mind.

Staring over the pasture, Eli contemplated his youngest child, wishing he could take away her pain. Losing Peter had been a blow to their family, but it was devastating to his sweet Sarah Rose. During Luke's time with them, however, Eli had seen Sarah Rose's genuine smile and heard her true laugh for the first time since Peter's death.

Eli leaned on the fence and considered how he could help Sarah Rose through this rough time. The girl had suffered enough after losing Peter. She deserved happiness.

"Busy up front?" a voice behind him asked.

Eli turned just as Timothy came up to him. "*Ya*. Very. I needed to step out and clear my head." He gestured back toward the shop. "How do you think production is? Jake mentioned he's swamped. I'm thinking about trying to hire another carpenter."

His son shrugged. "I think we're *gut*."

"Don't you think projects really piled up after Luke left? He was a *gut*, fast worker and a talented carpenter."

Timothy averted his eyes. "Luke is back where he should be. The shop is fine. We can handle it."

Eli studied his son. "Why do you look away when I mention Luke?"

"He hurt Sarah by telling her all of the stories about Peter's past. He should've quit while he was ahead. I encouraged him to go back to Ohio, away from us."

Anger boiled in Eli and his eyes narrowed. "Are you telling me you drove Luke away?"

"I didn't drive him away, but I encouraged him to go." Timothy folded his arms. "He lied about who he was when he first got here, and it just did more damage to Sarah, who was already in a fragile state. Besides, Sarah is going to marry Norman anyway."

"What did you say?"

"I said Sarah and Norman are going to get married. She doesn't need the distraction of her past around all the time when she's going to start a new life."

"No, they aren't getting married," Eli snapped. "She turned him down a month ago."

"She did? He never told me." Timothy grimaced. "I told Luke Sarah was going to marry Norman. They're *gut* friends, and it just seemed like they would."

"No wonder Luke left in such a hurry. He thought Sarah was going to marry Norman." Eli shook his head and stalked back toward the shop, fury roaring through his veins.

"*Dat!*" Timothy trotted up beside him. "Hang on." He tried to stop Eli, but Eli yanked away and kept walking. "Let me explain. Please."

Eli halted and glared at Timothy. "Do you have any idea what you've done? Sarah is miserable. She's almost as distraught now as she was after Peter died."

His son's eyes rounded like an animal caught intruding in a pasture of crops. "If you'll just let me explain." His folded hands pleaded for forgiveness. "I thought Norman was going to marry her. He told me he was going to propose, and I figured they belonged together. They were good friends, and it seemed natural for them to—"

"You thought wrong." Eli jammed a finger in Timothy's chest. "Do us all a favor and only think for yourself. You made the choice to be alone and not court after Miriam left you, but you have no business making Sarah Rose's decisions for her." He left his stunned son in the parking lot while he marched through the shop to his office.

Closing and locking the door, he sank into his desk chair and wracked his brain for a solution that would make Sarah smile again.

After several minutes, an idea lit his mind like lightning illuminating the midsummer sky. He fished the piece of paper with Luke's contact information from his jacket pocket, pulled out a notepad, grabbed a pen, and began to write a letter.

When he finished the letter, he folded it, deposited it into an envelope, and then sealed and addressed it. As he was angling a stamp in the upper corner, a soft knock sounded on the door.

"*Ya?*" Eli called.

"*Dat*, please let me in." Timothy's voice sounded humble on the other side of the door. "I need to talk to you."

Frowning, Eli rose and unlocked the door. Wrenching it open, he glared at his son. "You better be here to apologize."

Timothy nodded. "I am."

Eli studied him, waiting for an explanation.

"I thought I was doing what was best for Sarah," he said. "I wanted to protect her from enduring more pain. We all loved Peter, but seeing her suffer was the most horrific thing I've ever experienced." He sighed. "She's my baby sister, and I want her to be happy. I don't care about what happens to me, but I want to see my siblings happy."

Eli crossed his arms and rubbed his beard. "You had no right meddling between her and Luke. They love each other. Because of your actions, she may give up on love altogether and wind up alone."

"That's just it, *Dat.*" Timothy stepped into the office and leaned against the wall. "Norman loves her, and he'd be *gut* to her. I wanted to see them get together because I care about both of them. Norman is a *gut* friend, and Sarah is my sister. I thought they would make a good team since they've both experienced losing their spouses."

Eli shook his head in disbelief. "But that's not for you to decide. Sarah Rose has the right to choose her own husband."

"I see that now. My heart was in the right place, but I was making the wrong choices. I should've backed off." Timothy placed a hand on his father's shoulder. "I messed up. What can I do now to make it right?"

Eli held up the letter and shook it. "I'm hoping this will do the trick."

Timothy studied the address. "You wrote Luke a letter?"

"*Ya.*" Eli shook a finger at him as a warning. "Do me a favor and keep this between us. You've already done enough damage."

"*Ya.*" Timothy nodded. "You can trust me. I've learned my lesson."

"Say a prayer this works." Eli smacked his son's arm.

"I will, *Dat.* I will."

25

Luke leaned against his workbench and glanced across the empty shop, pondering what had possessed him to agree to come in to work on the weekend. Of course, it wasn't as if he had anything to do at the house.

He'd spent last night visiting with Mel and Sally, which meant he spent the entire evening eating too much and longing for the close, loving relationship his best friend shared with his beautiful wife. And those desires conjured up thoughts of Sarah that had haunted him all night long.

Taking a deep breath, he sauntered to the other side of the shop to Mel's work area where a half-finished cabinet sat. Grabbing a sander, he set to work, hoping to finish the project for his friend as another way to thank him for the delicious meal.

Luke was deep at work, struggling to tune out memories of Sarah and concentrate on the hum of the tool, when a tap on his shoulder startled him.

"You scared me half to death!" he hissed at the teenager who ran the front of the store. "What is it?"

"You have a visitor out front." The kid jerked his thumb toward the show room.

"A visitor?" Luke set the tool down on the workbench.

"Yeah." The kid shrugged. "Some girl."

"Girl?" Luke's stomach flip-flopped. Had Sarah come to see

him? Had she finally realized she belonged with him and not Norman?

Rushing out front, Luke stopped dead in his tracks when he spotted an English woman leaning on the counter. "DeLana?" he said. "How are you?"

"I'm good." She smiled. "How are you doing?"

"Fine. What brings you out here today?"

"I was hoping we could talk." She nodded toward the front door.

Luke glanced out the showroom window toward the large drops raining down on the pavement. "It looks a bit wet out there. How about we talk in the break room?"

She shrugged. "All right."

He led her through the shop and into the small room in the back, where she sat at the table. He fetched two cans of Coke from the refrigerator and sat across from her, handing her one.

"Thanks." She popped open the can, which fizzed and hissed in response. She then took a long drink before setting it on the table and meeting his gaze. "I had an interesting conversation with someone about a month ago. I've been meaning to stop by, but things kept coming up at work. Today I made it my business to come by and tell you about my special visitor."

"Anyone I know?" He took a long drink, enjoying the cool carbonation on his dry throat.

Her smile was smug. "Oh yeah. She's a pretty blonde who is all into you."

He looked at her with curiosity. "Who was it?"

"Sarah Troyer." She lifted her can and took another drink while he stared at her, unable to breathe for a moment.

"Sarah?" His voice was ragged. "How ... Where ..." He shook his head, trying to figure out what she meant. "I don't understand."

She grinned. "I gotcha."

"DeLana," he began with frustration. "I don't have the time or patience for games. How on earth did you meet Sarah?"

"She came to see me. She had some burning questions about Peter's past, so I filled her in." DeLana explained how they'd visited in a restaurant and she'd told Sarah the history of how she and Peter met and about the night he left.

Hurt radiated through Luke's soul at the realization Sarah had been a few miles from his shop only a month ago.

"She came all the way out here but didn't stop to see me," he muttered. He ran his hand through his hair as the truth sank in—Sarah never loved him, and he was kidding himself by thinking he'd ever had a chance with her. Maybe she really did love Norman.

And maybe she did hate him.

He swallowed a groan.

"That's where you're wrong." DeLana's smirk was back. "I drove her out here, but she was too afraid to get out of the car."

"Afraid?" He snorted. "Please. Have you ever known me to be intimidating?"

"No, but her feelings for you are."

He studied her eyes, finding no sign of a lie or a cruel joke. He needed to know more. "What do you mean?"

"It was obvious when she talked about you that she had feelings for you. I tried to encourage her to come and see you, but she insisted the feelings weren't mutual." She pushed back a lock of dark hair. "She was afraid you hated her since you had an argument the night before you left. She was in tears over you. It was difficult to watch her break down. She's such a sweet, innocent thing. I wanted to pull her into a hug."

The image of her crying in his arms twisted his heart. He pushed the memory away. Frowning, he shook his head. "It doesn't matter anyway. She's marrying someone else."

DeLana gave a look of surprise. "She is? She didn't mention that to me."

Luke nearly dropped his can. "She didn't mention a guy named Norman?"

She shook her head. "No, she didn't mention anyone named

Norman. But she was very emotional when she talked about you. It's obvious, Luke, that girl has the hots for you."

He frowned in disbelief, but his heart thumped in his chest at the possibility that DeLana was right. "She has 'the hots' for me? That's funny, because she accepted it when I told her I was leaving, and she hasn't contacted me. Her father has my information. She could get my number from him or look it up in the phone book at the library. There are ways to contact people. And you said it yourself that she went home without seeing me."

"You're just as stubborn as your brother was, Luke. You're not listening to me. She hasn't contacted you because she thinks you hate her." DeLana leaned forward, her eyes serious. "I got the feeling she would love for you to come after her. She needs the fairy tale, Luke. You have to ride in on your white horse and sweep her off her feet like a Disney movie."

He looked at her in confusion, and she snapped her fingers.

"I forgot." She chuckled. "You aren't allowed to watch movies or television. Just trust me on this. She wants you to come and save her, but she doesn't know how to reach out to you. I think she's afraid of being hurt again."

Luke leaned back in the chair and raked his fingers through his hair, letting her words soak into his mind. He crossed his arms and studied her expression. "Why are you telling me this?"

She placed the can on the table. "To be honest, I'm not sure what possessed me, but I've had a nagging desire to come and tell you all this. I guess it's because I let your brother slip through my fingers eight years ago, and I didn't want it to happen to you. I love my husband, and I don't regret marrying him. However, as I told Sarah, sometimes I wonder what would've happened if I'd run away with Peter the night he begged me to leave town with him. I don't want you to let the love of your life slip through your fingers too."

He narrowed his eyes, challenging her. "What makes you think she's the love of my life?"

DeLana snorted, lifting the can again. "It doesn't take a

rocket scientist to see your expression or hers and figure it out." She leaned forward and lowered her voice for effect. "Luke, don't be a dunce. You're wasting your life away living like a hermit here in Ohio. Go back to Pennsylvania and marry that girl."

His mouth gaped. How on earth had she figured out so much about him? While he studied her, she pulled an envelope from her purse.

"I brought photos of your nephew. He's almost nine now." She slapped a few photographs onto the table in front of him.

Luke flipped through the photographs, silently marveling at how much Cody looked like Peter. Warmth filled his heart. How could he have lived in the same town as his nephew for nearly nine years and never contacted him? He needed to be the uncle the child deserved and the uncle the twins deserved too.

"He's grown up so much," Luke said. "It's amazing how time flies."

"I'd love for you to meet him sometime."

He glanced up at her. "Really?"

She nodded. "Alex and I are going to tell him about Peter soon. We want him to know his other siblings, and Sarah promised to keep in touch."

"I'd love to meet him." He stared at the snapshots.

They chatted about old times, swapping funny stories about Peter. After nearly an hour, DeLana stood and said she had to get home. Luke walked her to the show room.

"It was great seeing you again." DeLana pulled him into a quick hug.

"You too." He rubbed her arm. "Thank you."

She gave him a wicked grin. "If you want to thank me, then go to Pennsylvania and tell Sarah how you feel about her before it's too late." She winked and then rushed out the door into the blowing rain.

Luke stood at the window while DeLana climbed into her SUV and sped through the parking lot, her tires leaving their wake in the puddles.

His stomach tightened while he contemplated all she'd revealed about her visit with Sarah. While it cut him to the bone that Sarah had visited DeLana without seeing him, he felt a ray of hope that she could possibly love him.

For a split second, he considered calling a taxicab, leaving the shop, and heading to the train station.

But how could he truly know Sarah wanted to be with him and not Norman?

It just didn't make sense. Why would Sarah share her true feelings with DeLana, a stranger who had shared an intimate love affair with her late husband, but not tell Luke how she felt?

He considered the thought. Then another idea struck him—why would DeLana come to see him after all of these years to share a lie?

A headache throbbed in his temple while he considered all of the possible motives for DeLana's visit. All he knew for sure was he was more confused than ever.

❊

On Sunday evening, Luke sank into a kitchen chair and flipped through the letters he'd piled up on the table over the past couple of days. He'd been so consumed with his conversation with DeLana he hadn't bothered to open his mail or read the newspaper.

He glanced through the usual bills without much interest and then stopped when he found a handwritten envelope with a Pennsylvania postmark. His heartbeat leapt when he read "Kauffman" in the return address.

Ripping it open, Luke held his breath as his eyes scanned the block handwriting.

Dear Luke,

I hope this letter finds you well. The shop has been busy since you left. We sure could use your hands around here these days. Please remember the job here is always available for you if you decide to come back.

The real reason why I'm writing isn't to tell you about the business at the furniture store. I wanted to tell you that the person who misses you most of all is Sarah Rose. She hasn't been the same since you left. I haven't seen her smile or heard her laugh in weeks. She spends most days in her room, reading her Bible and not talking to anyone.

If you can find it in your heart to come back to Sarah Rose, please do it as soon as possible. I'm sure she loves you. In fact, she admitted to Kathryn that she does. If you come back, I think you both would realize you're meant to be together.

May the Lord bless you and keep you in His tender care.

Sincerely,
Eli Kauffman

Luke stared at the letter, reading and rereading it until he'd committed it to memory. Eli's words were so similar to DeLana's.

Then it struck him like a ton of bricks — was God trying to tell him something? Was he, Luke, wrong to think Sarah belonged with Norman and not him? Was he wrong to think it was a sin for him to covet Sarah?

The questions rang through his mind all night and lingered into the early morning as he rode to work with his English driver.

Luke cornered Mel in the parking lot and filled him in on DeLana's visit and then handed him Eli's letter. He held his breath while he waited for Mel's reaction. When Mel met his gaze with a grimace, Luke's heart sank.

"Are you dense, Troyer?" Mel asked, handing the letter back to Luke.

"What do you mean?"

"What are you doing here?" Mel gestured around the parking lot. "What are you waiting for?"

Luke shook his head. "But isn't it a sin to covet my brother's *fraa?*"

His best friend raised an eyebrow. "A sin? Why would it be a sin? There's a verse about it. Let me think ..." Mel snapped his finger. "That's it! It's from Romans, and it goes something like, 'By law a married woman is bound to her husband as long as he is alive, but if her husband dies, she is released from the law of marriage.'" He shrugged. "So, where's the sin in coveting her? Peter was her past." He gestured toward Luke. "You could be her future."

Luke's stomach lurched with excitement. "You think so?"

"What are you doing waiting here?" Mel gestured toward the pickup truck sitting by the entrance to the shop. "Go! Get packed and rush to the train station. Go to Sarah before she marries Norman."

Luke gave Mel a quick hug. "*Danki*." He trotted toward the English driver. "I'll call you!"

26

Luke drummed his fingers on the door of the taxicab as it rolled down Route 340 toward Kauffman & Yoder. The train ride had seemed longer than the last time, due to his excitement. Even though Eli didn't mention a wedding in his letter, Luke prayed he wasn't too late to tell Sarah he loved her and not to marry Norman.

When the cab pulled into the furniture store lot, he tossed money to the driver, snatched his bag from the floor, and jogged into the showroom, finding Jake on the phone.

Jake looked up and grinned. Ending his call, he rushed around the counter and smacked Luke on the shoulder. "Hey, man! I knew you'd be back. You just couldn't stay away, huh?"

"*Ya.*" Luke forced a smile, anticipation bubbling in his gut. "Is Eli around?"

Jake shrugged. "Should be. Head on back. You know the way."

"*Danki.*" Luke hefted his bag on his shoulder and stepped into the shop. The familiar scents of wood and stain washed over him, and the booming sounds of tools rang through his head as he scanned the sea of men working on various projects. He missed the variety of building furniture.

Nodding greetings to his former coworkers, he steered to the back of the shop and knocked on Eli's office door.

"Enter," Eli called over the chorus of tools.

Luke wrenched open the door, which squeaked its protest.

When their gaze met, Eli's eyes rounded, and he jumped from his chair. "Luke!" Grabbing his hand, he shook it. "It's so *gut* to see you."

"I got your letter." Luke's voice trembled. *"Danki."*

The older man smiled. "I'm glad you came."

"How is she doing?" Luke's stomach clenched.

A knowing smile parted Eli's lips. "I think she'll be fine." He shrugged into his coat. "Let's call a driver and head to the house now. She'll be glad to see you."

❁

Sarah smiled and hugged her arms to her chest while she observed Jessica holding Rachel and Lindsay snuggling Seth. She was so glad Jessica had come to visit after finishing high school for the summer.

"He's so tiny," Lindsay said, running her finger over his hand. "Check out those teensy fingers, Aunt Trisha."

Trisha leaned over the chair and smiled. "So beautiful. Hey, little buddy."

Jessica grinned down at the baby girl. Rachel scrunched her face and yawned in response.

"You are just too cute." Jessica glanced up at Sarah and then back at Rachel. "She definitely looks like you. She has your chin."

Sarah chuckled. *"Danki."*

"I see Peter in him," Trisha said with a nod.

"You know what's weird?" Lindsay gave Sarah a serious look. "I see Luke in him. I guess it's the family resemblance."

Sarah's heart thumped at the sound of Luke's name.

"That's not weird," Trisha said, rubbing Seth's cheek. "My husband is a dead ringer for his uncle Poochie."

"Uncle Poochie?" Lindsay guffawed, and the baby squirmed.

"It's a long story," Trisha said. "I'll have to tell you some other time."

"Have you seen Jake yet?" Sarah asked Jessica.

Jessica shook her head and her face flushed. "Not yet. He thinks I have another week of classes. I'm going to surprise him at the shop."

"He'll be excited to see you," Lindsay said. "He always asks about you. He's still crazy about you."

"Don't rush it," Trisha warned with a serious expression. "You're young and have your whole life ahead of you."

"*Ya*. That's right," Sarah agreed with a nod.

An engine rumbled outside, and Sarah peered out the window as *Dat* and another man climbed from the cab of Mike Gray's pickup truck. "*Dat*'s home early."

Settling back in the chair, she took in the sight of the women cooing to her twins, who were almost six months old. It was hard to believe Peter had been gone nearly thirteen months.

Life had changed so much since the Christmas morning they'd been born. She'd lost her friendship with Luke and turned down a marriage proposal from Norman. It seemed things were changing daily.

She couldn't help but wonder what tomorrow would bring. She hoped she'd soon find happiness for her and the twins.

❄

Luke glanced around the Kauffman's kitchen, and his pulse pounded. He wondered if he'd made a mistake coming here.

"She's up in the nursery visiting with some out-of-town relatives." Eli gestured toward the stairs. "Go on."

Luke gnawed his lip, facing her father. "What if she's not happy to see me?"

Eli gave a knowing smile. "She will be. Trust me." Taking Luke's arm, he steered him toward the stairs. "Go."

"But we argued the last time we spoke. I said some awful

things to her." Luke adjusted his hat on his head. "She probably hates me."

"She doesn't hate you, Luke." Eli made a sweeping gesture toward the stairs. "Go tell her how you feel and listen to her."

With a deep sigh, Luke climbed the steps to Sarah's room. His heart was pounding so hard in his chest he was sure Sarah would hear it. Doubt mixed with worry swirled in his gut. What if she told him to leave?

What if she said she loved Norman?

Approaching her room, his palms trembled, and sweat beaded on his brow. The next few moments would change the rest of his life.

❧

Sarah had the nagging sensation of being watched. Glancing toward the doorway, her eyes focused on Luke. She gasped. "Luke?" she whispered, her voice quavering with a mix of shock, awe, and affection.

His handsome face displayed a tentative smile. "May I come in?"

"Please." She gestured toward the twins. "Your niece and nephew have missed you."

Misty-eyed, he stepped over toward Jessica, who held out Rachel. "I've missed them too. Hello, *mei liewe*."

Sarah's heart swelled when he called Rachel "my love." He did love the children.

But did he love Sarah too?

"Would you like to hold her?" Jessica asked with a smile.

He glanced at Sarah for permission, and she gave a quiet laugh. "Of course. You're her *onkel*."

Jessica passed the tiny bundle to him. He held her as if she were the most precious little person in the world, and Sarah's heart turned over at the sight. He looked so natural with Rachel in his arms. He looked like a father.

She suppressed the thought. He didn't love her.

Lindsay rose and handed Seth to Sarah. "We'll go downstairs and let you visit alone. We can run by the shop and see Jake." She motioned to Jessica and Trisha. "Luke, this is my sister and my aunt Trisha."

"Nice to meet you." He nodded as they exited the room. His eyes then met Sarah's, and the intensity in them caused her pulse to double. "It's so good to be back with you and the *zwillingbopplin* again."

"We've missed you." Sarah's mouth dried.

"They've gotten bigger. Rachel still looks just like you."

"Lindsay says Seth looks like you." She sidled up to him. He leaned over, and she inhaled his scent, so familiar, so warm.

"No," he said. "He's still my brother, through and through." He smiled at her, and her heart somersaulted.

She resisted the urge to touch his sweet face.

Questions swirled through her mind as she watched him with her baby. First and foremost, she wanted to know if he was back for good, but the answer scared her. She took a deep breath before she spoke.

"Why are you here?" Her voice was thick as fear slithered through her—fear that he'd say he wouldn't stay long.

"Your *dat* wrote me." He kept his eyes trained on the sleeping child snuggled in his large arms like a precious doll.

"What?" She studied him. "Why?"

"He asked me to come back and see you because you've been unhappy." He ran a large finger over Rachel's chin, and she sighed in her sleep. A loving smile graced his lips. "And DeLana came to visit me at the shop."

"DeLana?" Sarah's eyes popped wide open.

"She also said you missed me, and I should come back." He grinned. "She said I should ride back on my horse and sweep you off your feet like a fairy tale in some movie."

"Oh." She studied his eyes, trying to discern if he was laughing at DeLana's analogy or if he was saying he wanted to be with her. She had the sinking feeling that he was laughing, and he wasn't going to stay after all. She feared he was only here to visit and see the twins.

She needed to find out what his intentions were, but they couldn't talk with the children sleeping. Since Seth was already asleep, she placed him in his cradle. She then removed Rachel from Luke's arms, and placed her in the other cradle. Taking Luke's warm hand in hers, she led him into the hallway, gently closing the door behind her.

Still holding his hand, she guided him into her mother's sewing room, closing the door behind them. Once there, she stood before him. She knew she had to apologize to him, and she wracked her brain for the right words.

His eyes scanned her face, and she looked down, suddenly self-conscious.

"Why are you staring at me?" she asked, running her hand over her prayer *kapp* to be sure it was straight.

"I can't believe I'd forgotten just how beautiful you are." His face and eyes were serious.

"*Danki,*" she whispered, her body trembling at his intense expression. Squeezing his hand, she cleared her throat. She had to apologize before she lost her nerve. "I'm sorry, Luke." Her voice quaked. "I'm sorry for everything I said. You're not a liar, and I never meant to compare you to Peter."

His expression softened, and he touched her face. "No, I'm sorry. I was wrong to say you regarded me as gum on your shoe. I know you don't."

Tears began to drip down her cheeks. "You're so much more than that to me, Luke. So much more. I've missed you."

"I'm glad you feel that way." He swiped away a tear with his thumb. His touch was so gentle and so loving. "I didn't arrive here on a horse like the fairy tale DeLana mentioned, but I would like to sweep you off your feet."

Her pulse quickened in her veins, and her breath caught in her throat. "I think you've definitely swept me off my feet."

He cupped her face in his hands. "I'm here to ask you not to marry Norman." His eyes pleaded with her. "Please don't marry him, Sarah Rose. Please."

Her voice failed her for a moment. "What are you talking about? I was never going to marry Norman."

Luke raised his eyebrows in shock. "You weren't?"

She searched his eyes. "Who told you I was going to marry him?"

"Timothy said Norman was going to ask you when May arrived, and it was only natural for you to marry him since you're such close friends."

She groaned. "It wasn't true. There were no plans. Norman asked me to marry him the night I arrived back home after visiting DeLana, and I told him no. I said I only wanted to be friends."

She studied his brown eyes, drinking in the warmth she found there. "I told him I couldn't marry him because I didn't love him. When I looked into the eyes of my *kinner* I knew I couldn't raise them in a loveless marriage. They need so much more, and I do too."

Taking her hands in his, he pulled her to him. Her pulse pounded like a horse trotting through town.

"Sarah," he began, his voice ragged. "I'm miserable without you. I think of you day and night." Leaning down, he brushed his lips over her cheek, and her knees buckled. *"Ich liebe dich,* Sarah Rose. I want to come back here and stay. I already have a buyer for my land. He's been asking me for years to sell so he can build an English housing development." He released one of her hands and ran his thumb over where his kiss had fallen. "Will you marry me?"

She blinked back tears. "Luke, I love you too," she whispered, her voice quaking. "Yes, I'll marry you."

A smile broke out on his lips. "I am the happiest man on earth." He leaned down again. His lips brushed hers, sending her stomach into a wild swirl.

He pulled her to him, and she buried her head in his chest,

listening to the sound of his beating heart. She let the feel of his lips soak into her heart.

"At first I thought being with you would be a sin," he said.

"You did?" she asked. "What made you change your mind?"

A smile formed on his lips. "My best friend Mel. He reminded me of a verse in Romans." He rubbed her back. "He made me realize my brother was your past, but I could be your future."

"*Ya*." She buried her face in his chest again. "I'd like that, and so will the *kinner*." Closing her eyes, she said a silent prayer, thanking God for her beautiful twins and for Luke.

He held her close. "Your parents named you right. You're my beautiful rose. My perfect, lovely, sweet rose."

Sand Tarts

1 cup butter
2 cups sugar
4 eggs, separated
1 cup flour
1/2 cup cinnamon
1/2 cup almonds

Work in butter and sugar. Mix in 2 eggs. Use flour to make stiff dough. Roll thin, cut out small squares. Wet top with two beaten eggs, sprinkle with extra sugar, cinnamon, and chopped almonds. Bake on cookie sheet at 350 degrees for 10 minutes.

27

"This is the best chocolate cake I've ever had," Luke said, sitting across from Sarah at her parents' supper table later that evening. "It's so moist."

Sarah gave him a teasing glare. "I didn't make it. You better say it's not the best you've ever had or I'll never make you another chocolate cake."

"*Ack.*" He feigned a serious frown. "It's the second-best I've ever had."

"Well, that does it." Beth Anne gave him a mock glare. "You'll not have any more of my chocolate cake."

The rest of the Kauffman family laughed while a group of grandchildren raced through the kitchen on their way outside. Lindsay, Jessica, and Jake followed them out to the porch.

"Slow down," Robert called. "You don't want to fall down the porch stairs!"

"Luke," *Dat* said, forking more cake. "How long do you plan to stay this time?"

Luke gave Sarah a sideways glance. He was so handsome that her heart skipped in her chest.

"I was wondering if your offer of a job was still open." Luke wiped his napkin across his mouth and gave *Dat* a serious look. "Are you still looking for a carpenter?"

Dat's eyes rounded in surprise. "Are you here to stay?"

"I'll have to go home and take care of some things, but then I'll be back to stay." He met Sarah's gaze. "For good."

Beth Anne and Kathryn gasped and gave Sarah a surprised expression. Sarah's cheeks flamed.

Dat stood and crossed the room to Luke. "That's *wunderbaar*, son." He patted his shoulder. "You have a job. You know that."

Mamm stood and began gathering the dirty dishes, and Sarah and the rest of the women followed suit. The men headed for the porch.

Before stepping outside behind her brothers, Luke looked at her and gave her a loving smile. She mirrored his expression, and her heart warmed again.

He mouthed the words "I love you" and then disappeared outside. Joy flamed in her soul.

"It's so *gut* to see you smile again, Sarah Rose," *Mamm* said, wiping the counter.

Sarah smiled.

"She's glowing," Beth Anne chimed in.

"When's the wedding?" Kathryn asked with a grin as she filled the sink with soapy water.

"*Ya*." Beth Anne looped an arm around her shoulders. "We'll have to get started on a dress."

"You're marrying Luke?" Sadie asked, coming up to her. "I had no idea you were courting."

"Slow down." Sarah placed the dishes on the counter and then held out her arms. "We have no formal wedding plans."

"Not yet?" Sadie asked with a grin.

Sarah met *Mamm's* surprised expression. "We haven't set a date yet, but I don't see where there's any hurry. We can wait until fall if we need to. It will be a real transition with the *kinner*."

"I'm so happy for you, Sarah Rose," *Mamm* said, squeezing her hand. "I'm glad you listened to your heart."

Beth Anne, Sadie, and *Mamm* began to talk at once, commenting on Luke and their future. While they prattled on, Kathryn crossed the room to her.

With a smile, Kathryn pulled Sarah into her arms. "I'm so glad for you," she whispered. "You deserve happiness."

Cries erupted from upstairs, and Sarah pulled back. "I think the *zwillingbopplin* are hungry."

Kathryn chuckled. "*Ya*. I'd say so."

Sarah gestured toward the stairs. "Would you like to join me?"

"I'd love it." Kathryn looped her arm around Sarah.

She smiled. "Before you know it, my *kinner* will be running through the kitchen and out the back porch with the rest of them." Joy bubbled over in her heart at the realization of raising her children with her family, including Luke.

❀

Luke leaned on the porch railing and glanced over at Sarah's father, brothers, and brothers-in-law. While the men chatted about the furniture store, Luke smiled to himself, imagining his future with his Sarah Rose. His heart swelled at the thought of spending time with her and the twins.

Crossing his arms, his glance collided with Timothy's, who was studying him intently.

Timothy stepped over to Luke and nodded toward the stairs. "Can I talk with you for a moment? Alone."

"*Ya*. Why not?" Following Timothy down the steps toward the pasture fence, Luke dreaded Timothy giving him another lecture about how wrong it was to be back and spending time with Sarah.

They reached the fence, and Timothy leaned forward on it, resting his foot on the bottom rung while staring across the lush, green pasture.

Luke glanced back toward the house, his eyes focusing on the men visiting on the porch. He suppressed a smile while thinking of how he would be visiting with them more often — as a member of the family.

"So, you're back for good, *ya*?" Timothy asked, breaking through Luke's thoughts.

Luke crossed his arms and leaned back on the fence. "That's the plan."

"And you're courting my sister." Timothy kept his eyes trained across the pasture.

"*Ya.*" Luke rubbed his chin, wondering where Timothy was going with this.

"*Gut.*" Timothy met his gaze, his expression softening.

"*Gut?*" Luke raised his eyebrows, waiting for Timothy to say something negative.

Yet the man just nodded. "It's good to see my sister smile again. *Danki* for coming back."

"You're welcome." Luke tried in vain to suppress his surprise.

"I'm sorry about everything I did to make you leave." Timothy faced him.

"What do you mean?"

"I was wrong when I told you she was going to marry Norman. I assumed she'd marry him because they're good friends and have both suffered the same loss, but I was dead wrong." He paused and looked at his boots and then up at Luke. "I had no idea you and Sarah were so close. I was totally out of line. I'm sorry." He held his hand out. "I hope we can start over as future brothers."

A smile of relief curled Luke's lips as he shook Timothy's hand. "*Danki.* I appreciate your honesty."

"My sister has a right to decide who she'll court and who she'll marry, and judging by the smile you've brought to her face, I assume it will be you." Timothy smacked his arm. "*Danki* for making her smile again. She's been through a lot, but I think she's finally found happiness."

"*Gern gschehne.*" Luke crossed his arms. "It's my pleasure."

"Luke!" Kathryn called from the porch. "Sarah would like to see you upstairs."

"Duty calls." Luke turned to Timothy. "Thanks again." He trotted across the driveway, up the porch, through the kitchen full of women chatting, and up to the second floor.

Stepping into Sarah's room, he found her rocking Rachel and humming. Glancing up at him, she smiled, and his pulse skittered in his veins. She was the picture of beauty. He couldn't believe she'd agreed to marry him. He was more thankful than he could express in a prayer.

He lowered himself onto the hope chest next to her, rested his elbows on his knees, and smiled over at her. "Fast asleep?"

She nodded. "I just fed them, and they fell asleep."

Reaching over, he ran his finger down Sarah's arm. She looked at him, and her sapphire eyes simmered with an intensity that made his insides stiffen.

"My family is very happy you came back," she whispered.

"And are you?" he asked.

"What do you think?" She gave a coy smile. "*Ich liebe dich*, Luke."

"I love you, too, Sarah Rose. *Ich liebe dich*."

Her eyes grew serious. "I think I finally understand something my *mamm* told me a few months ago."

"What's that?" he asked.

"She said Scripture tells us 'Faith is being sure of what we hope for and certain of what we do not see.' When Peter died, I lost my faith. I was drowning in a deep abyss of sorrow and thought I would never find my way out." She paused, and her expression brightened. "Now I see God was with me all along. God had a plan for me, and His plan for me was you."

Reaching over, she cupped her hand over his. "Despite everything I thought was wrong, the Lord made sure everything was going to be all right for the *zwillingbopplin* and me. I should've had faith all along."

His heart filled with love for his future bride. "I know exactly what you're saying, Sarah Rose. The Scripture is true. I, too, was drowning in sorrow when I found out I'd lost my brother, and I was also envious of the family he had here. Now my faith in God is renewed, and I'm so thankful for what I've found in you."

EPILOGUE

While Luke trotted up the porch steps, Timothy leaned back against the fence and reflected on the conversation they'd shared.

A huge weight had dissolved from his conscience when Luke accepted his apology. He hoped Luke and Sarah had a long, happy life together. His younger sister deserved a life of joy after the pain she'd endured.

A buggy clip-clopped up the drive and stopped in front of the barn. Titus King climbed from the buggy and began to unhitch his horse. While *Dat* and Timothy's brothers gathered around to chat with Titus, his wife, Irma emerged. She greeted the men and then headed for the house while their children hopped out of the buggy behind them.

The youngest of them ran off to play with Timothy's nieces and nephews. Naomi leaned down and said something to her younger sister, Lizzie Anne, and handed her a large cake plate covered with foil. Lizzie Anne jogged toward the house with the plate, and Naomi turned, meeting Timothy's gaze. She waved, and Timothy nodded in response.

She walked over to him, and he noticed for the first time that she had the prettiest brown eyes he'd ever seen. Her expression brightened as she approached, and he spotted a dimple in her right cheek. Why hadn't he seen that before?

"Hi." Naomi hugged her apron to her body.

"Hi." Timothy smiled.

"Pretty night." She glanced across the pasture.

"*Ya*. Real pretty."

She gave him a shy smile. Why hadn't he ever observed how attractive she was? Too bad she was eight years his junior.

"I made an apple walnut cobbler." She jerked her thumb toward the house. "My sister carried it in."

He folded his arms and rubbed his chin. "Are you trying to get a job at my *mamm's* bakery?"

She laughed. "Somehow I don't think my *mamm* would let me leave the quilt business."

He nodded in agreement. "Don't blame her. You make a mighty fine quilt."

Her eyes lit up. "Really? You think so?"

"I saw the one you gave Luke. It was *wunderbaar*."

Her smile faded. "*Ya*, that was a bit immature of me. I thought Luke had wanted to court me." Her cheeks flushed, and he couldn't help but think she was adorable. "I was a bit silly with him. My *mamm* chastised me for being so forward. I'm embarrassed by it now."

"We all make mistakes." *I've sure made enough to last a lifetime.* He nodded toward the house. "Would you like something to drink? I'd love to try some of your cobbler."

Her smile was back. "That would be nice."

As they walked toward the house side by side, *Dat's* voice echoed in his mind. Perhaps Naomi King wasn't too young for him after all.

DISCUSSION QUESTIONS

1. As the story progresses, Sarah discovers more and more about her late husband's past. Her anger toward him grows throughout the book. She isn't able to forgive him until after her twins are born. Why do you think her children helped her forgive Peter?

2. Think of a time when you were betrayed by a close friend or loved one. How did you come to grips with that betrayal? Were you able to forgive that person and move on? If so, then where did you find the strength to forgive? Share this with the group.

3. Timothy assumes Sarah will marry a man she does not love. While his intentions are good, he is not taking into consideration what Sarah truly wants. Think of a time when you may have had misguided intentions for a child or loved one. Share this with the group.

4. Luke is overwhelmed when he discovers the life Peter has left behind. Although he wants to be a part of Sarah's family, he struggles to find his place. Think of a time when you felt lost and alone. Where did you find your strength? What Bible verses would help with this?

5. Peter feels he's saving Sarah from hurt by not sharing his past with her. However, after he dies, Sarah is left with lies and deception. Do you think Peter's intentions were justified?

6. Have you ever known anyone who lied in order to save someone's feelings? How did that situation turn out?

7. Read Nahum 1:7 (print out the verse). Has this verse ever helped you when you're struggling to accept a loss in your life?

8. Which character can you identify with the most? Which character seemed to carry the most emotional stake in the story? Was it Sarah, Luke, Elizabeth, Eli, Timothy, Naomi, or even DeLana?

9. Read 1 John 4:18 (print this out). What does this verse mean to you? How does it apply to the book?

10. What did you know about the Amish before reading this book? What did you learn?

ACKNOWLEDGMENTS

This book wouldn't have been created without the help of my fabulous plotting partner and best friend: my mother, Lola Goebelbecker. Thank you, Mom, for your patience with my incessant plot and character discussions. Also, thank you for all you do for our family. We would be lost without you, and we love you.

To my mother-in-law, Sharon Clipston: thank you for buying all the copies of my books in Hampton Roads, Virginia, and for sharing them with friends and family. I truly appreciate your support of my writing career. Thank you also for all you do for us.

Eric Goebelbecker is the coolest big brother in the world! Love you!

To my wonderful aunts, Trudy Janitz and Debbie Floyd: thank you for your love and encouragement.

Thank you also to my wonderful friends who were willing to edit, proofread, and critique for me—Margaret Halpin, Sue McKlveen, and Lauran Rodriguez. You all offered wonderful suggestions, and you cleaned up my endless typos. Love you!

There aren't enough words to express how much I appreciate all that Sue McKlveen has done for me. You're like a sister to me. Thank you also to Ruth Meily and Betsy Cook for their help with Lancaster County knowledge. I appreciate your friendship so much!

Thank you also Pastor Tim, PJ (Pastor John), and the rest of my wonderful church family at Morning Star Lutheran in Matthews, North Carolina. Your encouragement, prayers, and love mean so much to my family and me. Thank you also for making my book signings such a great success!

Thank you to John and Carol Ionescu, who offered guidance on twin pregnancies. Congratulations on your two beautiful baby boys, John Cristian and Nicolae Daniel!

Thank you also to my Old Order Amish friend who continues to share her friendship and the details of her life in Pennsylvania. You and your family are in my prayers daily.

I'm more grateful than words can express to the Zondervan team. Thank you to my amazing editors—Sue Brower and Becky Philpott. I appreciate your friendship and your fabulous talent polishing my books. I've learned so much from you both. I am also thankful to the amazing marketing team, especially Karwyn Bursma and Jessica Secord. Thank you also to Joyce Ondersma and Jackie Aldridge for your support and friendship. I'm so blessed to be a part of the Zondervan family.

To Mary Sue Seymour—you are the best agent in the world! Thank you for believing in my writing.

Zac and Matt, you are the most amazing boys on the planet. I love you with all my heart. Thank you for bringing sunshine into my life. There's nothing better than dancing in the garage to Michael Jackson and watching Disney Channel with you. And remember, the zombies in "Thriller" aren't real. If they were, then they wouldn't have any sense of rhythm!

To my husband, Joe: there aren't words to tell you how much I cherish you. Thank you for putting up with my mood swings and crankiness when I'm burning the midnight oil and writing until 3:00 a.m. You're my rock. Thank you for reminding me to always have faith. You handle your illness with more grace than I could ever fathom. I pray we have a matching kidney for you soon so you can get on with your life. You're my inspiration; you're my "Luke." I love you. Always.

I'm also eternally thankful to my readers. I appreciate the wonderful emails you send me telling me how much you enjoy my stories. Thank you also for praying for my husband during his illness.

Thank you most of all to our Lord Jesus Christ for granting me the words and the opportunity to share my faith through my books.

Special thanks to Cathy and Dennis Zimmermann for their hospitality and research assistance in Lancaster County, Pennsylvania.

Cathy & Dennis Zimmermann, Innkeepers
The Creekside Inn
44 Leacock Road—PO Box 435
Paradise, PA 17562
Toll Free: (866) 604–2574
Local Phone: (717) 687–0333
Fax: (717) 687–8200
cathy@thecreeksideinn.com

ENJOY THE KAUFFMAN AMISH BAKERY
SERIES AS AN E-BOOK COLLECTION!

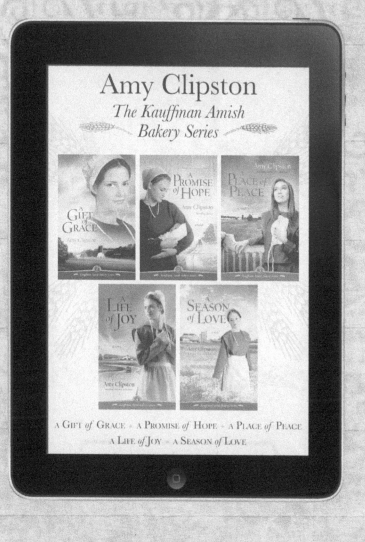

Available in e-book only

Naomi's Gift

An Amish Christmas Story

Amy Clipston,
Bestselling Author

Take a trip to Bird-in-Hand, Pennsylvania, where you'll meet the women of the Kauffman Amish Bakery in Lancaster County. As each woman's story unfolds, you will share in her heartaches, trials, joys, dreams . . . and secrets. You'll discover how the simplicity of the Amish lifestyle can clash with the English way of life—and the decisions and consequences that follow. Most importantly, you will be encouraged by the hope and faith of these women, and the importance they place on their families.

Naomi's Gift re-introduces twenty-four-year-old Naomi King, who has been burned twice by love and has all but given up on marriage and children. As Christmas approaches—a time of family, faith, and hope for many others—Naomi is more certain than ever her life will be spent as an old maid, helping with the family's quilting business and taking care of her eight siblings. Then she meets Caleb, a young widower with a seven-year-old daughter, and her world is once again turned upside-down.

Naomi's story of romantic trial and error and youthful insecurities has universal appeal. Author Amy Clipston artfully paints a panorama of simple lives full of complex relationships, and she carefully explores cultural differences and human similarities, with inspirational results.

Naomi's Gift includes all the details of Amish life that Clipston's fans enjoy, while delivering the compelling stories and strong characters that continue to draw legions of new readers.

Available in stores and online!

A Plain and Simple Christmas

A Novella

Amy Clipston

In the tradition of her widely popular Kauffman Amish Bakery Series, author Amy Clipston tells the tale of Anna Mae McDonough who was shunned by her family four years ago when she left her Amish community in Lancaster County, PA, to marry an Englisher and move with him to Baltimore. Now, eight months pregnant with her first child, she longs to return home for Christmas to reconcile with her family, especially her stern father, who is the religious leader for her former Amish church district.

So Anna Mae writes a letter to Kathryn Beiler, her brother's wife, to enlist her help. Kathryn asks her husband, David, if she should arrange Anna Mae's visit. David cautions her that a visit would cause too much stress in the family and instead suggests they visit Anna Mae and her husband in the spring. However, Kathryn arranges the visit anyway, believing in her heart that it's God's will for the family to heal.

When Anna Mae arrives in Lancaster for Christmas, the welcome she receives is nothing like what she had hoped for.

A book filled with love, the pain of being separated from one's family, and the determination to follow God's will regardless of the outcome, *A Plain and Simple Christmas* is an inspiring page-turner that will keep you guessing what happens next ... right to the very last page.

Available in stores and online!

READ AN EXCERPT FROM BOOK THREE OF THE KAUFFMAN AMISH BAKERY SERIES.

A PLACE OF PEACE

1

Miriam Lapp leaned over the counter and smiled at the little redheaded girl, her favorite patient at the Center for Pediatrics. "Good morning, Brittany. How are you feeling today?"

The four-year-old scrunched up her nose, causing her freckles to wrinkle. "My ear hurts."

Miriam swallowed a chuckle at the girl's adorable expression. "I'm sorry. I'm certain Dr. Sabella can help you."

Brittany's face was grim. "Yeah, but I don't want a shot."

Miriam leaned down, angling her face closer to the girl's, and lowered her voice. "I have a hunch he won't give you a shot. I bet he'll just look in your ear and make sure it's not full of potatoes."

"Pee-tatoes!" Brittany squealed a giggle, covering her mouth with her hand.

Glancing at Brittany's mother, Miriam smiled. "It's so good to see you today. How's Mr. Baker?"

"He's doing well, thank you." The woman pulled out her wallet. "How are you?"

"Doing just fine, thank you." Miriam straightened her purple scrub top. "I'll take your co-pay, Mrs. Baker."

"Thank you." The woman handed Miriam her debit card.

Turning, Miriam swiped the card through the credit card machine and snatched a pen from the counter.

"Miriam!" Lauren, the office manager, rushed over from the inner office. "Miriam, there's a call for you on line two."

"I'll be just a minute," Miriam said, punching the keys on the credit machine. "I'm running through Mrs. Baker's co-pay."

Lauren took the pen from Miriam's hand. "I got it." Frowning, she nodded toward the inner office. "Use my phone."

Arching an eyebrow in question, Miriam studied her coworker's worried face. During the year Miriam had worked for Lauren, she'd never seen her look so concerned about a phone call. "Who is it?"

"Go on," Lauren said, nodding toward the office again. "I'll take over up here. You take your time."

"Who is it?" Miriam asked again.

"Hannah," Lauren whispered.

"Hannah?" Miriam's mind raced, wracking her brain with thoughts of who it could be. She only knew one Hannah ... "My *sister* Hannah?"

Lauren gave a quick nod. "Yes. Now go."

Miriam's stomach twisted. In the nearly four years since she'd left her family in Lancaster County, Pennsylvania, not one member of her family had ever called her. Only Hannah had written her, but called—never. Miriam had made it a point of giving Hannah her cell, home, and work numbers, and Hannah said she would only use them in case of an emergency.

Something is wrong.

Her thoughts moved to Hannah's eldest daughter, Lena Joy, who'd been born with a genetic disorder. Had something happened to her?

Her eyes widened with worry.

"Go!" Lauren nudged her toward the office. "Take all the time you need."

Taking a deep breath, Miriam rushed to the inner office, dropped into Lauren's chair, lifted the receiver to her ear, and punched the button for line two.

"Hello?" Miriam held her breath, waiting for her sister's familiar voice.

"Miriam," Hannah said. "How are you?"

The voice was sweet and familiar, bringing tears to Miriam's eyes as memories assaulted her mind. She'd treasured those nights long ago when they would lie awake late into the evening in the room they shared, whispering their future plans. Funny how it all came true for Hannah—she'd married the love of her life and had a family. Miriam, on the other hand, was the disappointment of the family. She'd left the community and never joined the Amish church or married.

Hannah was the only one who'd seemed to understand when Miriam made the choice that changed her life forever—when she left the love of her life, her family, and the only community she'd ever known. Hannah forgave her when the rest of the family did not.

Oh, how Miriam had missed her sister.

"I'm good. You?" Miriam stared absently at the date and time glowing on the phone while winding the cord around her finger.

"*Gut.*" Hannah's Pennsylvania *Dietsch* brought another flood of family memories crashing down on Miriam.

"It's so wonderful to hear your voice, Hannah," Miriam said. "How is your family? How are the children?"

"Oh, the *kinner* are *gut, danki,*" Hannah said. "They grow so fast."

"And Lena Joy? She's doing well?" Miriam asked and then held her breath in anticipation of the response.

"She has good and bad days, as to be expected. If only there were a cure ..." Hannah paused for a moment as if collecting her thoughts or perhaps censoring her words. "Miriam, I'm afraid I have bad news." Her voice was cautious, causing Miriam's heart to thump in her chest.

"What is it?"

"*Mamm ...*" She paused. "*Mamm iss gschtarewe.*"

"What?" Miriam gasped. "Mom died?" She groaned and covered her face with her hands. "No. No, no, no. Hannah, you don't mean that."

"*Ya*, I'm sorry to say I do." Her sister's voice trembled. "I can't believe it either."

"When?"

"Last night. In her sleep, from complications due to pneumonia. *Daed* found her this morning. He didn't know that she'd . . ." Her voice trailed off, the unspoken words hanging between them like a thick fog.

Miriam wiped the tears trickling down her hot cheeks. "How can she be gone? I was planning a trip home over the holidays to try to make everything right."

"I'm so sorry to call you at work and tell you this."

"No, no." Miriam plucked a tissue from the box on Lauren's tidy desk and dabbed her eyes and nose. "I'm glad you let me know. I'll go home and pack and then get on the road. I'll be there as soon as I can." She glanced at her watch and then mentally calculated the trip from her home in LaGrange, Indiana, to Gordonville, Pennsylvania. "I should be there before midnight."

"Oh, *gut*. I was hoping you'd come."

"Of course I will. We're family."

"*Ya*. We are." Hannah's voice trembled. "Drive safely. *Ich liebe dich, Schweschder.*"

"I will." Miriam tried in vain to stop the tears flowing from her eyes. "I love you too, Sister."

After dropping the receiver into the cradle, Miriam cupped her hands to her face and sobbed while memories of her mother flooded her mind. The last time she'd seen her mother was the night she snuck out of the farmhouse and left the community to move to Indiana and live with her cousin Abby.

Lifting the receiver to her ear again, Miriam dialed Abby's office and groaned when voicemail picked up.

"You've reached the voicemail for Abigail Johnston, paralegal with Wainwright, Morrison, and Rhodes," Abby's voice sang into the phone line. "I'm either on the phone or away from my desk. Please leave a detailed message, including your name, the time and date of your call, your phone number, and the nature of your call, and I will call you back as soon as I return. Thank you."

After the shrill beep ended, Miriam took a deep breath. "Abby, it's me." Before she could stop them, the tears started, and her voice was thick. "Call me. I just got the most horrible news. Hannah called me, and my *mamm* ..." Her voice trailed off; she couldn't say the word. "I'm heading home to pack up and leave for Gordonville right away. Call me. Bye."

She slammed the phone down and stood. After explaining the situation to Lauren, she rushed to the apartment she'd shared with Abby since Abby's husband left her two years ago.

Miriam was drowning in memories and packing when the door to her bedroom whooshed open, dragging across the worn tan carpet.

"What's going on?" a voice behind her asked.

Miriam turned to find her cousin standing in the doorway, clad in her best blue suit. Her light brown hair was cut in a short, stylish bob, perfect for a professional climbing the corporate ladder. She looked the part of an aspiring lawyer.

"Abby," Miriam said. "What are you doing here?"

"I left the office as soon as I got your voicemail." Her eyes were full of concern. "What did Hannah say?"

"Mamm passed away last night." Miriam's voice broke on the last word. Covering her mouth with her hands, she choked back a sob.

"Oh no." Abby encircled her in a hug. "I'm so sorry."

"I can't believe it," Miriam choked through her sobs. "I was going to surprise her with a visit over Christmas and try to work things out. I wanted to make things right. I wanted to see her and talk to her in person. But, now ... Now she's—"

"Shhh." Abby patted her back. "It's going to be all right."

"But how?" Miriam swiped her tears away with the back of her hands.

A somber smile turned up her cousin's lips. "Remember what you told me when that snake of a husband of mine left me for his perky secretary?"

Miriam shook her head. "Not really."

"You reminded me of a very important verse from Isaiah — 'those who hope in the Lord will renew their strength.'" Abby's eyes were serious. "We'll get through this. I promise."

Biting her bottom lip, Miriam nodded.

"I'll pack a few things, and we'll get on the road." Abby headed for the door.

"You're coming with me?"

Abby gave a little shrug. "Of course I am. Did you honestly think I'd let you face the family alone after nearly four years?"

Miriam let out a sigh. "I'd hoped not."

Abby gestured toward the suitcase. "Get packed, and we'll get on the road. With any luck, we'll be there before midnight. I imagine your dad and my parents won't welcome us with open arms. I guess we'll stay with Aunt Edna?"

Miriam nodded. "I was thinking that. As far as I know, she's still living alone in that little house on my *daed's* farm."

"I should have said *Aenti* Edna." Abby smiled. "Guess I better brush up on my Pennsylvania *Dietsch*, huh? Man, how long has it been since I've been back there?"

"Six years, right?" Miriam lowered herself onto her double bed next to her suitcase.

"Yeah, I guess so." Abby shook her head and stepped toward the door. "Well, we have a long ride ahead of us. We better get on the road."

Taking a deep breath, Miriam rose from the bed and fished a few blouses from her dresser. Closing her eyes, she whispered a prayer for strength and courage as she embarked on this painful trip to her past.

CPSIA information can be obtained
at www.ICGtesting.com
Printed in the USA
LVHW040709100121
676121LV00010B/129